GIRLS CAN SUCCEED IN SCIENCE!

Antidotes for Science Phobia
in Boys and Girls

Linda S. Samuels

CORWIN PRESS, INC.
A Sage Publications Company
Thousand Oaks, California

For information:

Corwin Press, Inc.
A Sage Publications Company
2455 Teller Road
Thousand Oaks, California 91320
E-mail: order@corwinpress.com

SAGE Publications Ltd.
6 Bonhill Street
London EC2A 4PU
United Kingdom

SAGE Publications India Pvt. Ltd.
M-32 Market
Greater Kailash I
New Delhi 110 048 India

Printed in the United States of America

Library of Congress Cataloging-in-Publication Data

Samuels, Linda S.
    Girls can succeed in science!: Antidotes for science phobia in boys and girls /
by Linda S. Samuels.
       p.   cm.
    Includes bibliographical references and index.
    ISBN 0-8039-6730-6 (cloth: acid-free paper)
    ISBN 0-8039-6731-4 (pbk.: acid-free paper)
    1. Women science students—Study and teaching. 2. Science
teachers—Training of—Handbooks, manuals, etc. 3. Science—Study
and teaching (Secondary)—Activity programs. 4. Science—Study and
teaching (Higher)—Activity programs. I. Title.
    Q181 .S19 1998
    507.1—ddc21
                                                  98-19664

This book is printed on acid-free paper.

99 00 01 02 03 04 05 7 6 5 4 3 2 1

Corwin Editorial Assistant: Kristen L. Gibson
Production Editor: Astrid Virding
Editorial Assistant: Nevair Kabakian
Typesetter: Christina M. Hill

Contents

PART 2: SPECIFIC TACTICS FOR CLASSROOM SUCCESS

PART 3: CLASSROOM ACTIVITIES

My Dana Hall Colleagues and Students, 1972 to 1999
My Husband, Martin
My children, Marilyn and Charles
My parents, Esther and Robert Garber and Jean and Sydney Samuels

CORWIN
PRESS

The Corwin Press logo—a raven striding across an open book—represents the happy union of courage and learning. We are a professional-level publisher of books and journals for K–12 educators, and we are committed to creating and providing resources that embody these qualities. Corwin's motto is "Success for All Learners."

Over the past 25 years as a science instructor at the Dana Hall School, I have developed a clear teaching philosophy and effective strategies for teaching science. These are designed to counter misconceptions about science and gender that students have learned from various sources, including parents, other teachers, and popular culture, before entering their first junior high or middle school science courses. I have taken this approach because far too often, by the time girls reach my 7th, 10th, and 12th grade classes, they have already "learned" that they are "not good at science." Often, lack of confidence precipitates poor performance, which, in turn, convinces students that their initial self-doubts were justified. Bolstering self-confidence in these students is the crucial first step for parents and teachers.

A considerable body of evidence suggests that some young women actually fear science and mathematics. There are myriad reasons for this fear: American culture teaches young women that they should be well-mannered, quiet, and passive (Gleason & Snow, 1991). Girls are told both explicitly and implicitly that by being assertive (even by being and acting intelligent), they will scare boys away (Sadker & Sadker, 1994). Both peers and adults discourage feminine assertiveness, calling it by the negative terms "pushiness" or "nagging." Instead, girls are encouraged to be passive, supportive, and irrational, and to avoid competition (dumb down) in favor of personal relationships. Obviously, these stereotyped traits directly conflict with the rationality, perseverance, and competitive demeanor expected of scientists.

Likewise, images from TV, movies, magazines, and even textbooks imply that women need men to explain scientific, mathematical, or technical concepts. Although women have made major scientific contributions, the icons we use to represent "the scientist" remain male: Edison, Einstein, Salk, even Frankenstein. Only a few short years have passed since TV medical dramas began to showcase female doctors. Even more disturbing, in a study conducted at American University, students had difficulty naming 20 famous women in American history who weren't athletes, entertainers, or Presidents' wives (Sadker & Sadker, 1994). Women still grace magazine covers more often in bikinis than in business suits or lab coats. Unfortunately, the preponderance of these gender stereotypes influences the way young women perceive themselves and damages their self-esteem.

Nevertheless, things have changed, and they continue to change. The politically correct 1990s have called serious attention to the persistence of sexism in the United States. Although the feminism of the 1970s helped to eliminate, in large part, explicit discrimination, women of the 1990s continue to grapple with countless implicit inequalities. Major victories have been won in employment, education, and the mass media. However, in the struggle for gender equality, educators have sometimes been overlooked as valuable resources.

Educators have a special opportunity, even an obligation, to counteract expectations of failure and to nurture self-confidence in their female students. A teacher can be an important role model for students, offering a constant source of support and guidance. Through encouragement and supportive relationships with teachers, girls can develop the skills necessary to be competent and successful in any scientific endeavor. Furthermore, by encouraging independent, creative thinking, teachers can inspire female students to greater intellectual heights and even change the courses of their lives. For these reasons, it is critical for science instructors to help young women learn that they can succeed in science.

Girls Can Succeed in Science! illustrates effective teaching strategies that really work! Although my teaching methods were developed to help young women who are apprehensive about science, they will benefit students of both genders. In addition, students who already enjoy science will find the approach and the activities interesting and engaging.

The book is divided into three parts. Part 1 presents an overview of the factors that discourage many young women from studying science and details the roles of students, parents, and most important, teachers in helping young women recognize their unique potentials as individuals. It defines the problem and details my new philosophy for confronting these issues. Part 2, "Specific Tactics for Classroom Success," combines the current literature on science for girls and my own successful experience. I discuss the tools needed to build a classroom that teaches boys and girls to love science. I introduce a general approach to course design and classroom atmosphere and describe the specific classroom procedures and activities that make the philosophy work. The specific techniques and strategies outlined provide successful ways to elevate self-esteem and promote student competence.

Creative activities tailored for classes in life science, biology, and advanced biology follow in Part 3. Some activities are also integrated into the text. My innovative class activities and laboratory exercises demonstrate how to implement the new philosophy of science education to create independent, self-assured problem solvers! This book is designed to help students, parents, and teachers eradicate the obstacles young women face in science education by changing the methods we use to teach. It does *not* advocate teaching a watered-down quasi-science for girls and requires no significant change in the subject matter. My hope is that, with consistent implementation of the techniques and strategies outlined here, many students will not only perform well in class but will develop a passion for scientific inquiry.

Acknowledgments

I would like to thank Eric Chaisson, Director of the Wright Center, and Ronnee Yashon, Educational Coordinator, Elaine Betts, Headmistress of Dana Hall School, and Blair Jenkins, Head of the Dana Hall School, for their guidance and care. To my students and colleagues at Dana Hall: Many thanks for a lifetime of learning. Special thanks to Professor Carl A. Huether, University of Cincinnati, my mentor and initial inspiration. To my husband, Martin, and to my children, Charles and Marilyn: You are my life. To my parents, Robert and Esther Garber and Sydney and Jean Samuels, I owe the world!

For their editing help, I am grateful to Jason Overdorf, Elizabeth Tua, Tanya Rubins, Jeannie Wang, Emily Chin, and Liz Howar.

About the Author

Linda S. Samuels is known for her passion for science and her dedication in teaching girls to stretch beyond academic and societal limits and pressures to claim their own places in the science field. For 25 years at Dana Hall School for Girls in Wellesley, Massachusetts, Linda has faithfully encouraged her students through process, not memorization.

In 1994, she was nationally recognized as the Outstanding Biology Teacher in Massachusetts by the National Association of Biology Teachers and awarded Norfolk County Science Teacher of the Year by the Massachusetts Association of Science Teachers. In 1996, she was awarded the Distinguished Alumni Award from the University of Cincinnati; in 1996-1997, she was named a fellow at the Wright Center at Tufts University. In 1997, she received the Award for Excellence in Encouraging Equity (sponsored by the National Association of Biology Teachers); and she is President for 1998 of the Massachusetts Association of Biology Teachers.

She continues to expand her love of learning by taking courses or attending workshops and symposia at Tufts, Harvard, MIT, Wellesley, Boston College, Boston University, and Syracuse. Her undergraduate degree was in biology-zoology and her master of science degree was in population genetics, both at the University of Cincinnati.

She is married and has two college-age children.

Part 1

Identifying and Overcoming Barriers to Success

[If we, as parents, teachers, and members of society,] stop trying to change girls and . . . let a feminine approach to science inform our pedagogy, we may see some exciting results for boys and girls and for science and technology.

—A. Pollina (1995, p. 33)

Catherine Joyce
Kathryn Whelan
    Dana Hall students

SOURCE: Printed with permission.

Jordana Kosow
Lia Lopez
    Dana Hall students

SOURCE: Printed with permission.

1

Barriers to Success in Science

The underrepresentation of girls in science and science-related fields has been seen primarily as a "girl problem" (Campbell, 1993, p. 3). That is to say, educational systems have blamed women for the difficulties they have had with science. Experts have even gone so far as to speculate that women are genetically encoded for scientific incompetence! Because we have defined the problem this way, most of our solutions have been designed to make girls "more compatible" with science (Campbell, 1993) and have largely ignored the many environmental factors that affect the way women view themselves and even the way their personalities develop. Before we can do anything, we must realize that young women face many obstacles, both inside and outside the classroom, that may discourage them from excelling in science: These include stereotyping, low self-esteem, and poor preparation.

Young women face many obstacles, both inside and outside the classroom, that may discourage them from excelling in science.

Stereotypes

Stereotypes and metastereotypes say science is a "male" endeavor. Current stereotypes about science and science-related professions are particularly discouraging to young women (Wolfson, 1993). Many of these stereotypes suggest that science is a "masculine" discipline and, therefore, unsuitable for women. Stereotypes and folk history also suggest that scientists, like virtuoso violinists or tennis greats, are so-called geniuses or prodigies and must be discovered early in life. Perhaps even more discouraging to young women, conventional wisdom asserts that scientists must be rigid and analytical, never creative or open.

One of the most common scientific stereotypes— Doctors are male and nurses, female. This stereotype has been well-entrenched by many long-running television drama series.

Stereotypes in Movies and TV

From the science fiction movies of the 1950s onward, scientists have been portrayed as men in white coats. Women have been screamers.

Stereotypes in Magazines

As Naomi Wolf (1991) points out in her book *The Beauty Myth,* take a look at any magazine rack and you'll see women in bikinis and men in business suits. The contrast suggests to young women that they will be valued for their physical attributes, whereas men will be recognized for their abilities.

Role Models

Too few teachers and textbooks call attention to successful women in the sciences.

Peer Pressure

Junior high and high school is the time of "the great leveling," when to be different is to be wrong. It's not cool to be smart, particularly for girls, particularly in science. Many girls believe that being smart is in conflict with being popular (Sadker & Sadker, 1994).

Low Self-Esteem

When was the last time a woman made a magazine cover for her achievements?

Low self-esteem predicts failure. In adolescence, boys begin to base self-esteem on their accomplishments, whereas girls base self-esteem on beauty (American Association of University Women [AAUW], 1991). Because you're either born beautiful or you're not, girls "begin to attribute their success to luck and not to skill," particularly in math and science (Skolnick, Langbort, & Day 1982, p. 21).

Poor Preparation

Few elementary school teachers teach science effectively. Science receives less emphasis among the so-called basics of reading, writing, and arithmetic. Few elementary school teachers have science training. As a result, some students enter middle school with no science background!

Overcoming the Barriers

How Can the Barriers Discussed in Chapter 1 Be Overcome?

Generally speaking, we must do three things:

1. Combat gender stereotypes and stereotypes about science
2. Build young women's self-esteem to defeat "science phobia"
3. Continue to work for curriculum reform

My philosophy of science education accomplishes the first two of these goals and effectively teaches science to both boys and girls. Science is a discipline of ideas, not just facts. Therefore, courses should be designed to encourage independent thinking, problem solving, and scientific inquiry. In addition, teachers must strive to make science more "girl-friendly" by emphasizing collaboration over competition; valuing teamwork; and incorporating presentations, essay exams, and written reports into the science curriculum. Note that these changes not only build on the communication and interpersonal skills for which girls have traditionally been known but also more fully prepare students for college science courses.

Perhaps the following quote from a former student best expresses how this philosophy works:

> Mrs. Samuels somehow manages to raise self-esteem, inspire students and eliminate fear, and provide a relaxed, happy environment without sacrificing rigor and very high standards. . . . I remember wanting to study hard because I was inspired and happy in the course, not because I was afraid.

The following chapters help clarify the "somehow." If parents and teachers consistently implement these suggestions, students will realize that science can be fun and doesn't have to be intimidating. The principles discussed here help eradicate students' fear of science and help prove to young women, and young men, that they can do science.

The Philosophy

For the best results, we need the cooperation of students, parents, school systems, communities, and teachers. Students must be willing to put in the time and effort necessary to succeed. Parents must provide positive reinforcement and express a belief in the students' ability to understand complicated ideas. The school system and community must work to provide a gender-neutral curriculum. Last, the teacher must strive to adapt his or her teaching style to the needs of the students.

3

The Role of the Student

Strategies for Student Success

- ◆ Work Hard
- ◆ Develop Good Study Habits
- ◆ Complete All Assignments
- ◆ Ask Questions

Ownership

Although students may not necessarily be part of the problem, they are definitely part of the solution. Students should take responsibility for their performances (it's the teacher's job to make them want to do so!). When students take control of their education, they no longer feel they are being bossed around or that it is their parents' job or the teacher's job to see that they do their homework and pass tests. Some ways students can participate actively in their education include accessing textbook and library resources, taking detailed notes from classroom lectures and readings, and making outlines of material covered in each chapter for review. Furthermore, students should not feel dumb asking questions about material they do not understand: The only stupid questions are those not asked!

Of course, the first step is for the student to realize that it is in her or his interest to work hard, because she or he will be the one to benefit from a good education or suffer from a poor one. Students may resist taking this responsibility, but effective teaching can do a great deal to overcome even the most stubborn opposition.

There is, of course, no guaranteed way to convert students, but consistently demonstrating that you care about the indifferent student's performance can often initiate a turnaround.

Design Your Course so Students Can Succeed

Courses should be designed to encourage students to become involved in the material, work hard, and ask questions. For all age groups and ability levels, assign a variety of activities that require independent thinking and problem solving. In contrast to the old listen-memorize-regurgitate model, these exercises force students to think about questions for which the answers are not readily available. To ensure that you meet each student's cognitive strength, present material in diverse ways: textbook and supplementary readings, lectures, worksheets, laboratories, and visual aids.

Of course, teachers cannot expect students to take responsibility for their education until they teach them how. Initially, set guidelines for what students should do to succeed. Make it clear that you expect them to prepare for class daily.

One way to train them to do so is to assign and collect daily homework assignments. That way, students who prepare receive immediate gratification. Also, quiz students (both formally and informally) on reading assignments, explaining to them that they must read before the class discussion so that they can participate. You can emphasize the importance of note taking by teaching students how to take notes and occasionally collecting students' notes to check them. Everything you do should be designed to set a quantifiable, immediate reward for taking responsibility. Later, when they see their performances on tests and class work improve, students learn that the long-term rewards are much higher!

One way to emphasize that learning science requires discipline is to require that students complete all assignments for course credit. Although some students may need to work after school to complete assignments, it will help them learn to manage their time wisely. If a student is absent, expect her or him to get class notes and assignments from a peer. In general, make sure students understand what you expect from them: persistence and hard work!

4

The Role of the Parent

Parenting Strategies

◆ Maintain a Positive Attitude and High Expectations
◆ Encourage Success
◆ Provide At-Home Activities
◆ Support Good Study Habits

The explicit and implicit messages parents send can radically affect the way children perceive themselves and their abilities (Skolnick et al., 1982). Even a single negative comment, such as, "I was never any good at science either," may have lasting repercussions, whereas consistent positive reinforcement from parents can make the difference between an underachiever and an overachiever. Just how important are parents as mentors and role models? A survey conducted by the Group Independent Study Project at Brown University indicated that the most important factor determining whether a young women would pursue a career in science was the vocation of her parents (New England Consortium for Undergraduate Science Education [NECUSE], 1996).

Of course, parents can't change careers to inspire their daughters, but there are several things they can do. Here are some key points teachers should communicate to parents:

Parents can affect their children's attitudes toward science by taking an interest in projects, science fairs, class presentations, and other school activities.

Be Involved

By showing the child that they are genuinely interested in what she or he is doing in science, parents can reinforce the child's belief in her or his ability to "do" science. Attending PTA meetings, science fairs, and class presentations and keeping up on school activities are all important ways parents can show they care!

Maintain High Expectations and a Positive Attitude

> Encourage, don't discourage.
> Don't badger.
> Don't say, "I could never do science, either."

Avoid Stereotypes

> Be aware of gender issues.
> Show confidence in your daughter's ability to understand how machines, electricity, and technology work.

Encourage At-Home Science Activities

By scheduling and participating in science-related games, trips, and adventures, parents can show their children that learning can be both informative and fun. Parents should be reminded to tell their kids that they're doing science.

ACTIVITIES

✓ Museum or Library Trip

Take your daughter(s) to the museum or library and investigate a scientific topic. Most natural history museums offer interesting exhibits on anthropology or biology. Make it fun!

✓ Zoo Trip

A trip to the zoo is fun *and* educational. Emphasize that zoology is a science by getting an identification book from the zoo office or from the bookstore and organizing an Explorer's Journal for your kids. Kids can pretend to be explorers or naturalists and write observations about animal adaptation or animal behavior. Find a full description in Chapter 15, p. 180.

✓ Internet Scavenger Hunt

Help your child learn to apply the technology of the Internet (or let your child help you!). For specific sample scavenger hunts and web sites, see Chapter 15, p. 192.

✓ Nature Hike

Identify trees, plants, wildflowers, and rock formations. Once you learn the area, you can organize scavenger hunts or identification contests. Be sure to carry identification books for the flora and fauna of your area. See Chapter 15, p. 179.

✓ Camping, Fishing, and Outdoor Sports

If mom or dad loves the outdoors, be sure to include daughters as well as sons! Believe it or not, simple activities, such as cleaning fish or filtering camp water, can teach science. See Chapter 15, p. 184.

✓ Home Experiments

There are numerous books of science experiments you can do at home. But experiments don't have to be so formal. Why not take car trouble or mowing the lawn as an opportunity to discuss how engines work? Use an encyclopedia or even an owner's manual for reference. Encourage your daughters to get greasy!

5

The Role of the School System

School System Strategies

- ◆ Support Student Independence
- ◆ Bridge Gaps in Curriculum Between Middle School, High School, and College
- ◆ Avoid Gender Bias
- ◆ Recognize Developmental Needs
- ◆ Communicate With the Scientific Community

What "Acting Out" Means

A recent study conducted by the American Association of University Women (AAUW) Educational Foundation (AAUW, 1996) found that young girls use many different strategies to establish their individualities and meet academic challenges. Clowning, talking loudly, adopting radical styles of dress or body ornamentation, and other behaviors often interpreted as "trouble making," "defiance," or even signs of hormonal imbalance are, in fact, strategies for establishing power and independence. It is likely that these behaviors are a rebellious response to constrictive interpretations of what is "proper" behavior for young women. We can identify a harmful cycle: Society discourages girls from being assertive, so they "act out" or "rebel"; society responds with reprimands and punishments, making rebellion even more necessary.

Clowning, talking loudly, adopting radical styles of dress or body ornamentation, and other behaviors often interpreted as "trouble making" are, in fact, strategies girls use for establishing power and independence.

The first step in breaking the cycle is to recognize assertiveness, even in its most radical forms, for what it is: an attempt to gain or express independence. After teachers, administrators, and parents understand that, they can channel that energy into more productive avenues.

Education must be connected to girls' and boys' personal experiences and developmental needs (AAUW, 1996). Traditionally, schools have focused on students' academic skills, without acknowledging the developmental challenges they may be facing. School officials, guidance counselors, and teachers alike should recognize that, especially for adolescent students, school is a place for both academic and psychological development. Schools should design programs to help their students deal with developmentally critical issues, such as separation, individuation, autonomy, and responsibility.

Turning Rebels Into Leaders

School systems should create leadership opportunities for students and encourage girls, in particular, to take advantage of them. Changing class and student council presidents to copresidents (one of each gender), requiring that student councils comprise both males and females, and giving important duties to all-female organizations are all ways to encourage women to be leaders.

In addition, exposing young girls to women in visible leadership positions helps foster girls' senses of competence and allows them to try out new roles. Schools should try to invite women leaders to speak at school functions and meet with girls in smaller groups.

Bridging Curriculum Gaps

Bridging the gap between the middle and high school years and easing the transition between high school and college are crucial if we are to interest girls in science and keep them interested in scientific careers (Spragg, 1993).

Middle School

From infancy to adulthood, children learn by observing particular phenomena and inferring things about the more general world from those observations. Thus, before they can understand abstract concepts (those that cannot be directly observed), children must have a firm grasp of the concrete phenomena those concepts seek to describe. In other words, it's much easier for a student to understand parabolic motion, for example, if she or he has played softball or thrown the shot put.

In middle school, science moves rapidly from concrete, easily observable phenomena, such as evolutionary adaptation, to more abstract concepts, such as DNA structures and genetics. Not coincidentally, it is at this time that the gulf between girls' and boys' performances widens. Boys, who in many cases have more play experience with concrete phenomena, have an easier time extrapolating abstract conclusions. To compensate, each lesson should be designed to derive the abstract concepts being taught from concrete examples. Girls must be given the opportunity to develop the hands-on understanding of the world that boys gain through familiarity with traditionally masculine toys.

High School

High schools should design their curricula to teach students how to prepare for college-level science courses. This goal can be achieved by broadening the focus of your science curriculum and integrating science with math and other disciplines, such as history, social studies, and English. Because interest and ability often varies with a student's age, schools should offer science courses at all levels of challenge.

IDEAS:
Things That Should Be Posted
Around Your School

☛ Information about national prizes for young women
☛ Information about camps and activities for young women
☛ Articles and displays honoring female "firsts"
☛ Profiles on successful women in the community

College

School systems should ensure that high school students receive good information about colleges and careers. Guidance counselors should be required to meet with students throughout their high school years, even when there are no problems, to offer advice about the future. Likewise, schools should make resources available for teachers to arrange mentor programs with nearby colleges and universities and invite college professors and administrators to talk to students.

Avoiding Gender Bias

Schools also need to pay attention to the social context and bias in science fields. School officials might consider offering gender-sensitivity training seminars for teachers and staff to improve overall opinions about women's academic capabilities. Schools might also want to participate in science workshops or outreach programs in an effort to confront debilitating stereotypes.

Advertise Women's Issues

Schools should make gender issues visible at all levels of a school system—in the school district offices, classrooms, and hallways (AAUW, 1996). Some ways to do so include displaying pictures of local women who have achieved prominence within the community or in a larger arena; establishing awards for outstanding female students; and posting information about national prizes, camps, and activities for young women. Articles and displays honoring female astronauts, politicians, and other "firsts" should be placed in prominent locations.

Create Forums to Discuss Gender Issues

School officials need to create regular opportunities for gender issues to be discussed among parents, staff, community members, and students. Public forums and PTA meetings are excellent venues for the discussion of crucial issues facing young students and can help to shape school policies, programs, and activities that are acceptable to all.

In addition to offering meetings, school systems might also consider forming committees of students, parents, and school staff to examine, on a regular basis, how well the school is meeting the needs of its female students. To prevent ideas from getting mired in a single committee, create a professional network among staff, teachers, and guidance counselors.

Forge Ties With Community Groups

Another solution is to forge an ongoing connection with existing community organizations devoted to gender and women's issues. These groups can be excellent resources, providing mentors for female students and educating the school and community about gender issues.

6

The Teacher's Role

Teachers' Strategies

- ◆ Raise Students' Self-Esteem!
- ◆ Relate Science to Life Outside the Classroom
- ◆ Establish Close Relationships With Students
- ◆ Continue Professional Development

Educators are invaluable in the struggle to keep girls interested in science. Teachers must inspire an interest and enthusiasm for science among their pupils, emphasizing that "making the grade" is of secondary importance. Teachers who successfully retain girls in science maintain classrooms that are attractive, orderly, and well-equipped (Kahle, 1991). These highly effective educators encourage students to enjoy science beyond the classroom, emphasize careers and further education in science and related fields, and use educational techniques that encourage creativity (Kahle, 1991). In short, successful teachers have a positive attitude and present girl-friendly science.

Building Self-Esteem

The first hurdle to be overcome is students' low self-esteem, especially common among young women. Like parents, teachers have a great impact on students' visions of themselves and the world. If a teacher believes his or her students are capable, they will begin to believe in themselves. If the teacher suggests, implicitly or explicitly, that he or she does not have confidence in the student, the student is likely to adopt the same attitude.

Low self-esteem prevents many students from succeeding in science.

Women, more than men, tend to base their opinions of themselves on what others think of them (NECUSE, 1996). A women is also more likely than a man to perceive her performance as worse than it really is and is more likely to interpret this supposed poor performance as evidence of her own inadequacy. Teachers, as authority figures, can have a dramatic effect on young women's self-perception. Encouraging words can last for years (NECUSE, 1996). Here are some ways for teachers to make sure they are providing positive reinforcement:

QUICK TIPS

☞ Use stickers with encouraging messages to support students.
☞ Talk to each student one on one. Tell them they can succeed.
☞ Demonstrate you care by taking an interest in students' performances, remembering in what areas students did well or poorly, being available, and offering to help.
☞ Give extra credit for supplementary projects and outstanding performances.
☞ Work with students individually to correct wrong answers on tests. Explore *why* they made the mistakes.

Look girls in the eye when you call on them in class, and congratulate them on work well done (Sanders, 1994).

Make a conscious effort to call on girls as often as boys. Always respond with articulate verbal encouragement, not just "uh-huh" or "mmm."

Take an active interest in your students' futures. Ask them about their plans for college, and provide information about careers in science.

Establish limits, and follow through. If you expect your students to behave in a particular fashion, they will! On the first day of class, make it clear that you expect all students to participate.

Develop guidelines with your students. Devise a "learning bill of rights" aimed at helping students overcome anxiety about science-related subjects (Tobias, 1985, p. 68). To alleviate the science phobia prevalent among young girls, assure students that they have the right not to understand and to speak up when they don't, to learn at their own pace and to ask whatever questions they may have (Tobias, 1985). With consistent help from supportive teachers, these students will realize that they are capable of learning any subject, including science!

Reform your approach. Courses should focus on collaboration, not competition. Teachers should teach study skills and present materials in numerous formats so they hit each student's cognitive strength. Likewise, educators should provide students with adequate opportunities for expressing their individuality and creativity.

Girls thrive when cooperative learning is stressed over competition.

Develop and recommend support systems. Good support systems for young women can also help bolster their self-confidence. For example, schools could establish a Women in Science program or an extracurricular club to alleviate feelings of isolation and self-doubt, to provide encouragement, and to address the many other personal and academic issues facing young women (NECUSE, 1996).

Adopt a class motto. Class mottoes, such as "I Can Do Science!" and "Don't Ever Give Up!" help students maintain self-esteem and confidence in their abilities to perform well. Mottoes foster a sense of teamwork, which, in turn, implies that students can rely on classmates and teachers for support. A good way to make sure students accept the motto and buy into the program is to have the students choose the class motto themselves.

Relating Science to Life Outside the Classroom

Ask any girl why she doesn't like science, and she's likely to tell you, "It doesn't relate to my life." Of course, nothing could be further from the truth. Science, because it describes the physical world and how it works, relates to everyone's life! What the girl who says otherwise really means is, "My science class doesn't relate to my life," and that's what teachers have to change.

> Use the framework of science to address issues important to your students.
> Teach science outside the classroom, with field trips or nature walks.
> Relate activities and class discussions to current ethical and theoretical issues in science.

Presentations from science professionals, field trips, and off-site classes are all excellent ways to relate science to life outside the classroom.

In addition, teachers must help students look ahead by discussing courses and college majors that lead to different careers in science.

Establishing Close Relationships With Your Students

Many students feel that teachers are too busy to talk or to meet with them outside of class. As part of the effort to build self-esteem and because knowing your students personally has its own benefits, you should combat that notion.

Make Yourself Available

Set aside specific hours when you will be available to meet with students in your office or classroom. Remind students throughout the year that their questions and visits are welcome.

Give students your E-mail address, if you have one. E-mail works well with shy students who may have questions but don't like to speak up. In addition, it encourages students to think of your classroom as "professional," and sends the message that their thoughts are important. Remember to respond to questions promptly!

In large classes and for older students, require an office visit from each student within the first few weeks of class. Meeting privately with your students tells them right away that you are willing to treat them like adults and that you value their opinions and individuality.

Encourage students and parents to meet with you by appointment whenever they need help or want to confer about the students' progress. The students need to know that their teachers are there not only to provide them with an education but also to act as mentors to whom students can turn when they have a problem.

The best way to motivate students is to show you care.

QUICK TIPS

✓ **Raise Self-Esteem**
   ☛ Look girls in the eye
   ☛ Call on girls as often as boys
   ☛ Give articulate verbal praise
   ☛ Show interest in students' futures

✓ **Relate Science to Life Outside the Classroom**
   ☛ Address issues important to your students
   ☛ Teach outside the classroom
   ☛ Relate science class to current ethical and theoretical debates

✓ **Establish Close Relationships With Students**
   ☛ Make yourself available
   ☛ Give frequent feedback
   ☛ Make personal contact every day

✓ **Continue Professional Development**
   ☛ Keep up to date
   ☛ Present yourself as a fellow student

Give Frequent Feedback

Teachers can build relationships with students by correcting and responding to assignments frequently. Teachers should try to initiate a dialogue with students through comments on homework and class assignments. Keep in mind what you have written on each student's papers in the past, and draw attention to trends and improvements.

In particular, after correcting tests or assignments, teachers should meet with students who have performed poorly (NECUSE, 1996). This gives the student an opportunity to determine why she received a low grade and to discuss different study strategies for the future. The teacher can also direct the student to tutoring facilities and other support systems.

Make Personal Contact With Each Student Every Day

Talking with your students personally assures them that their education is important to you. Of course, every teacher's time is limited, but there are many little ways you can recognize each student. It can be as simple as calling each student by her first name (Sandler, 1991). Making an effort to remember what extracurricular activities your students are involved in and recognizing their achievements in their other classes and outside of school are excellent ways to show that you care.

Continue Professional Development

It is important for all educators to be aware of changes in educational theory and in their subject areas. New research constantly revises and adds to what we know about science; therefore, it is especially crucial for science teachers to stay current.

Science teachers should attend university lectures or seminars, subscribe to science journals, and even take university courses to keep up on the latest advances. Presenting yourself as a student as well as a teacher reinforces a central message about science: It is a never ending process of discovery, not a series of memorized facts. Knowing that their teacher also studies, takes tests, and makes mistakes reduces students' anxiety.

ROLE FULFILLMENT REVIEW

✓ **Role of the Student**

- ▦ Work Hard
- ▦ Develop Good Study Habits
- ▦ Complete All Assignments
- ▦ Ask Questions

✓ **Role of the Parent**

- ▦ Have a Positive Attitude and High Expectations
- ▦ Encourage Success
- ▦ Provide Activities at Home
- ▦ Support Good Study Habits

✓ **Role of the School and Community**

- ▦ Support Student Independence
- ▦ Bridge Gaps in Curriculum Between Middle School, High School, and College
- ▦ Avoid Gender Bias
- ▦ Recognize Developmental Needs
- ▦ Communicate With Scientific Community

✓ **Role of the Teacher**

- ▦ Raise Students' Self-Esteem!
- ▦ Relate Science to Life Outside the Classroom
- ▦ Establish Close Relationships With Students
- ▦ Continue Professional Development

Part 2

Specific Tactics for Classroom Success

Any educational strategy is useless unless teachers can put it into action. This requires concrete, applicable teaching techniques that teachers can put into effect in their classrooms right now.

Kim Maloomian

Jessica Bradley

Amanda Sherman

Dana Hall students

SOURCE: Printed with permission.

7

Setting the Stage for Success in Your Classroom

Simple Rules

These simple rules effectively help students, and particularly young women, overcome some of the everyday obstacles to pursuing their interest in science.

◆ Create a Relaxed, Secure Classroom Atmosphere
◆ Teach Study Skills
◆ Implement Alternative Assessment Measures
◆ Assign Independent Projects
◆ Provide Women Role Models
◆ Present Age-Appropriate Material
◆ Discuss Current Issues
◆ Set Clear Classroom Guidelines and Procedures

Chapters 8 through 10 present effective tactics for teaching science to any grade level. Chapter 7 provides guidelines for designing a safe and productive classroom environment in which even the most reticent student can succeed.

How to Create a Secure Environment

Be Positive

One of the most important ways you can make your students feel relaxed and secure is with your personal demeanor. It's unrealistic to expect teachers to change their personalities, but everyone can make an effort to be more tolerant and supportive. Remind yourself to be positive.

Be Aware of Stereotypes

In most societies, for most of recorded history, women have been perceived as having neither the discipline nor the intellectual ability to succeed in science (Gornick, 1995). Unfortunately, although women have come a long way, many of the old sexist stereotypes still affect today's young women. Negative or narrowly defined

TABLE 7.1

Stereotyped Activity	Stereotype-Free Activity
Cheerleading (for women)	Debate
Class secretary (for women)	Class president
Auto mechanics (for men)	Cooking
Home economics (for women)	Building trades
Child rearing (for women)	Animal husbandry
Parabolic motion of a football (for men)	Parabolic motion of a softball
Chemical reaction of a combustion engine (for men)	Chemical reaction of baking bread
Fishing (for men)	Hiking

images of scientists, which female students learn from the media, pop culture, and their parents and peers, often deter them from considering science as a career (NECUSE, 1996). In one study, a majority of high school students depicted "nerdy" white males with beards, glasses, and a white lab coat when instructed to draw a scientist (Skolnick et al., 1989).

To counteract years of conditioning, learn to recognize stereotypes and consciously avoid them. Likewise, keep a constant watch on how you interact with students. Do you treat boys and girls differently? Have you called on boys and girls equally often? Keeping an eye out for nonverbal cues is also important, because many girls tend to think first before answering (NECUSE, 1996; Sandler, 1991). Girls may take longer to raise their hands, so you should watch for signals such as leaning forward or making eye contact, which indicate that they are ready to participate. Teachers should also keep track of students who frequently contribute to class discussions and those who participate less often, and make an extra effort to encourage shy students. Making students feel comfortable with participating in class is essential!

Take Action

Girls may be slower to raise their hands than boys, so be aware for other cues that they want to contribute.

Being aware of stereotypes is not enough. Teachers must also combat them. Educators should choose activities that are free from sex-role stereotypes (Blake, 1993). Encourage students to pursue their interests, not just what society deems appropriate for their gender (see Table 7.1 for some examples of stereotyped and stereotype-free activities).

Make a conscious effort to acknowledge the contributions of female students to class discussions. To make certain the student hears and understands your praise, you should offer substantial and precise responses instead of merely nodding or mumbling "uh-huh" (Sandler, 1991). Educators should make eye contact with both male and female students and should not look exclusively at male students for responses to questions or for ideas.

When discussing the contributions of scientists to a particular topic, teachers should mention the work of both male and female scientists (see Table 7.2) and always refer to the scientists by first and last names so that students do not assume the scientist is a man. Likewise, avoid using the male pronoun to refer to both men and women. Try to use *humankind* or *humanity* instead of *mankind* (Sandler, 1991).

TABLE 7.2

Women Nobel Prize Winners

1903	Physics	Marie Curie
1911	Chemistry	Marie Curie
1935	Chemistry	Irene Joliot Curie
1947	Biochemistry	Gerty Radnitz Cori
1963	Physics	Marie Goeppert Mayer
1964	Chemistry	Dorothy Crowfoot Hodgkin
1977	Medical Physics	Rosalyn Sussman Yalow
1983	Medicine or Physiology	Barbara McClintock
1983	Medicine or Physiology	Rita Levi-Montalcini
1988	Biochemistry	Gertrude B. Elion

Although it sometimes leads to syntactical quagmires, use "he or she" and "him or her" instead of using the masculine pronoun to represent both genders.

Another way to assert the importance of women to science is to be sure to present data on both males and females when discussing laboratory experiments, whether the subjects are animals or humans. Aside from all its more subtle effects, being conscientious about how you convey information indicates to your female students that you are aware of, and concerned about, women's issues.

As already discussed, the attitudes and expectations of teachers strongly affect students' sense of themselves and their abilities. What is vital to remember in class is that you express these attitudes and expectations not only with what you say but also with what you don't say and with your body language. That means that to ensure you communicate the right message, you should always respond verbally. Responding to female comments with negative body language (averting eye contact; shuffling papers; appearing bored, annoyed, or disinterested) reinforces students' beliefs that their comments are dumb, irrelevant, or not worth addressing (Sandler, 1991).

It is important to emphasize the achievements of women in scientific careers.

ACTIVITIES FOR GENDER AWARENESS

✓ Gender Difference in Problem Solving

Students separate into all-male and all-female groups. With one group member acting as an observer, each group works to solve a series of problems. The observer writes down how the group solved the problem, and afterward, the class discusses different solutions and identifies gender difference (if any).

✓ Mother of the Year

Students discuss a set of women who engage in both traditional and nontraditional activities. They then decide which woman is most qualified to win the "Mother of the Year" Award and develop an argument supporting their choice. Class discussion follows. See also Chapter 12, p. 78.

Control Your Classroom

Don't tolerate students who interrupt or dismiss others' answers.

As important as your reaction to comments, is the reaction of students to each other. Teachers must not tolerate interruptions or rude, dismissive "evaluations" from the class at large. In particular, because adolescent girls are very sensitive to how boys react to them. Teachers should monitor how their male students behave towards their female students.

Establish a Noncompetitive Atmosphere

Competition among students, although it has some benefits, disastrously reinforces the low self-esteem of students who are having trouble. Cooperative group learning, on the other hand, is effective for all students.

Specific steps teachers can take to foster noncompetitive environments include encouraging the use of study groups; assigning collaborative projects; and designing relaxed, user-friendly labs, which require interdisciplinary skills (Spragg, 1993).

Encourage Group Work

Group work provides opportunities for evaluation, revision, and expression of ideas among peers without fear of "looking dumb" in front of the teacher or entire class.

Collaboration or cooperative learning in small groups helps students to learn from each other (Applegate, 1995). Group work requires students to ask questions, integrate information from past experiences, and decide what information is important and relevant.

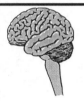

ACTIVITIES

✓ **Collaborative Projects**

Puzzle Piece Investigation (Life Science)

Students learn how collaborative thinking and the scientific method are vital to science. Each student has one piece of a puzzle. He or she formulates a hypothesis about the whole picture based on that piece. See Chapter 13, p. 89.

Jelly Genes (Biology)

Students make peanut butter and jelly sandwiches by following three different sets of "genetic" instructions. Each student acts as one genetically ordered process, following instructions read by the narrator. See Chapter 13, p. 104.

Group Lab Experiments (Advanced Biology)

Students work in small groups to design and implement a laboratory experiment on a topic of their choice. Requires writing and desk research as well as traditional laboratory skills. See Chapter 13.

✓ **User-Friendly Labs**

"Your Baby" Adoption (Life Science)

Students "adopt" a baby, made from a sack of flour. They use creativity to dress and decorate their baby, then use interdisciplinary skills of writing and research to create teaching aids for the baby to learn science. See Chapter 12, p. 77.

Living Thermostats (Biology)

Students measure the effects of the external environment on body temperature using warm water and ice to simulate environmental conditions. See Chapter 13, p. 111.

Playing Card Meiosis and Mitosis (Biology)

Students make circles with yarn on their desks to represent cells. Then they put the 2, 3, 4, and 5 of hearts and the 2, 3, 4, and 5 of clubs into the circles to represent chromosomes. Following the directions of the teacher, they reenact meiosis and mitosis. See Chapter 13, p. 94.

QUICK TIPS

✓ **Do**

Experiment with various types of groups:

- ☛ Vary group size from 2 to 5 members.
- ☛ Assign groups using random selection.
- ☛ Allow students to choose their own groups.
- ☛ Designate groups yourself.
- ☛ Mix students of varying skills and backgrounds together.

✓ **Don't**

Place students together who you know are friends when you assign groups

Group work provides opportunities for evaluation, revision, and expression of ideas among peers without fear of "looking dumb" in front of the teacher or entire class. Assigning groups gives students the opportunity to work with students with whom they might otherwise never interact. Furthermore, consultation with others in a group can provide helpful feedback, and the sharing of ideas that characterizes group projects improves students' negotiation skills. Small groups encourage active and cooperative participation (Spragg, 1993).

Group work also allows students to become comfortable with informal evaluations of each other's work. This technique teaches students, girls in particular, to help their colleagues improve and to feel comfortable evaluating their peers' efforts. Group work also helps develop students' interpersonal skills: Students learn effective and appropriate methods of reaching consensus and contracting agreements acceptable to all members.

Female students in particular thrive on working in small groups to do collaborative, independent research. They enjoy coupling science with so-called social skills and studying in a noncompetitive arena.

Encourage Students to Teach

Allow students to be "experts" by assigning students to give presentations and lead class discussion for particular sections of a chapter or unit. The student is responsible for preparing the lessons, worksheets, and assignments. Student-taught classes are indispensable in building self-confidence, because they empower students and give them opportunities to demonstrate their knowledge to their teachers, their peers, and to themselves. Handing over control of your class to a student sends a strong message that you believe in his or her abilities.

Choose Discussion Format Instead of Lectures

Class discussions in which everyone participates remove much of the pressure of being dictated to and alleviate the stress of being expected to know all the answers.

ACTIVITIES

✓ Group Work

Research Projects

See Chapter 11.

Lab Experiments

See Chapter 13.

Ethical Problems

Students work together in a group to come up with answers to ethical problems dealing with genetics, gender roles, Darwinism, environmental protection, and more (e.g., see "Send in the Clones," Chapter 12).

Review for Exams

Teacher assigns study groups and distributes study guides. Students work together to prepare for the test.

Skits and Other Class Presentations

See, for instance, "Born Free," "mRNA Translator," and "Your Baby Adoption" in Chapter 12.

Displays and Posters

See for instance, "Diversity of Life" in Chapter 12 and "Your Genetic Family Tree" in Chapter 13.

Social Activism

Students work with community organizations that deal with problems associated with classroom subjects (ecology, medicine, recycling). For instance, see "Mother of the Year Contest" and "Investigating the Ebola Virus" in Chapter 12.

Research projects, lab experiments, class debates, skits and class presentations, and art projects are all excellent opportunities for collaborative work.

Teacher Evaluations

Teacher evaluations are also a way to promote a secure learning environment. Asking students to give you feedback about your lectures, laboratory exercises, projects, and class discussions shows them that you value and respect their opinions. Ask for student input frequently, and try to put some of the suggestions into effect.

Likewise, you can use lesson evaluations to gauge how well you presented the material and whether students understood it. Use 1-minute essays to draw students into the course material (Spragg, 1993). After the end of each lesson, ask students to write down anonymously on a piece of paper their answers to the following three questions: What was the most important point of the lecture? What aspect(s) of the material were least clear to you? What information do you think should be included to make the information presented more clear?

These 1-minute essays give students opportunities to make suggestions for the class without fear or embarrassment. In addition, they help the students focus on the lecture, help the instructor quickly understand what points need further attention or more explanation, encourage students to think critically and analytically about their own learning, and allow even the shyest student to feel as though he or she is being heard.

How you respond to these essays is very important, too. You should assure students that it is natural for them to be confused about some of the material. Confusion is a normal part of learning. But most important, you should listen to what your students have to say and take their concerns seriously!

REVIEW

✓ **How to Create a Safe, Secure Classroom Environment**

- Give positive reinforcement.
- Fight stereotypes.
- Control how students treat one another.
- Stress group collaboration instead of competition.
- Encourage students to teach.
- Choose discussion format.

8

Clear Goals and Study Skills for Self-Esteem

Set Goals and Guidelines

Setting clear guidelines is a crucial step in reducing students' anxiety and building self-esteem. By presenting your expectations clearly and methodically, you give students specific goals to work toward and benchmarks against which to measure their progress. As they meet these incremental goals, students feel a sense of accomplishment that bolsters their self-esteem and propels them toward the overall goal: a successful science education.

State Course Objectives Explicitly and in Writing on the First Day of Class

Providing students with a blueprint of all you plan to teach them in your course takes the pressure off and gives them an immediate answer to the nagging question: Why are we doing this? A written syllabus is indispensable; it sends a message about your professionalism, students can refer to it throughout the year, and you can even distribute it to parents by mail or at parent-teacher conferences. (If parents are to take part in their children's education, teachers have to give them the tools they need to do so!) The syllabus should include brief descriptions of assignments and note the percentage of the final grade they are worth.

Teachers should explain their grading criteria and discuss class rules and what they expect from students. Before each assignment, it is helpful to review these expectations when you give instructions. Always answer these questions: Why are we doing this? What will students be graded on? How much of the grade does this account for? When is it due?

Post a Calendar Listing Assignments, Discussion Topics, and so on, for Each Month

A calendar helps students look ahead to organize their time. Most middle school and high school students don't use appointment books or monthly planners.

SAMPLE COURSE OBJECTIVES

✓ **Goals of the Course:**
- ☛ 1. To complete an extensive survey of life science in preparation for biology
- ☛ 2. To understand the methods of scientific inquiry
- ☛ 3. To learn to work independently—projects and laboratories
- ☛ 4. To learn to work collaboratively in groups
- ☛ 5. To learn to think conceptually and support all statements with examples and details
- ☛ 6. To develop essay-writing skills
- ☛ 7. To develop accurate and organized note-taking skills
- ☛ 8. To learn how to select key ideas from reading assignments
- ☛ 9. To learn to organize and summarize ideas
- ☛ 10. To learn to take precise measurements and organize and analyze data
- ☛ 11. To demonstrate the relevance of life science to everyday life
- ☛ 12. To encourage every student

✓ **Class Motto**

Science is fun! "I can do science!"

✓ **Evaluations**

Students will be evaluated on the basis of homework accuracy, test results, cooperation with peers and teachers, lab skills, and oral class participation. Attitude and effort are also important. Students are expected to be responsible, conscientious, and contributing members of the class.

TABLE 8.1 Sample Calendar (for 1 Week)

BIOLOGY ASSIGNMENTS

Monday, May 6: Start PLANTS!!

1. Read and Underline Ch. 25 Reproduction in Seed Plants.

2. Report on a biological news article about immunity, drugs, or disease due.

Tuesday, May 7:

1. Read and underline Germination and Growth Lab and Extra Credit Library Assignment (due May 21). We'll start the lab in class!

2. Read and underline photocopied sheets—An Introduction to Plants, Wonderful Plants and the entire thick packet called Plants! Read carefully, very carefully.

3. Check the Mystery Seed Lab for germination. Write-up of lab due at end of class.

Wednesday, May 8: Complete these worksheets:

1. Life Cycle of Angiosperms

2. Artificial Vegetative Reproduction

Thursday, May 9:

1. Read and underline Fruit Packet and Cute Fruit Lab—due at end of class! Bring in unusual fruit!

2. Creative writing on fruits and flowers due—one page!

Friday, May 10:

Ch. 6, Respiration and Photosynthesis—Read and underline.

What Should Teachers Expect From Students?

It is also useful to have a written handout that states your expectations and class rules. These are mine:

> > Arrive to class on time.
> > Respect materials and equipment.
> > Complete reading assignments before class discussions.
> > Homework assignments must be turned in on time; late papers will be marked down.
> > Be courteous to teachers, guests, and fellow students.
> > After a test, students must correct their mistakes and turn in the test again.
> > Keep an organized notebook, including notes from lectures, discussions, and readings. (This notebook will be collected and evaluated periodically.)

Teach Study Skills

General study skills must be an integral part of any curriculum, but they are particularly helpful for students of science. Improving a student's ability to concentrate on a task, to take in new material, and to understand (not just memorize) information is extremely important. Good study skills build confidence and get students of all ages started out on the right foot.

To ensure that your students benefit fully from your course, you should teach them early in the school year the study skills they will need to succeed. Spend the first week of school on study skills. For some students, it will be a review, but reinforcing good study habits with helpful study hints at the beginning of a semester can enhance a student's performance throughout the entire school year. Many students, out of laziness or forgetfulness, will have abandoned study skills they've learned in the past, even if they know they work!

All of these suggestions for improving study skills can work for students of any age. However, teachers may need to tailor specific study hints to match the course level. For example, it may help upper-level biology students understand many of the scientific terms used throughout the year to review the Greek and Latin prefixes, suffixes, and roots commonly found in scientific jargon. This exercise especially capitalizes on female students' verbal abilities and helps them see how science and language are intimately connected. For students who will be required to complete an independent library research project, review the steps involved in writing a scientific research paper (once again, setting clear guidelines). In short, a two-plank plan is effective in improving students' study skills: (a) Teach general study skills (reading, writing, listening, note taking, organizing material) at the beginning of the course, and (b) teach specialized techniques (report writing, reviewing for exams) as the need for them arises.

Reading

Because reading is a primary route for conveying information, any study skills lesson should begin with tips for improving reading skills. Using a tool such as Allyn and Bacon's (1987) SQ3R (survey, question, read, recite, and review) approach shows students how to read to understand and formulate questions about information they are learning and allows them to reflect on material that has been presented both in class and in the textbooks.

One of the key lessons of the Allyn and Bacon (1987) study skills program is that students should adjust their reading speeds to match the difficulty of the material. Short reading-comprehension exercises allow students to experiment with different reading speeds and to help them determine when scanning, skimming, rapid reading, or slow and careful reading is best suited to the material. Students should practice finding the main idea in their readings. Focusing on the most important idea in a paragraph, chapter, or scientific article helps students absorb and retain information more quickly and can serve as a starting point for summarizing or making outlines.

Before starting classroom activities or assigning homework, familiarize students with their textbooks and lab workbooks. Becoming familiar with the textbook at the beginning of a course makes it easier for students to find necessary information later in the semester. To help students become more efficient researchers, explore their textbooks with them, showing them how to use and get the most from the table of contents; illustrations; graphs, tables, and charts; chapter reviews; glossaries; appendices; and indices.

Laboratory Procedures

Before doing a laboratory experiment, familiarize students with the laboratory procedure and the steps involved in the scientific method. Understanding the concepts applied in a lab experiment and the problem to be investigated are crucial for conducting an experiment correctly and safely. To ensure that everyone understands the purpose of the experiment, go over the introduction to the lab together. Also, examine the directions, study the flow charts, and make note of any cautions or warnings about materials to be handled during the laboratory exercise.

At the outset of any science course, the teacher should introduce or review the scientific method. Although students in advanced classes should remember it from prior years, the review reasserts one of the key messages about science. It is not about facts, it is about investigation.

Many introductory textbooks present the scientific method as a kind of mantra that students should learn by rote: Identify the problem, collect information, suggest a hypothesis, design an experiment, perform the experiment, analyze data, draw conclusions, repeat or revise the hypothesis. Although this shorthand effectively describes a complex process in a (relatively) easily assimilable form, unfortunately, it also can be threatening to students. It is just one more thing they have to memorize, and it sounds clinical. On the contrary, when teachers present the scientific method, they should stress that it is a natural tool for problem solving, which humans have used from time immemorial.

To make the scientific method more accessible, accompany terminology with specific examples. In introductory classes, the "Black Box Investigation" helps give the students a hands-on illustration of how the method works. The black box, inside of which is a marble, a paper clip, or some such item, presents a concrete "scientific problem" that they can define, observe, form hypotheses about, and investigate. Students remember terminology better when they can apply it immediately to a concrete example.

Along with your introduction, discuss techniques for formulating hypotheses. In particular, teach students how to accurately predict the possible relationships between variables. You should also describe how to go about designing a controlled experiment to test the hypotheses, emphasizing the importance of establishing

Short reading-comprehension exercises allow students to experiment with different reading speeds and help them determine when scanning, skimming, rapid reading, or slow and careful reading is best suited to the material.

Understanding the concepts applied in a lab experiment and the problem to be investigated are crucial for conducting an experiment correctly and safely.

Teaching the Scientific Method

✓ Black Box Investigation (Life Science)

Students formulate hypotheses about what is inside a sealed black box. The teacher explains the metaphor: The black box represents every scientific problem. See Chapter 13, p. 91.

✓ Mystery of the Alpine Slide (Biology)

Students read a description of incidence of allergic symptoms with no explanation of the cause. They analyze the data and form hypotheses about what is causing the reaction in class discussion. See Chapter 12, p. 85.

✓ Hepatitis Case (Advanced Biology)

Students read a description of hepatitis symptoms and underline whatever data they think are important clues. They form groups and investigate four lab stations to gather more information. Last,

each group writes a hypothesis, with evidence. See Chapter 11.

✓ The Scissors Game (Life Science)

Students and teachers form a circle. The teacher passes a pair of scissors to the student to his or her right and says either "crossed" or "uncrossed." Students then try to guess the accuracy of crossed or uncrossed as the scissors pass around the room. The real criteria is whether the holder's legs are crossed or uncrossed. See Chapter 13, p. 92.

✓ Investigating Ebola Virus (Biology)

Students read descriptions of how Ebola virus first manifested in Africa. Then, they provide written answers to questions designed to help them formulate hypotheses about the disease. See Chapter 12.

well-controlled conditions and demonstrating how to manipulate the independent variables.

In advanced classes, recall students' attention to laboratory projects they conducted in the past and reassert the connections between the steps in the lab and the steps of scientific inquiry.

Taking Notes and Outlining

To ensure that students retain and understand the information you will present, first teach them how to take notes from classroom lectures, from textbooks, and from library resources. The best way to teach note taking is to provide written outlines of your lectures and readings, then gradually begin to require students to fill in the blanks until they're ready to take notes "from scratch." For at least the first few weeks, you should collect notes occasionally to be sure they are adequate.

As part of this lesson, show students how to use chapter headings, main ideas, and verbal cues from lecturers to make outlines to organize new material. Emphasize that outlines serve as valuable tools to illustrate the connections between points and how particular facts or data are comprised in a system of information.

Excessive anxiety can actually cause poor performance, which causes greater anxiety the next time around, and can result in a nasty downward spiral.

Interpreting Graphs, Diagrams, Tables, and Charts

As another important part of the study skills lessons, provide students with opportunities to read and construct graphs, diagrams, tables, and charts so that they understand how to collect and record data accurately and are able to recognize the many ways scientific data can be communicated.

EXAM PREPARATION

Studying for the Exam

- Exam preparation is as important as taking the exam.
- Organize materials (notes, quizzes, tests).
- Schedule your review: Select what you will review. Decide whether you will review one or more subjects each day.
- Make summaries or outlines of what you will need to know to get "the big picture."
- Ask questions of teachers and peers.
- Go over notes, review sheets, and books.
- Know the format of the exam.
- Select the items you need to memorize. Don't try to memorize *all* the material.
- Study with a friend or a group of friends. Quiz each other orally from your class notes or the text.

Physical Preparation for Exams

- Be sure to keep eating healthily, sleeping, exercising and *relaxing!*
- Study in places where you don't get distracted. Don't study near a phone, TV, or radio. Choose a place with good light and keep all the materials you need handy.
- Take reasonable breaks.

Before the Exam:

- Get a good night's sleep.
- Have an adequate breakfast (not too large, not too small).
- Wear comfortable clothes (layers are good if you tend to get hot).
- Bring necessary materials (extra pencils, tissues, watch, calculator).
- Avoid the company of panicky friends.
- Arrive with enough time to spare but not so much time that you lose focus or become anxious.

Taking the Exam:

- Read directions thoroughly before you begin. Ask for clarification if you don't understand.
- Determine in which order you will answer the questions. Answer the easy questions first.
- If you get stuck on a question, skip it and return to it after you have answered the others.
- Answer the question specifically. Adding extra information probably won't help your score.
- Attempt to answer every question.
- Write as legibly as possible.
- Label all answers with the appropriate number or letter.
- Allow time to go over your answers.

Don't expect to feel fully prepared. Rarely do people have enough time to feel totally in control of it all. Concentrate on doing your best.

Writing Lab Reports and Papers

Taking students step by step through the writing of several lab reports can help improve their writing and organizational skills. To write a good report, students must understand both scientific concepts and laboratory procedure. Carefully review how to organize information to construct a title page, introduction, and procedure section, and show them how to include data, calculations, charts, and graphs correctly in their reports. Review techniques for appropriately documenting sources used and for constructing a reference page. The in-class practice lab reports help identify potential problems before they occur so students never have the chance to "fail." In some cases, it is also helpful to arrange a computer tutorial, to make it easier for students to type their reports.

Reviewing for Tests and Exams

Tests make students nervous. A low level of nervous energy is productive if we can harness it to make students work hard to succeed. When that nervousness becomes acute, however, it can turn into science phobia. In addition, excessive anxiety can actually cause poor performance, which causes greater anxiety the next time around, and can result in a nasty downward spiral.

The good news is that it's easy to reduce students' anxieties by making sure you prepare them for exams. Before the test, you should familiarize students with the types of questions that may be asked and encourage them to organize their thoughts (and check to see they've done so). After the test, you should discuss the correct answers, identifying frequent mistakes and why they may have occurred. Show students how to learn from their mistakes. It will improve their future performances and reinforce the message that tests are tools for learning, not simply opportunities for you to make judgments about the students. Eventually, your review methods will become an automatic part of the students' study routines.

Another way to alleviate anxiety about tests is to provide alternative assessment measures (see Chapter 9). This makes tests less ominous, because students know there are many other factors influencing their grades.

9

Implementing Alternative Assessment Measures

Educators should not focus on trying to change the ways female students approach mathematics, science, or technology but should identify the unique ways young women learn (Pollina, 1995). Girls may learn differently from boys, but that does not mean that the ways girls learn are either wrong or inappropriate for science. Part of this change in approach is changing the way we assess student performance. First, we must be aware that how well a student does on an exam doesn't always indicate how well the student understands the material. It may indicate nothing more than how the student responds to that particular exam style (NECUSE, 1996). For example, girls tend to do better on essays than on multiple-choice formats. Then, we have to adapt our assessment methods so that we effectively test the students' knowledge of the material, not just their test-taking skills.

Understand What Tests Mean

The standardized tests and the tests supplied by publishers primarily assess students' abilities to memorize facts, terms, and concepts and do not evaluate their reasoning, experiential understanding, or problem-solving abilities (Harmon, 1993). Because these tests do not tap procedural knowledge and do not emphasize hands-on, real-world science, they are a serious obstacle to science education reform. In response, educators should assess students' abilities in a number of different ways and should encourage students to choose which way they prefer to be evaluated. Tests, for example, should give students a choice among multiple choice, short answer, and essay questions.

Expand Your Definition of Lab Work

Reform of assessment measures cannot be limited to tests; instead reform must extend to all of our measurement tools. Because many girls enter science classrooms

ALTERNATIVE LABORATORY ACTIVITIES

✓ Your Genetic Family Tree

Students interview relatives about the family's inherited traits and diseases. They write down responses and then graph their family trees, indicating dominant and recessive traits. See Chapter 13, p. 103.

✓ A Jug of Wine, A Loaf of Bread, and Yeast

Students bake bread, changing variables and predicting the effects of the changes. Use conventional cooking measurements instead of "laboratory" measurements. See Chapter 13, p. 121.

✓ Tide Eats Jello

Students learn about biotechnology by investigating proteases found in laundry detergents. They assay each detergent to find out which ones contain the enzyme protease by testing them on jello substrate. See Chapter 13, p. 107.

✓ Immunization Analysis

Students obtain copies of their immunization records and evaluate them. Then, they research diseases and vaccinations and make conclusions about what immunizations are currently necessary. See Chapter 15, p. 177.

ALTERNATIVE ASSESSMENT MEASURES

✓ Take-Home Exams

Questions should require problem-solving skills. Because students can use their book and notes, take-home tests do not evaluate their abilities to memorize and regurgitate.

✓ Independent Laboratory Projects

Independent laboratory projects require students to demonstrate that they understand the scientific method. Topics should be designed to build on knowledge from class work. See examples in Chapter 11.

✓ Research Projects

Research projects give students the opportunity to apply the concepts learned in class to more complex problems. Reports should demonstrate the student's ability to analyze data and evaluate the accuracy of hypotheses. See examples in Chapter 11.

✓ Laboratory Tests

One way to evaluate students' understandings of concepts is to ask them to solve a laboratory problem without specific instructions. In a short time, they must design and conduct an experiment and tabulate their results.

✓ Oral Exams

Oral exams are another way to vary your testing style. Have each student prepare for a specific subject, then ask him or her a series of questions. Questions should be designed to use problem-solving skills, not test memorization.

✓ Student-Taught Classes

To teach, we have to understand the material we present. Therefore, it follows that for students to teach a chapter or unit of the class, they, too, must understand the material. Students don't think of this activity in the same way they think of a test or a report, even though they do receive a grade. For an example, see "Born Free" in Chapter 12.

with less hands-on or technical experience than boys and thus, are at a disadvantage when it comes to laboratory work, it is particularly important to provide female students with alternative activities where the playing field is more level (Spragg, 1993), such as written reports, surveys, or social-interaction-type laboratory studies, and so forth.

Present Material in Diverse Ways

Presenting material through written, oral, and visual media takes into account each student's cognitive strength and allows students to learn at their own paces. Employ lectures, worksheets, laboratories, readings from the textbook and supplementary sources, and class discussions. By monitoring what learning techniques work best for each student, you can learn to develop lesson plans that help every student to succeed.

Improve Existing Measurement Methods

In addition to adopting alternative modes of assessment, you should also strive to improve existing measurement methods. For example, you can modify multiple-choice tests to include questions about why students responded as they did (Bailey, 1992). Or teachers might construct exams that place more emphasis on essay questions and explanation rather than simple parroting of facts. Experiment with how you administer tests and evaluations (Pollina, 1995). Consider untimed or take-home tests. Alleviating the time constraints on exams may help reduce students' anxiety and emphasize logical, organized thinking and more in-depth analysis of the material (NECUSE, 1996). Varying the exam structure might also help. Using a combination of multiple-choice, true-false, problem-solving, and essay questions may provide students with better opportunities to demonstrate their understandings of the course material by allowing them to present their knowledge in a variety of ways.

IMPROVING EXISTING MEASURES

✓ Sample Short-Answer Question (Biology)

Answer two out of three of the questions carefully and thoughtfully.

1. Anatomy—Structure of cells

   a. Describe the cell theory.

   b. Are cells alive? Explain.

   c. Compare and contrast eukaryotic and prokaryotic cells. Draw, label, and describe 5 major structural differences.

2. Physiology—Mechanisms and control of entrance and exit of materials

   a. Draw and label cell membrane structure.

   b. Describe osmosis and give examples (hypertonic, isotonic, hypotonic solutions).

   c. Describe facultative diffusion and give examples.

   d. Describe active transport and give examples.

3. Evolution—Discuss cell specialization. Give examples in your discussion. Speculate about future specialization.

   a. Unicellular

   b. Colonial

   c. Multicellular

   d. Diversification

✓ Essay Questions (Advanced Biology)

1. Based on your study of genetics and evolution, write a one-page essay on how new species, such as Darwin's finches, could form and succeed on the Galapagos Islands. Use specific details, examples, and definitions.

2. Using the levels of organization of life as a backbone, write an essay on your concept of biology as the study of life. Use concrete examples from your reading, labs, worksheets, and articles. Include all of the major topics we have studied: genetics, evolution, anatomy, physiology, development, and ecology. You certainly can include labeled drawings and activities.

3. Using your knowledge of genetics and evolution, write a detailed two-page essay supporting the existence of biotechnology companies and outlining the significance of molecular biology research.

10

Making Science Relevant

Students frequently believe that science classes are too difficult or too time-consuming. Likewise, they often fail to see the potential benefits of science and how science fits into the so-called big picture (NECUSE, 1996). As a result, many students never take even a single science course.

Scientific Careers

Educators must emphasize the value of science education. Teachers must explain why it is imperative that all high school graduates have some science experience before entering college. Many of the available job opportunities in the 21st century will be in science, technology, and related fields. Even in nontechnical fields, scientific skills will increasingly be necessary as computers and technology permeate every facet of society. More important, teachers must emphasize the vast career opportunities available to professionals with science-related degrees and advise students about the science courses that serve as prerequisites to those careers.

It is also important that we refute the notion that the only option open to students of science is to become laboratory researchers. Teachers should point out that scientists work for governmental agencies, are employed in industrial professions, and do not merely work with test tubes and beakers. Nor is science exclusively a technical field; it informs disciplines, such as psychology, that are intimately connected with ethics, human relations, the legal system, and so forth. To make this point, call attention to people who majored in science but went on to nonscientific careers for which a solid understanding of scientific principles can be valuable such as law, education, science writing, and public policy (NECUSE, 1996).

Some type of science education is necessary for astronauts, anthropologists, architects, doctors, psychologists, software engineers, and veterinarians.

Women Role Models

Female role models, whose confidence and achievements demonstrate that women can attain positions of power and prestige within the scientific community, inspire and motivate young women.

Female role models, whose confidence and achievements demonstrate that women can attain positions of power and prestige within the scientific community, inspire and motivate young women. Teachers (with the aid of school systems, it is hoped) should work to provide these role models in several ways. Here are eight possibilities:

1. Incorporate profiles of women who have succeeded as scientists, inventors, anthropologists, biologists, computer technicians, astronauts, chemists, or physicists into class lectures, discussions, and activities. Emphasize that it is possible to balance a career in science with a family or other serious life commitment. Provide young students with examples of both women and men who are able to pursue their interests outside the lab without sacrificing their careers.

2. Choose a textbook with pictures, not just brief mentions, of women scientists. Images are much more powerful in communicating (and combating) stereotypes.

3. Select female teacher assistants whenever possible.

4. Invite guest speakers. Invite young women studying or working in technical fields, female scientists, even female financial planners to discuss ways of paying for college (Sanders, 1994). Whether scientists, researchers, or graduate students, guest speakers provide young girls with opportunities to speak informally with women and men in science-related fields and learn about their lives (Campbell, 1993).

5. Assign students to research female scientists. In conjunction with the greater effort to implement alternative assessment measures and to incorporate ways of exploiting girls' linguistic aptitudes, teachers can assign students to research a female scientist and then to present to the class the woman's contributions to modern science. The project has a dual effect: It teaches the class about one woman's accomplishments, and it places another woman (the female student) in a position of authority.

6. Decorate your classroom. Teachers should post photographs, drawings, or portraits of female as well as male scientists in their classrooms (Mosca & Shmurak, 1995). It is also useful to pin up a calendar that celebrates the achievements of women scientists and call students' attention to it at the beginning of each new month.

Help students find mentors among parents, professionals, or even older students.

7. Help students to find mentors. Nothing is more important to girls' developing sense of self than a mentor (AAUW, 1996). Both male and female mentors can be effective, but it is particularly important to expose female students to women who are successful in science and related fields. Seeing someone like themselves who has succeeded in a given career affirms girls' notions that that occupation is appropriate for them (NECUSE, 1996). This mentor could be an older student, a teacher, or a volunteer from the community.

8. Support the hiring and retention of female faculty. One important, but frequently overlooked, solution is the hiring and retaining of female faculty who can serve as role models. The presence of women teachers communicates a strong message, according to the National Resource Council: It signals to female students that women are respected and treated fairly.

Teachers are students' most important academic role models. Share with your students how you yourself became interested in science and discuss what your life as a scientist is like.

WOMEN IN SCIENCE

Gladys Anderson	Diane Fossey	Emily Howard Stowe	Dr. Sylvia Mead
Melitta Bentz	Dr. Rachel Fuller Brown	Christine Jones-Forman	Lise Meiter
Elizabeth Blackwell	Lillian Gilbreth	Martine Kempf	Maria Mitchell
Annie Jump Cannon	Dr. Alice Hamilton	Mary Leakey	Bette Nesmith
Gerty Theresa Cori	Elizabeth L. Hazen	Rita Levi-Montalcini	Cecilia Payne-Gaposchkin
Jocelyn Crane	Edith Hinkley Quimby	Lady Ada Lovelace	Marje Sklodowska
Carrie Matilda Derick	Dorothy C. Hodgkin	Dr. Maria G. Mayer	Rosalyn Yalow
Marie-Josee Drawn	Dr. Leta S. Hollingworth	Christa McAuliffe	
Dr. Gladys A. Emerson	Grace Hopper	Barbara McClintock	

Independent Thinking and Problem Solving

Every part of a science course should require students to think independently and solve problems, because these are the basic skills of scientific inquiry. Designing your course with independent work at its center also benefits your students psychologically: You encourage them to express themselves, which tells them they do have something important to say; you trust them to choose topics and design projects.

Here are some ways you can encourage independent thinking and problem solving:

Use Research Papers and Independent Laboratory Experiments

Library research papers and independent laboratory projects are great ways to give students ownership of their educations: They choose topics that interest them, and they take responsibility for meeting incremental deadlines and monitoring their own progress.

Independent projects also help students develop and refine the methods of laboratory inquiry. Independent laboratory projects foster self-expression and self-confidence and assess precision of thought and execution of tasks. Because the students design the entire experiment, rather than simply perform an activity described in a textbook, they must apply the principles of scientific investigation. To solve the problems they set for themselves, they must consider the types of data they have collected and choose a method for their analyses. Often, they select and apply sophisticated techniques for analyzing statistics.

Allow Students to Select Topics and Activities

Try to give students a choice of topics or activities whenever possible. It encourages them to take ownership of their educations and ensures that (at least, within the given subset) you are working with the topic that interests them most. Likewise, it allows students to select activities commensurate with their cognitive strengths so they have more confidence of their success.

Student-selected independent projects that provide opportunities for hands-on learning keep students motivated and involved.

EXAMPLES OF INDEPENDENT LAB EXPERIMENTS

✓ **Effects of Alcohol and Aspartame on Alaska Peas (Nutrition)**

Students divided plants into three groups: Group A, the control; Group B, treated with alcohol; Group C, treated with aspartame. Students charted growth of leaves and drew conclusions. See a full description in Chapter 11, p. 62.

✓ **Study of Left-Handedness and Right-Handedness in Homo Sapiens (Genetics)**

✓ **Drug and Alcohol Use of Teenage Girls (Drug Use)**

Students developed hypothesis from desk research, then designed survey for peers at other schools. They tabulated and analyzed results, drawing conclusions about reasons for discrepancies between data and their original hypothesis.

Opportunities for Experiential "Hands-On" Learning

Hands-on activities are vital supplements to a standard lecture format, because they allow the student to grasp hold of the concepts being presented. No other method ensures as effectively that students engage the material. Laboratory work is only part of hands-on science; remember, we want to teach students that science is not restricted to the lab and that science is relevant to the world and their lives!

As Jim Applegate (1995), Professor of Natural Resources at Rutgers University, points out, students accustomed to a traditional, memorize-and-regurgitate model of education can find the transition to one emphasizing hands-on activities frustrating. To ease this transition, educators should provide students with arrays of activities and projects to choose from. That way, they can choose those that reflect their interests and strengths.

Field trips, projects, movies, and guest speakers, aside from their intrinsic benefits—making science more interesting and raising social awareness—are excellent opportunities for teachers to segue into hands-on activities.

Creative Projects (All Ages)

Hands-on activities can be combined with field trips, multimedia presentations, guest speakers, and outside reading assignments to make them more effective.

Kevin Collins (1981), a science teacher at Stidwell Junior High in Idaho, suggests independent or group projects consisting of plant or insect collections, algae or tree specimen collections, or microscope photography projects. Spragg (1993) recommends designing and building musical instruments when studying sound and researching musical instruments from different cultures. Explore the technology involved in hair care, design new and improved hair care or beauty products or futuristic inventions. Build compound machines from simpler ones. Have students design their own inventions. Use journals or record keeping of natural phenomena such as seasons or movements of clouds. Students might consider projects in astronomy or horoscopes.

HANDS-ON ACTIVITIES

Use in Conjunction With . . .

✓ **Greenhouse Field Trip (younger students)**

Students receive seeds or seedlings for plant of their choice (from selected set). They plant the seeds in greenhouse or window box, and each tends his or her own throughout year. They chart growth and observe how their plants respond to different stimuli (how much water, light, etc., it needs). See Chapter 14.

✓ **The Animal Project (younger students)**

Students select from among several animals that can be purchased for the class (rats, mice, guinea pigs, gerbils, chameleon, iguana, etc.), then research, care for and observe the animal throughout the year. See "Animal Project" in Chapter 11, p. 57.

✓ **Cell Models (younger students)**

Students construct plant or animal cell models out of materials such as clay, styrofoam, macaroni, yarn, beads, or wood, or whatever materials they can come up with themselves. I have found that students really enjoy this activity as it lets them be creative and artistic. See Chapter 13, p. 93.

✓ **Creative Writing (all ages)**

Inspired by scientific topics studied in class, students write essays, stories, poems or plays.

✓ **Nature Hike, Movie About Photosynthesis, Trip to Botanical Gardens or Arboretum.**

Use to teach photosynthesis and basic life cycle.

✓ **Zoo Trip, Movie about Animal Behavior, *Born Free*.**

Use to teach evolutionary adaptation, biological classification or basic observation skills.

✓ **Science in Literature**

Read excerpt from Henry David Thoreau's *Walden*, watch performance of *Inherit the Wind*, or read poems inspired by science.

Age-Appropriate Topics

Today's young people face a variety of stressful and confusing issues: teenage sex and pregnancy, drug and alcohol abuse, depression, suicide, and eating disorders are more prevalent than ever before. Consequently, the task confronting educators is monumental: We must not only present students with the information they need to make the right decisions regarding these issues but also convince them that it describes their situation; it isn't just dry statistics in a book. On the other hand, because adolescents are brimming with curiosity and energy (stimulated in large part

ACTIVITIES TO TEACH HUMAN SEXUALITY

✓ Pregnancy Testing

Demonstrate how an over-the-counter pregnancy test works. Discuss accuracy, the actual biochemistry, and how the product was engineered. See Chapter 13, p. 106.

✓ AIDS and Epidemiology

Each students has a test tube of colored water. One of the test tubes contains a low concentration of acid. Each student mixes his or her tube with one other student's. Then, all students test the pH of their tubes in a mock HIV test. Nearly 90% of the tubes will be infected, demonstrating how rapidly sexually transmitted diseases can be spread. See Chapter 13, p. 137.

✓ Television Critique

Watch and discuss segments on teen pregnancy from the popular media. Assign students to write essays about what they learned.

✓ Book Report

Assign students to write book reports on teenage sexuality as it appears in works of fiction of their choice. Reports should focus on the messages the books present about sex.

✓ Magazine Evaluation

Examine teen magazines. What kind of messages do they present about sex and dating? Assign students to compare and contrast information about pregnancy, abortion, or dating presented in a popular magazine to what they've learned in class.

by these very same issues), the teacher also has a tremendous opportunity to excite them about science.

Human Sexuality

Teaching human sexuality has never been easy, and now it is harder than ever: Sound-bite politics has polarized Americans over AIDS, homosexuality, abortion, and rape—all issues science teachers haven't traditionally been expected to discuss. If we are to combat the notion that science isn't relevant to life, then we can no longer pretend that sex is only a biological phenomenon.

The biological aspects of sex are the easiest to teach. An excellent way to show teens that their science classes are allies in their quests for self-discovery is to integrate some of the "popular" sources into your classroom activities. These can include novels, nonfiction books for teens, TV shows, and magazines. Ask students what books or articles they've read or TV shows they've seen in recent weeks that dealt with sex. Assign them to write essays about the presentation of sex issues within the story. What knowledge from science class can they apply to the text? Videos of *The Oprah Winfrey Show* or *Sally Jesse Raphael*, where pregnant teens discuss their motivations and problems, are excellent points for the class to discuss. Episodes of popular TV dramas also often address social issues such as abortion, rape, and pregnancy. After obtaining parental consent, show scenes from these programs to your class, and discuss the views presented and whether or not they are valid. MTV's *Real World* showcased a gay character who was HIV positive (he eventually died of AIDS). The program, though clearly not high art, presented the issues of epidemiology and civil rights effectively.

ACTIVITIES TO TEACH HUMAN DEVELOPMENT

✓ "Your Baby" Adoption (Life Science)

Students "adopt" a baby, made from a sack of flour. They use creativity to dress and decorate their babies, then use interdisciplinary skills of writing and research to create teaching aids for the baby to learn science. See Chapter 12, p. 77.

✓ Embryology of the Chick (Biology)

Students each receive and dissect a fertilized hen's egg. They answer questions about the development of the zygote. See Chapter 13, p. 123.

✓ Skull and Bones: The Inside Story (Advanced Biology)

Students dissect a boiled mammal skull, examine skull and bones from human skeleton, and answer questions about the purposes of each bone. See Chapter 13, p. 113.

✓ Abortion Debate (Biology)

The teacher presents neutral scientific evidence of fetal development at various stages of pregnancy. Students work in small groups to prepare arguments either for or against abortion during first, second, or third trimesters in various extenuating circumstances. Afterward, each group presents its arguments to the class.

Human Development

Human development is especially relevant to teens because, being in various stages of puberty, they are witnessing some of the most radical stages of development in their own bodies. Likewise, it demonstrates that biological concepts relate directly to humans, not just to simple organisms. Girls, especially, are interested in prenatal human development because it builds on the foundations of traditional "motherhood" toys and games with which many of them played.

Alcohol and Drug Abuse

Discussing with teens the risks involved with drinking alcohol and taking drugs helps students better understand how drugs affect their bodies. Teaching students about the dangers of drugs and alcohol can help them steer clear of bad choices and feel more comfortable saying "No."

Authorities from professional or volunteer organizations can lend credibility and seriousness to your discussions of complicated issues, such as alcohol and drug abuse.

Nutrition and Eating Disorders

Discussing the signs of anorexia and bulimia helps students become aware of issues they face every day and teaches them what to do if they or a friend are in trouble—how to get more information and where to get help. Eating disorders are of particular interest to girls, because many more women than men suffer from them (males account for only 5% to 10% of cases).

Our increasingly appearance-obsessed culture is driving more and more teenage girls into anorexia and bulimia.

FIGHTING ALCOHOL & DRUG ABUSE

✓ Peer Education

Students watch peer educators from a local college present a skit on drug or alcohol abuse, then participate in class discussion led by the educators.

✓ Alcoholics Anonymous

A speaker from Alcoholics Anonymous presents information about the dangers of alcohol.

✓ Poster Campaign

Students make posters against drug or alcohol abuse.

✓ Teenage Alcohol and Drug Use Survey

Students create a survey about teenage drug and alcohol use. The teacher arranges for it to be administered in area schools. The class tabulates and discusses results.

✓ State Police

A speaker from the state police visits the classroom to discuss either the dangers of drunk driving or the risks of drug abuse. In either case, the officer brings home the seriousness of the problem with anecdotes and statistics.

✓ Group Research Project

Students break into small groups to research teenage drinking and drug addiction. Some groups should search for statistics; others should seek out information about specific teens, to attach faces to the numbers.

ACTIVITIES TO TEACH NUTRITION

✓ Draw Your Body Image (all ages)

Students draw pictures of their bodies and submit them, anonymously, to the teacher. Then, the teacher passes out overhead-projector slides and markers for the students to draw their "ideal" bodies. Show samples on overhead projector. Class discusses what are healthy and an unhealthy body images. See Chapter 13, p. 131.

✓ Cafeteria Lab (all ages)

Students observe and catalog what other students are eating at lunch. Each meal should be evaluated. Is it nutritious? Does it signal an eating disorder? See Chapter 13, p. 132.

✓ Eating Disorder Watch (all ages)

The teacher introduces and discusses anorexia and bulimia, with statistics on the numbers of teenagers who suffer from them. Invite speakers from local support groups.

✓ Food Fair (all ages)

Students and the teacher bring in samples of various types of food (fast food, "down-home" food, ethnic cuisines, etc). Students prepare balanced meal from selections on various tables. The teacher evaluates meals and provides approximate calorie, fat, and vitamin counts. See Chapter 13, p. 136.

✓ Intestinal Report (all ages)

Students write a story, play, or poem about nutrition or eating disorders. They are encouraged to personify foods, vitamins, and the gastronomic track. See Chapter 12.

✓ Independent Lab Projects (Advanced Biology)

Students study the effects of diet pills, aspartame, or various foods on animal or plant life, through an experiment of their own design. See Chapter 11.

Current Trends in the Field

Discussing current ideas in science with your students helps show them that science is not a list of facts they have to memorize but instead, a constantly evolving field. Molecular biology, computer applications, environmental issues, and new treatments for diseases all interest students. Because they will become increasingly important, computer applications, biotechnology, and neuroscience must be emphasized in today's science courses. Neuroscience and biotechnology, the human genome project, DNA sequencing, and cloning can also spark students' interests because of their intrinsic interest value and also because they receive so much attention in the media.

Because technological and scientific advances almost inherently raise ethical issues, discussions about current events in science can be good opportunities for students to apply argumentative reasoning and communication skills they've developed in other areas of study. In addition, emphasizing that science must, at least in part, be governed by political, ethical, and practical rules underscores our argument that science is not sterile and limited to the lab..

There are unlimited ways to bring current scientific developments into your class discussions:

Cutting-edge scientific developments, such as the successful cloning of sheep, provide opportunities for ethical as well as theoretical discussions.

The Internet

The Internet may not yet have lived up to its hype, but it is still an incredibly useful tool for students and educators. It is inexcusable for a science teacher to be afraid of this new technology: If we are afraid, how can we ask students not to be afraid of science?

Especially in upper-level biology classes, teachers should make sure all of their students gain experience working with computers. They should learn how to connect to servers and browse some appropriate web sites. They should also learn to execute particularized searches to find information about specific topics.

Internet exercises, such as scavenger hunts, help students use the latest scientific tools to access the most up-to-date information. Likewise, web sites where scientists exchange ideas and hash out arguments show that science is always changing and alive. Some of these online debates require students to bring to bear the analytical skills they've acquired in the course to understand and evaluate the various arguments.

The Internet is a great resource for articles, pictures, and discussions on current scientific topics.

CURRENT SCIENCE ON THE INTERNET

✓ Internet Scavenger Hunt

Students search for articles and Web sites relating to classroom topics and print search results. They then choose a site and write a "Web Site Review" or article summary. See Chapter 15, p. 192.

✓ E-mail "Lab Partners"

Students exchange notes with E-mail pen pals from other science classes around the country. The teacher works with students to develop survey questions for pen pals. Chart data for laboratory analysis.

✓ Web Sites and Scientific Forums

Students choose a scientific ethical issue and post a comment in Web site chat room or forum. See Chapter 15.

QUICK TIPS

✓ Do
- ☞ Provide articles of varying scientific sophistication and for all reading levels.
- ☞ Bring in "Guaranteed Hit" articles you find in the newspaper or on TV and focus on them for class discussion.
- ☞ Push students to think and evaluate the articles: What's the writer's point of view? Is it logical? How could you argue against it?
- ☞ Connect science to politics and ethics.

✓ Don't
- ☞ Repeat, *don't* allow students to get away with busywork. Their reports should demonstrate that they've thought about the articles, not just rephrased them.

✓ Publications to Watch

FDA Consumer Magazine
Population Today
The American Biology Teacher
Science
Scientific American
National Wildlife
National Geographic
National Geographic World
Sierra Club
Self
Seventeen
Glamour
Harper's
The Atlantic Monthly
The New York Times
The Discovery Channel
The Public Broadcasting System

Supplementary Readings

Keep a notebook in your classroom of supplementary articles about current developments, research methodology, and related topics. Students should read articles and write reports according to a schedule you devise. They can also refer to these articles for information for their experiments or research papers. Encourage students to bring articles they stumble on at home or in the library so other students will have a chance to read them.

Some examples of recent "current science" opportunities include discussions of DNA-identification techniques in conjunction with articles about the O.J. Simpson case, discussions of eugenics and "laws of nature" in relation to successful sheep cloning, and discussions of "Olestra" fervor in the context of lessons on nutrition and eating disorders. Keep your class in the back of your mind as you read the newspaper and watch TV, and ideas will leap out at you!

Science Outside the Classroom

Perhaps the best way to show that science relates to the real world is to go out and observe science in action.

Social Activism

Many people are reluctant to become involved in social activism. Students may be unsure about what they can do to help, how to get involved, or where to get information. It is helpful to provide concrete suggestions for what they can do about world and community problems and even to make some type of activism a class requirement.

One of the best ways to connect science class to the outside world is to conduct class outside the classroom— the world is your laboratory!

Links Between Students and the Scientific Community

Creating links between students and scientific professionals reinforces the message that science is a practical area of study (Wolfson, 1993). Schools should form partnerships with the scientific community (libraries, professional laboratories, universities), bring professionals into the classroom, and take students to visit scientific organizations. Exposing students to science work settings (professional laboratories, engineering facilities, computer centers) can be extremely helpful; seeing scientists, both men and women, demonstrating applied science at work in the real world lets students know that science is practical and can help reverse stereotypes or mistaken beliefs about what scientific work is really about (Wolfson, 1993).

As already mentioned, indicating to students the correlation between actual research in the field and their course work can increase interest in a particular area of study. Demonstrations of the application of principles learned in your course can include, but needn't be limited to, trips to local factories and businesses. You can also bring examples to class. For instance, when you discuss the skeletal system, bring in a human skeleton and various X rays, casts, and splints from a local hospital.

SOCIAL INITIATIVES

✓ **Recycling Experiment**

Students develop plans for home recycling, then try to implement them. Afterward, they write a report on efficacy and draw conclusions about potential impediments to larger recycling efforts.

✓ **Would You Drink This?**

Students conduct purity tests of local tap and rain water.

✓ **Write Your Congressman**

Students write lobbying letters to congressman about issues of their choice: conservation, pollution, genetic cloning, wetlands, and so forth.

✓ **Campus Cleanup**

Class volunteers to pick up trash around the school grounds. Teacher should take the opportunity to discuss biodegradability.

✓ **Conservation Center Visit**

Class learns about conservation efforts going on in your area. Trip to wildlife refuge, habitat preserve, or even waste-water treatment plant.

✓ **Plant a Tree**

Students receive seedlings for various types of trees. They plant the trees in locations of their choice. Class discusses deforestation and global warming.

REVIEW: TACTICS THAT WORK

These techniques prove essential in implementing an approach to science that emphasizes individuality, inquiry, and improvement.

1. Provide a relaxed, secure environment.
2. Develop effective study skills.
3. Because learning differs for each student, alternative assessment measures and varied approaches to each unit will ensure that information reaches every student. Whereas some students learn through reading, others need to hear and repeat lessons, and still others may learn most effectively through written work. Lectures, worksheets, laboratories, review books, coloring books, and current articles address the many different learning styles present.
4. Emphasize the value of science education.
5. Provide women role models.
6. Encourage independent thinking and problem solving and independent projects.
7. Unique activities and projects keep science interesting and fun. Field trips, projects, movies, and guest speakers make science more real.
8. Include group work and collaboration.
9. Age-appropriate topics help students relate better to the material presented in class.
10. Clear guidelines give students goals to work toward and show them how to reach them.

With effective guidance, students realize that learning is not automatic but is a precise and methodical process.

a. Students must complete all assignments to receive course credit. Establishing a standard of hard work presents science as a learned discipline, not an innate talent given to only certain people.
b. Requiring corrections on tests convinces students that they learn from their mistakes as well as their successes.
c. Assign, collect, and evaluate written work every day. Students embark on a kind of dialogue through their written work as well as through their participation in class. Grading and evaluation become less stressful if they occur regularly.

11. Present science outside of the classroom to connect classroom lessons to everyday experience. Field trips, projects, movies, and guest speakers make science more real and raise social awareness.
12. Discussing current trends in science reminds students that the process of learning is never ending. Computer applications, biotechnology, and neuroscience should be emphasized, because these are the frontier interdisciplinary fields of the 21st century.

Scientific Skills Are Life Skills

Science education should emphasize life learning and life skills (Gardner, Mason, & Matyas, 1989). The perceived relevance of science to everyday life experiences is a crucial factor in facilitating interest and participation at both the precollege and college levels. Lab sections, in particular, are often effective places to stress such applications if they relate directly to the course work. As students learn how science affects their lives, they are given incentives and are empowered to act. Thus begins the process of asking questions—the first step in the scientific method!

Part 3

Classroom Activities

By encouraging independent, creative thinking and effective use of natural strengths, teachers can inspire female students to greater intellectual heights, encourage well-founded self-confidence, and equip them with vital skills for dealing with the world of the 21st century.

Let the fun—and the excitement and the successful learning—begin!

Elizabeth Winter

Jessica Bradley

Rachel Lifter

Katharine Sidell

Devon Ciampa

Dana Hall students

SOURCE: Printed with permission.

SOURCE: Printed with permission.

11

Independent Projects

Chapter 11 begins Part 3 with the presentation of independent projects covering three areas of study. The first, the Animal Project, is described in detail and includes a sampling of extracts from student reports to give you an idea of the enthusiasm and thoughtfulness that can be evoked through use of these and similar activities. Chapter 11 is composed of the following projects:

Scientific Method: Animal Project

Encourages Taking Responsibility
Fosters Collaboration
Enhances Process Thinking
Relates to the Real World

Purpose:

- To learn to apply scientific methodology
- To learn to collect, organize, and analyze data
- To learn to take accurate measurements
- To gain specific insights into an animal's growth and development
- To learn to work with others in a group
- To explore your own capabilities
- To learn to handle long-range responsibility

Materials:

Mice, guinea pigs,
    hamsters, rats, gerbils
Animal cages
Food (laboratory pellets)
Wood shavings
Water bottles
Metric rulers

Method:

1. Divide students into groups of 3 or 4.
   a. Each group must have at least two members who can take the animal home for weekends and holidays.
2. Select an animal. Rats, mice, guinea pigs, gerbils, or hamsters are best because of size and ease of handling.
3. Decide where the animal will be purchased (pet store or friend).
4. Visit library to get information about caring for the animal; a written report is required (see guidelines to follow).
5. Choose an animal cage in the animal room.
6. Make a list of 10 questions to be answered during the year. Narrow it down to five answerable questions. Here are some examples:
   a. How much food does a hamster eat each day?
   b. What kinds of food do hamsters eat?
   c. Do a hamster's ears continue to grow?
   d. Does a hamster gain weight every day?
   e. How does the animal respond to bright light? Can it tell the difference between different colored lights?
   f. Can your animal learn to remember its way through a maze?
7. Design charts for feeding and cleaning schedules and for data taking. The group is responsible for taking care of the animal.
   a. Cleaning and feeding are to be done before or after school or during study periods.
   b. Data is recorded every other day or after school or during the first few minutes of class. Each student must have a copy of the data for the animal group. Metric units are used.
8. Progress reports will be due once per month.
9. Each group writes a final report that includes purpose, method, results, and conclusions (approximately 20 pages in length).

Each Day:

Change the water.
Feed the animal every afternoon.
Remove used litter from cage.
Remove ruined food from the cage.
Check to see if animal is healthy and lively.

Each Week:

Clean the cage completely.
Check to make sure you have all needed supplies. If not, stock up!

Results:

Results should include the following:

1. Data tables (length of body, ears, feet, weight, maze time, amount of food, etc.)
2. Graphs of data; use the date of measurements for the x axis and values of measurements for the y axis.

3. Written observations about the animal's daily behavior. Here are some examples:
    a. When (or how much) does the animal sleep, exercise, eat, or play?
    b. What playthings does the animal like or dislike?
    c. What pleases or frightens the animal?
    d. Write down everything the animal does.

Conclusions:

This section contains an interpretation of numerical and observational information. What has been learned about the animal's growth or behavior or feeding or cleaning? What has been learned about responsibility and peer interaction? This is a very detailed section! What would you change if you could do this activity again?

We can learn a lot by studying animals. Animals can be used for testing basic concepts in psychology, medical testing, and even to discover new things about how our bodies work.

Animal Project Report Guidelines

Check grammar, organization, clarity, amount of data taken, accuracy of graphs, title page, table of contents . . . *everything!!!*

Note for the Teacher

It takes about 3 weeks to get the students organized. Begin the project in the fall and make the final paper due in the winter.

Frequent Questions and Answers Concerning the Animal Project

Q: Who pays for the animal?

A: The Science Department will reimburse parents who buy the animals. The students, however, must bring the receipts for the animals to the Science office or to class. A maximum of $15 is allotted to each group for buying its animal.

Q: Who supplies cages, food, and materials for the animals?

A: The Science Department will supply cages for the animals while they are at school. Students will be allowed to take the cages home with their animals for weekend and vacation visits. Rabbit cages, however, cannot be taken home, so students with rabbits must supply cages if they plan to take their rabbit home. The department will furnish food and bedding for the animals.

Q: What happens if the animal dies?

A: When this happens, an effort will be made to replace the animal with one from another group. If another animal must be bought, the students in the group that lost the animal must share the expenses for replacing the animal.

Q: What happens to the animals at the end of the year?

A: Homes must be found for the animals. This is the responsibility of the students.

Q: What are students expected to learn from this project?

A: The project involves caring for and studying the development and behavior of animals. This offers the students an opportunity to learn about responsibility, getting along with peers, graphing, using a balance, the metric system, long-range planning, and how a scientist learns new things.

Q: Where can I go for more information?

A: See the following list of resources.

Resources

Barrett, K. (1986). *Animals in action.* Berkeley, CA: University of California Press.

Barrett, K. (1987). *Mapping animal movements.* Berkeley, CA: University of California Press.

Holley, D. (1994). *Animals alive!* Niwot, CO: Roberts Rhinehart.

Moore, R. (1989, April). Inching toward the metric system. *The American Biology Teacher, 5*(4), 213-218.

National Association of Biology Teachers. (1990). *The responsible use of animals in biology classrooms.* Richmond, VA: Byrd.

Orlans, F. B. (1977). *Animal care from protozoa to small mammals.* Reading, MA: Addison-Wesley.

Settel, J. (1985, May). Study of animal behavior in zoos. *The American Biology Teacher, 47*(5), 270-274.

Zim, H. S., & Hoffmeister, D. F. (1987). *Mammals.* New York: Golden.

Sample Project Excerpts

Mice (Algernon and Q-T-Pie)

Purpose

The purpose of this experiment is to learn about different kinds of animals, learn how to work in groups, and learn long-range responsibility. We will use scientific investigation to answer some questions we have about our animals. Weight, body length, tail length, distance traveled, maze time, and body length without tail were measured.

Conclusions

Cleaning: We needed to clean a bit more than we did. We didn't really follow the chart, which made it hard for us to remember whose turn it was.

Feeding: The mice liked to eat cheese, lettuce, and sunflower seeds best. They didn't seem too appealed by the cereal and oatmeal.

Measurements: In the beginning, Algernon weighed more than Q-T-Pie but Q-T-Pie got pregnant and gained weight. Algernon was more consistent in the maze and took a shorter time to do it. Algernon's tail was longer. Q-T-Pie's grew and shrunk. Pregnancy didn't stop Q-T-Pie from climbing the tightrope. Her width increased a lot due to her pregnancy.

Observation: The two mice got along very well but had to be separated when Q-T-Pie became pregnant. They both despised being picked up by the tail and being kissed. At first, Algernon bit people until he learned that he wouldn't get hurt.

Organization: When we first started, we thought it would be very easy to get organized. How wrong we were!

Purpose: (Hypothesis); 2 pages

(e.g., To learn and use metrics, group skills, responsibility, scientific method, about animals, etc.)

Method:

Drawings and sample; charts and description! Very detailed! 5 to 10 pages

Results:

Graphs, data tables, daily observations; 5 to 10 pages

Conclusion:

Interpretation of data and results; 4 to 5 pages

Mice (Wooly and Loco)

Purpose

The purpose of doing this animal project was so that we could get a sense of responsibility and learn to divide the responsibility and our time. We also wanted to see how animals grew and developed, behaved and ate. We were to learn this by gathering data and turning the information into graphs. By measuring and weighing, we learned how our animals developed. We learned how they behaved by daily observations. We learned what and how much they ate. Length and weight were measured.

Conclusions

Introduction and responsibility: Our group assigned a different person each day to feed and clean the mice, but it turned out that each person came in every day to help and play with the mice. Everyone was responsible in taking their turns and doing their shares.

Feeding: To maintain a healthy diet, we fed the mice food and water daily. We started with rodent pellets, then tried different cereals. The mice liked Shredded Wheat best and were fed it regularly. Cheerios and milk made the mice a little sick.

Measurements: We measured length and weight once a month. The length of the mice were very close throughout and was continually increasing. However, their weights were often very different although neither were starving.

Behavior: Loco was a little more playful than Wooly, who liked to sleep longer. They were intelligent, never bit anyone, and became less afraid. They did not fight with

each other and even showed behaviors of caring for each other, such as one mouse bringing the sick one food and playing together.

Mice (Buttercrunch and Nestle)

Purpose

There are many reasons to do the animal project. We learn how to measure and weigh. We are responsible for food and cleaning. We learn to do experiments and learn participation. We learn watching skills. Length, weight, body length, tail length, leg length, and ear length were measured.

Conclusions

Feeding: Feeding is very important in helping the animals survive. We created schedules, which were successful but sometimes, required a little reminding. The mice enjoyed the sunflower seeds most and sometimes astonished us by eating a whole bowl of food.

Cleaning: Mice can get a very strong odor if their environment is not cleaned regularly. This job was not as fun as the feeding, but we made schedules, which everyone followed.

Measurements: The only measurement that showed no change was the mice's ears. Weight and length varied but generally increased. Nestle was shorter than Buttercrunch but weighed more.

Responsibility: The essential parts of responsibility were feeding, cleaning, measuring, and observing. We made charts to organize each responsibility. We followed these charts pretty well and ran into no problems.

Hamsters (Archie and Betty)

Purpose

The purpose of this project is to answer 10 questions: How much weight do the hamsters gain; what kind of food do they eat; which one will grow more; how can someone tell the difference between a boy and girl hamster; how many hours do they sleep in a day; how many times do they mate; do they fight; what to do if they fight; once the hamsters have been separated, can they be reunited; and what is the maximum number of babies a female can have in one year. Weight and number of sunflower seeds eaten were measured.

Conclusions

At the beginning, we thought the animal project would be tons of fun and pretty easy. It's still tons of fun but not as easy as we anticipated. We all needed to be responsible and cooperate. In our group, this was not always done. We did not act as responsible as we thought we could be.

Cleaning: At the beginning of the project, charts were made as to who would come in when. This was not followed a lot of the time. One person that did the best job of cleaning was Alea. When it was not even her day, she cleaned up.

Feeding: This part was not hard; the hamsters were with food 95% of the time. Our hamsters ate very nutritiously, including seeds, dry corn, vitamins, cereal, and hamster treats.

Measurements: This part of the paper was the hardest. We all could have helped by going to the animal room as scheduled to take measurements. Both hamsters had huge increases in weight. Betty went from 28 to 156 grams and Archie went from 29 to 142 grams. The hamsters grew a lot in length for the first 3 months, then did not change. We decided that they stopped growing.

Behavior: We found that the hamsters disliked loud noises, being with strange hamsters, water dropped on them, milk, and hot areas. Hamsters liked being held, attention, humans, yogurt, cereal, and graham crackers.

Hamsters (Peanut and Acorn)

Purpose

The objectives of the seventh-grade animal project were to gain specific insights into an animal's growth and development, to learn how to make scientific observations, to learn how to present data in graphs, to develop an understanding of teamwork and responsibility, and to have fun learning. Weight, breadth, length, length of ears, and maze time were measured.

Conclusions

Responsibility: The first thing we did was make a schedule. This helped us to organize ourselves and be responsible. Our animals' lives depended on it.

Group work: We fought, we yelled, we laughed, we learned. One of the most important reasons for doing this project is to work together with our peers. Not only will we use this skill in school but also in our careers. We thought our group did very well in this part of the project.

Organizing: We had to make schedules for feeding and cleaning. A few times, we did not stick to the schedule, especially at first, but luckily, this was not often.

Cleaning: We always thought it would not be so pleasurable to clean a hamster's cage. Now, we realize that it takes only 5 extra minutes and is no hassle.

Feeding: It is very important to feed your hamsters the right amount. It is a good idea to give them a little more food than usual so they won't starve.

Behavior: We learned about the different objects in the cage and the way each had its function. Our group learned about the hamsters' comfort. We learned where they like their house, food, exercise wheel, and where they go to the bathroom.

Measurements: Both hamsters grew in ear length, breadth, and length. Peanut did not improve in the maze. Acorn did, a little. The hamsters enjoyed the bird seed treat best of all.

Designing Experiments:
Independent Laboratory Experiments

Fosters Self-Expression and Self-Esteem
Teaches Scientific Method
Fosters Responsibility and Task Ownership

Purpose:

- To learn how to design and monitor a scientific experiment
- To research a topic of your choosing and apply lessons from science class
- To refine library skills, statistical analysis techniques, accuracy in measurement, and critical thinking

Materials:

Some, but not all, of the following equipment is necessary for independent laboratory experiments. Students and teacher should work together to adapt experiments to suit available materials.

Laboratory space (greenhouse, animal room, classroom, home, etc.); students must be sure that their experiments can be completed without interruption or interference from outside forces.

University, college, or municipal library

Traditional laboratory equipment (Bunsen burners, test tubes, beakers, filtration pipette, etc.)

Additional equipment: Students can buy or make additional equipment. When possible, school can allocate a budget of $60 for each group of four students.

Method:

1. Defining your experiment (4 weeks)
   a. Your teacher will distribute a list of potential topics. Look them over to see whether one of them interests you. If not, speak to the teacher about choosing another topic.
   b. Go to a local library (preferably, a college or university library) to gather information about your topic. You should try to gain as much knowledge of your topic as possible and start to think about what questions you could answer with an experiment.
   c. Write up a proposal for your experiment. Follow the same format used by your lab book. Each experiment should be designed to prove or disprove a hypothesis about a topic. Develop a pilot study (a shortened, simplified "test" of your experiment).

   d. Order any necessary materials, arrange for surveys to be conducted, and so forth.
2. Preparing for your experiment (2 weeks)
   a. Implement your pilot study. Your teacher will evaluate the project's success and suggest any changes you may need to make before you conduct your actual experiment.
   b. Write the relevant and important information you learned from your library research into a brief report. This report is called a *literature review*. It is due before you proceed to Step 3.
3. Design your actual experiment and implement it.

Results: (3 weeks)

1. Analyzing the experiment
   a. Graph your results to make them easy to read and understand.
   b. Calculate χ^2 values.
   c. Determine conclusions.
2. Final report due
   a. Review of literature: As an introduction to your experiment, write a brief report (5 typed, double-spaced pages) summarizing the current knowledge about your topic. Describe any similar experiments to the one you designed and what aspects of your research prompted you to choose your experiment.
   b. Pilot study: Write a description of your pilot study, including a brief synopsis of your purpose, method, and results. Describe in your conclusions any modifications you made for your actual study.
   c. Actual study: This part of the report should be a complete laboratory report, including purpose, method, results, and conclusions. Be sure to explain why your experiment proved or did not prove your hypothesis and what steps you would take in further experiments to correct any errors.

Notes for the Teacher

The most difficult part of independent laboratory assignments is ensuring that students choose experiments that (a) are manageable and (b) teach them an important scientific lesson. Students' descriptions of five tried-and-tested project ideas follow:

1. Sleep Deprivation in Mice
2. Biochemical Links Between Plants and Animals
3. The Effects of Alcohol and Aspartame on Height, Number of Leaves, and Dry Weight of Alaska Peas
4. The Effects of Ethyl Alcohol on White Lab Mice
5. The Influence of Varied Light Allowances on the Feeding Behavior of Carassius Auratus

1. Sleep Deprivation in Mice

Purpose

Studying sleep deprivation in mice reflects the effects of sleep deprivation in people. By measuring food intake, attitude, respiration, timed maze, energy, and weight averages, we shall be able to draw conclusions about sleep deprivation.

Materials

60 Mus Musculas mice: 20 per group.
20 cages with bedding: 3 per cage
Mouse food
1 maze simple enough for a mouse
Stopwatch
Three colored markers
Light with timer
Vibrating mechanism
Scale

Method

1. Setup: We divided the mice into three groups: Group 1, the control group; Group 2, the "loss of sleep" group; and Group 3, the "movement" group.
   a. The control group was fed regularly and left undisturbed so that they could sleep whenever they wanted.
   b. Group 2, the "loss of sleep" group, was fed regularly, on the same schedule as Group 1. We kept the mice in Group 2 awake, using lights and, when necessary, by shaking their cages, for most of the day. We only left them undisturbed for 4 hours of each 8 a.m. to 9 p.m. period.
   c. Group 3, the "movement" group, was fed regularly. Their sleep was partially disturbed by vibrating mechanisms attached to their cages. No extra lights were added.
2. Observations: We developed criteria for observation and a schedule for which a group member would observe the mice at each scheduled point in the day. Because we could not observe the mice at night, the experiment ran from 8:00 a.m. to 9:00 p.m. Observation criteria were
   a. Body weight (recorded daily)
   b. Behavior (recorded daily)
   c. Maze time (recorded daily)
   d. Hourly tables of sleeping habits
   e. Amount of food consumed (recorded daily); each group received one cup of food per day. Observers recorded whether previous day's food has been consumed before adding additional food.

Results:

Data tables showing the criteria as observed over a 5-day period.

Conclusions:

Chi-Squares and Percentage Differences in Weight

According to the chi-squares, the biggest weight increase occurred in Group 3 (movement group), with a total percentage difference form Day 1 to Day 5 of 9.27, which gives us a p value of .001. This shows us that the weight change from Day 1 to Day 5 was significant in this group. The least weight change occurred in Group 2 (light group), which disproves our hypothesis of increased food consumption in sleep-deprived mice. This figure came out to a .5072 total percentage difference from Day 1 to Day 5, which gave us a p value of .50, showing that the overall difference from beginning to end was insignificant.

The chi-squares also show us that there was no significant difference in weight between the light and control group or between the movement and control group. The biggest total percentage difference in weight on the last day was between the light and vibrations group. Because both of these groups were sleep deprived, this difference disproves our hypothesis that there is a difference between sleep-deprived mice and rested mice.

Chi-Squares and Percentage Differences in Maze Times

The biggest total percentage difference from Day 1 to Day 5 was in Group 2 (light group). The maze times in the light group had a 156.44 difference, which gives us a p value of .001. This makes the difference significant statistically. This is compared to a 14.69 total percentage difference in the control group and a 4.05 total percentage difference in the movement group. Neither of these figures are significant. This shows us that the light on the mice may have been more of an irritant or stimulant than the movement was.

The total percentage difference among groups shows us that the most significant difference in maze times on the last testing day was between the light and movement group. This may support the conclusion that there is a difference between the performance of mice in the light and movement groups.

Examples of Advanced Biology Projects
Undertaken at Dana Hall School

1. "The Effects of Alcohol and Aspartame on
   Height, Number of Leaves, and Dry Weight of
   Alaska Peas" (1992)
2. "A Study of the Characteristics of Left- and
   Right-Handedness in Homo Sapiens" (1985)
3. "Water Analysis" (1988)
4. "The Influence of Light Exposure Periods
   Upon the Feeding Behavior of Carassius
   auratus" (1980)
5. "Finding a Biochemical Link Between Plants
   and Animals: An Advanced Biology Laboratory Experience"
6. "The Effects of Cigarette Smoke on Alfalfa
   Grass and Bean Plants" (1989)
7. "Adolescent Sexual Behavior" (1994)
8. "Drug and Alcohol Research Project" (1994)
9. "The Relationship Between Smell and
   Memory" (1996)
10. "Drug and Alcohol Use of Teenage Girls"
    (1996)
11. "Effect of Abscisic Acid on Zinnia Plants:
    Design of an Advanced Biology Laboratory
    Experience"

2. Biochemical Link Between Plants and Animals

Purpose:

The plant hormone *abscissic acid* (ABA) and the animal
hormone *diethylstolbesterol* (DES) are very similar chemi-
cally. Do they have similar effects on wheat seed germination?

Conclusion:

Abscissic acid inhibits germination of wheat seeds at high
concentrations and DES inhibits germination of wheat
seeds at low concentrations. Overall, however, there was
no significant difference in the total effects of ABA versus
DES at any given concentration.

3. The Effects of Alcohol and Aspartame on Height, Number of Leaves, and Dry Weight of Alaska Peas

Purpose:

To show the effects of alcohol and aspartame on the
height, number of leaves, and dry weights of Alaska pea
plants

Method

3 Groups:

Group A = Control
Group B = Alcohol
Group C = Aspartame

Results:

Control: 975 cm
Alcohol: 712.37 cm
Aspartame: 766.56 cm

Alcohol stunted growth; alcohol prevented normal leaf
growth. Dry weight of alcohol group was below normal.
Aspartame group had fewer leaves than control group.

Conclusion:

Alcohol and aspartame both stunted the growth of the
plants and the number of leaves grown. The alcohol affected the plants more than the aspartame.

4. The Influence of Varied Light Allowances on the Feeding Behavior of Carassius auratus

Purpose:

To determine the qualitative influences and precise quan-
titative effects of differing exposure periods to artificial
light on the feeding activity of Carassius Auratus. We
sought to ascertain whether there is a significant difference between the feeding motivation exhibited by dark-
adapted fish and that of light-adapted or normal animals.

Conclusion:

In all instances, the sequence of chi-square values indicated definite significant differences between the feeding
behaviors of dark-adapted goldfish, light-sensitized goldfish, and control or "normal" organisms. Those fish receiving only 6 hours of light per day appeared to deviate
most from the norm established by the control fish.

Research:
Advanced Biology Research Papers

Fosters Taking Responsibility
Incorporates an Alternative Assessment Measure
Is Interdisciplinary

Purpose:

- To learn to collect and analyze information from secondary sources.
- To learn more about a biology-related topic of your choice.
- To practice writing a research paper on a scientific subject.

Method:

1. Choose a topic that deals with some area of life science. Be sure the topic is specific and focused so that you can treat it fully in a 10-page report. Also, do some preliminary research to ensure that there are significant scientific studies for you to use for reference. Present your topic to your teacher for approval.

2. Use a minimum of 20 reference sources (science journal articles only). Take your notes on index cards so that before you begin writing, you can organize your findings. Be sure to keep accurate records of bibliographic information on your note cards.

3. Make an outline of your proposed report. It should have the following parts:

   I. Introduction
      A. Opening statement (introduces the topic and gets reader interested)
         Example: "Hepatitis-B is as prevalent among Americans living at or below the poverty level as it is in the hardest-hit areas of the Third World: China, India, and Africa."
      B. Thesis (an argumentative statement, or opinion, that the evidence you collected will prove)
         Example: "The response of the American health care system to the increased volatility of Hepatitis-B has been inadequate."

   II. Major Point
         Example: Only 5% of inhabitants of poverty-stricken areas currently experiencing Hepatitis-B epidemics receive immunization injections.
      A. Supporting data
      B. Supporting data
      C. Supporting data
   III. Major Point
         Example: The public transit advertising campaign intended to raise awareness about Hepatitis-B in urban areas has been sadly ineffective.
      A. Supporting data
      B. Supporting data
      C. Supporting data
   IV. Major Point
         Example: The steady increase in Hepatitis-B cases treated in inner-city hospitals suggests that even "bursts" of public awareness campaigns and immunization drives have had little impact.
      A. Supporting data
      B. Supporting data
      C. Supporting data
   V. Conclusion
      A. Restatement of Thesis
      B. Summary of Main Points
      C. Expansion of Thesis

4. A first copy of your paper is usually turned in sometime during the last week of November or the first week of December.

5. This paper is to be completely footnoted or endnoted with a thorough bibliography, title page, and report cover.

6. A research paper is a synthesis of all the past and recent knowledge accumulated on a given topic. In the course of your library work, you will find key names and experiments. (Concentrate on them!)

7. Come in for help as needed!! Have fun!

Writing in Science

The activities included in Chapter 12 are designed to join students' developing skills in English usage with their increasing scientific knowledge, thereby enriching and furthering both. These 10 activities fall into six topics as follows:

**Classification:
Diversity of Life**

**Fosters Creativity
Is Interdisciplinary
Incorporates Alternative Assessment**

Purpose:

- To demonstrate your knowledge of the diversity of organisms through creative writing
- To show a link between science and arts
- To have fun!

Method:

Based on your concept of the diversity of organisms, choose one of the following writing assignments. You have read over 15 chapters. . . . You have a tremendous amount of information from which to draw inspiration.

- The writing should be approximately three pages long.
- Be sure to include scientific terms that you have learned from class.
- Check grammar, spelling, and accuracy!
- Be prepared to share with the class!

1. Make a classification tree.

   a. Draw or build a visual aid that illustrates the branches of biological classifications (kingdoms, phyla, orders, etc.). Each "branch" of your classification tree should include drawings, photos, or other representations of the types of organisms it includes.

   b. Demonstrate your knowledge of how the classification system works with some kind of "key" to your display. Your key should explain why each branch of the tree differs from the others.

   c. Be as creative as you like. Your tree will be graded based on accuracy, creativity, and the amount of information you present (i.e., its value as a tool for learning).

2. Write a play.

   a. Dramatize an aspect of the diversity of organisms in a short play. For example, you could demonstrate how the food chain works in a particular ecosystem. Each of your characters could be organisms from different kingdoms, phyla, and so forth of that system (blackberries, fir trees, a deer, a human).

   b. Your play should include a description of the setting (the ecosystem, for instance), the performers (organisms), and stage directions (illustrating biological processes and plot twists).

   c. Be creative! What if microscopic organisms could talk about pollution? How does a parasite feel about its host? What do trees whisper about? Be sure to demonstrate your knowledge of biology. Your play will be graded based on accuracy, creativity, and the amount of information about biology you present.

3. Create an illustrated storybook.

   a. Write a children's story about one of the biological processes we have studied. Maybe you want to write about mitosis or meiosis as though the cell were a community of thinking beings (like a town, for instance). Maybe some of the cell's inhabitants revolt and refuse to fulfill their biological roles (making it a cancerous cell!). Or you could write about an animal and its mother, describing the processes of biological development—"The Ugly Duckling" and "Horton and the Egg" are good examples to follow, but you need to be more scientifically specific. Come up with your own idea!

   b. Write and illustrate your story for a fourth grader. How can you render the biological concepts you've learned into simple terms that a kid could understand? Clear drawings will help a lot!

   c. Remember, this is *your* assignment. Have fun with it. You'll be graded on creativity as well as on the accuracy and amount of information about biology processes you present.

4. Compose some poetry.

   a. Part of a poet's job is to catalog the world around him or her (usually, exclaiming in awe or amazement; sometimes, crying out in protest). Look, for example, at Walt Whitman's "Song of Myself," or any poem from *Leaves of Grass.* Write a poem that describes a natural process or laments a natural disaster. Be sure to use your knowledge of biology to make your poem accurate and convincing. Play with biological terminology—see if, removed from the textbook and placed into art, it can become funny or moving.

b. You can imitate one of your favorite poems (or even make fun of it!) or come up with a poem that is entirely your own. You will be graded based on your creativity and the accuracy and amount of information you present about biology.

5. Create a newspaper.

   a. Using whatever materials you like (clippings from real magazines and newspapers, drawings, photos, beads, string, glitter, etc.), make a science newspaper. Maybe you want to pretend your paper is *The Underwater Social Journal*, read exclusively by high-society frogs. Maybe it's a scandal sheet about pol-lution and other environmental abuses (a wetlands advocate called *The Muckraker*, for instance).

   b. Include both "hard" science articles—articles that describe scientific processes and problems—and ethical articles—about social problems that relate to science.

   c. Make sure your newspaper is visually interesting, with lots of illustrations. Remember, the newsstand is crowded, and you'll go out of business if the paper doesn't sell.

   d. Don't be limited by these suggestions. There's no limit to the assignment or what you can do with it. Just remember that you'll be graded on creativity and on the quality and quantity of biological information you present.

6. Select your own writing assignment, but it must be approved by the teacher. Make sure that it will allow you to prove you know a lot about biology!

**Ecology:
Born Free**

Purpose:

- To practice reading comprehension, outlining, and taking notes
- To learn about conservation and animal behavior.

Method:

1. Read and discuss *Born Free* (Adamson, 1960)

Day 1: Read and underline the important ideas in pages 1-39 of *Born Free* ("Preface," "Cub Life").

Discussion Questions:
a. What is anthropomorphism?
b. What evidence does the writer of the preface see in Elsa's story to suggest that animals do have complex feelings and intelligent responses beyond instinct and conditioning?
c. What do you think a *conditioned reflex* is? What about a *release mechanism*?
d. Were George and Joy Adamson right to adopt the lion cubs?
e. What is a *pride*?
f. What are some ways that the Adamson family used to "train" the lion cubs?
g. What are some of the games the lion cubs played? What was the purpose of these games?
h. What is Joy Adamson's opinion about race? Explain.

Day 2: Read and underline the important ideas in pages 40-56 of *Born Free* ("Elsa Meets Other Wild Animals").

Discussion Questions:
a. What anti-instinctual behavior did Elsa demonstrate in this chapter? Why do you think she acted this way?
b. What are some examples of instinctual behaviors?
c. What are some of the species of animal you learned about in this chapter?
d. When Elsa "played" with the elephants, was it an example of instinctual behavior or not? If you think

it was, why do you think lions do this? If not, why did Elsa do it?
e. Can you think of a reason Elsa's paws became damp when she was nervous?

Day 3: Read and underline the important ideas in pages 57-79 of *Born Free* ("Elsa Goes to the Indian Ocean" and "The Man-Eating Lions").

Write one or two key themes or ideas in the margins of each page that you read.

Think about possible ideas for a skit based on a scene from *Born Free.*

Discussion Questions:
a. Why did Pati die? What were the symptoms of her ailment?
b. Do you think it was right for George to kill the "troublesome" lion? What kind of lions should be allowed to live? Who should decide?
c. Why did George have to kill the goat Elsa caught for her? What does this tell you about lions and hunting?
d. Did you notice anything in "Elsa Goes to the Indian Ocean" about race?
e. What did you learn about the Boran tribe in "The Man-Eating Lions?" What do you think Joy's attitude toward the Boran was? Was it sophisticated or simplistic?
f. How did George Adamson deal with man-eating lions? Can you think of any other way the problem could be solved? Why do some lions attack and kill people?
g. How big is a lion's heart?
h. How did Elsa feel about the death of the man-eating lions? Was she angry with George and Joy?

Day 4: Read and underline the important ideas in pages 80-109 of *Born Free* ("Safari to Lake Rudolph").

Write one or two key themes or ideas in the margin of each page that you read.

Write a poem or draw a picture of your favorite scene from *Born Free.*

Discussion Questions:
a. What are the anal glands ? What do you think they are for?
b. How did the Adamsons manage the close cohabitation of Elsa and the donkeys on the safari to Lake Rudolph? What does this teach you about the instinctual behaviors of lions?
c. Why did Joy have to grease Elsa's paws? What does this say about the environment lions ordinarily live in?
d. What are poachers? Why is it important to stop them? Are there poachers in the United States?
e. What do you think are the causes of poaching? How can poaching be stopped?
f. Were the Adamsons right to beat Elsa for attacking the donkey?

Day 5: Present skits on *Born Free*.

Day 6: Read and underline the important ideas in pages 110-125 of *Born Free* ("Elsa and the Wild Lions").

Take at least one page of notes on the chapter.

Discussion Questions:
a. Why did Elsa run away to the wild lions? Are lion mating behaviors similar to or different from human mating behaviors? Do you think Joy is right to describe rival lionesses as "jealous"?
b. Why did Elsa return to the Adamsons? Were they right to try to lure her back?
c. Why do you think "the call of the wild" became stronger as Elsa grew older?
d. What type of area did the Adamsons choose to release Elsa? Why?

Day 7: Read and underline the important ideas in pages 126-145 of *Born Free* ("The First Release").

Go to any library and find out three interesting facts about lions.
a. What do you think about Joy Adamson's attempt to imagine the male lion's thoughts, "Don't you know lion etiquette? How dare you, woman, interfere with the lord while he is having his meal . . . "?
b. What are some ways the Adamsons tried to get Elsa to socialize with wild lions? Think of several of the failed attempts. Why did they fail? What does this tell you about the way lions form prides?
c. What was the Adamsons' second strategy for getting Elsa to socialize with wild lions?
d. How did the Adamsons try to train Elsa to hunt? What does this tell you about the way mother lionesses rear their young in the wild?
e. What did Elsa's virus suggest to the Adamsons?
f. Why did the Adamsons decide that the game reserve was not an appropriate place to train Elsa to survive in the wild?
g. Why didn't Elsa become pregnant from her mating with male lions while in season?

Day 8: Read and underline the important ideas in pages 146-171 of *Born Free* ("The Second Release").

Make a one-page outline of the chapter.

Discussion Questions:
a. How did George teach Elsa to kill?
b. What is some evidence that Elsa had instinctual knowledge of how to kill?
c. Why do you think Elsa had such an extreme reaction to the water buffalo George shot?
d. How did Elsa protect the carcass of the water buffalo from the hyena? What do you think a wild lion would have done?
e. Why did Elsa drag the carcass of the buffalo through the river? Was this an example of instinctual or learned behavior?
f. Later, Elsa drags the recently killed waterbuck across the river. Would a wild lion do this to bring a kill to its pride?
g. What do you think it means when Joy writes of Elsa's mating, "It was obvious she was in love?"

Day 9: Read and underline the important ideas in pages 172-196 of *Born Free* ("The Final Test").

Take at least one page of notes on the chapter.

Discussion Questions:
a. What was Elsa's first kill? Why do you think she chose that species?
b. Did Elsa adopt any curious hunting behaviors she learned from the Adamsons?
c. Why do you think Elsa allowed Nuru to cut the throat of her buffalo kill? Can you think of an example of a similar behavior that might occur in the wild?
d. Why do you think Elsa returned to the Adamsons after she found a pride? Why did she finally leave them?

Day 10: Read and underline the important ideas in pages 197-220 of *Born Free* ("Postscripts," "L'envoi").

Write one or two key themes or ideas in the margins of each page that you read.
a. Why didn't Elsa join a lion pride?
b. Should the Adamsons have released Elsa? What were the potential dangers to Elsa and to the people living around her?
c. Were the Adamsons right to continue visiting and observing Elsa after she was released? Do you think that their visits prevented Elsa from fully adjusting to life in the wild?

2. After finishing the book, a test can be given or, as an alternative assessment, a final project may be done.

Fosters Creativity
Is Interdisciplinary
Incorporates Alternative Assessment

Purpose:

- To discuss the process of protein synthesis, the ultimate function of DNA
- To demonstrate your knowledge in a creative way

Method:

Your job is to "translate" the scientific knowledge you've acquired into writing. You may choose any of the following assignments. There is no minimum length for the assignment, but you *must* present all the steps of protein synthesis. Have fun!

1. Write a play, using performers, setting, and stage directions, to show how DNA works to synthesize proteins.
2. Write journal entries about your "Voyage Through Protein Synthesis." Describe the molecules involved and the places you visit. Maybe you'd like to look at Jules Verne's *Journey to the Center of the Earth* for inspiration.
3. Pretend that you are the factory manager for protein synthesis. Make connections between each step of protein synthesis and the steps of an assembly line.
4. You have entered the Mr. or Ms. Protein Synthesis Contest. Who can make the protein first?
5. Write a personal letter to a human friend about how you, his or her protein pen pal, were born.
6. You are a traffic police officer trying to prevent a traffic jam during protein synthesis. Describe what you have to keep straight for protein synthesis to take place.
7. Write a poem, "Ode to Protein Synthesis." Your poem should include the complete process.

Genetics:
Another Type of Fingerprint

Teaches Analytical Thinking
Is Interdisciplinary
Fosters Collaboration

Purpose:

- To practice reading and analyzing scientific writing
- To think critically about scientific arguments
- To explore how science is changing criminal investigation

Method:

1. Read the following passage:

We are all aware that each of us has unique fingerprints caused by the pattern of ridges that cover the skin of our fingertips. Almost every detective show on television has a line about "dusting for prints." But advances in forensic science may well make dusting for prints a thing of the past. Forensic scientists can now examine a new kind of evidence left at the scene of the crime and tell with almost certainty whether it came from a particular individual!

The evidence can come from a drop of blood, a piece of skin, or even a strand of hair left at the scene of the crime. The evidence is obtained using a technique called *restriction fragment length polymorphism* (RFLP) analysis, also known as DNA fingerprinting. DNA fingerprinting takes advantage of the differences in the sequence of bases in the DNA of different individuals. The DNA at certain places, or loci, in the human genome shows significant variability. This variability makes the DNA of each person unique. By analyzing the sequence at these particular spots, a pattern can be established that will be unique for each individual, no matter what the source of DNA. So DNA extracted from a hair left at the scene of the crime will give the same RFLP pattern as DNA from a drop of blood drawn from a guilty suspect.

The technique is a fairly simple one. DNA is digested, or chopped up, using a restriction enzyme. These enzymes recognize a particular sequence of bases within a piece of DNA and cut the strand of DNA at the place where that sequence occurs. Because of genetic variation, these sequences occur in different places along the DNA in each individual. The pieces generated by the enzyme can be separated according to their sizes in an electric field. The separated fragments are then probed with pieces of DNA that bind to specific sequences within the fragments. Depending on where the enzyme cuts the DNA, that sequence may be part of a large fragment in one person's DNA and a small fragment in another person's DNA. Repeating the technique with different restriction enzymes and different probes generates a "map" that is unique for each person. By comparing the map from a piece of evidence to that obtained from a suspect, it can be determined whether the two DNA samples came from the same person. When four different probes are used, the odds of obtaining an identical pattern from two unrelated samples are 13.5 million to one!

2. Based on the preceding reading, answer the following questions. If the answer cannot be determined from the passage, simply write "Answer not given."
   a. From what kind of evidence can scientists collect data for DNA fingerprinting?
   b. What are the odds that scientists will make a mistake when performing DNA analysis?
   c. What kind of difference do scientists observe in DNA from different people?
   d. Will a sample of skin yield a different DNA structure from a sample of blood?
   e. What are the odds that the DNA from two unrelated samples will match?
   f. How do scientists know the odds against matching DNA from unrelated samples?

3. Using investigative reasoning (on a separate sheet of paper), develop hypotheses to explain each of the following scenarios. Explain why you think your hypotheses are reasonable, and suggest ways (if they exist) your hypotheses could be tested.

a. Donald P. Hockstraw is the prime suspect in a murder investigation in Miami. The victim, Susie Hockstraw, was his wife. Police have established that Donald was the beneficiary of his wife's $2 million insurance policy.

When interviewed, Donald claimed that he could not have murdered his wife because he was sailing his yacht (alone) from Nassau to Miami on the day she was killed. His business associate, Marv Druger, reported receiving a radio message from Donald, apparently aboard ship, on the day of the murder, and the marina on Nassau reported that Donald's yacht, Insider Trader, did leave its slip at the marina at 9 a.m. on the day in question. Because it takes a full day to sail from Nassau to Miami, the police know that if Donald really was on board Insider Trader, he couldn't have murdered his wife.

Susie Hockstraw's body was found dead, from a fatal gunshot, in a Miami hotel room. Police found no physical evidence (fingerprints, skin cells, blood, etc.) that anyone but the deceased had been inside the room. They did find hair and traces of blood on Insider Trader. DNA analysis showed that the hair and blood belonged to Donald Hockstraw.

If Donald killed his wife, how can you explain the presence of his DNA aboard Insider Trader ? How can you explain the absence of evidence at the crime scene? Do you think there's enough evidence to prove, beyond a reasonable doubt, that Donald did it?

b. You are a defense attorney, and Nigel Peabody is your client. He is on trial for stealing almost $100,000 from the First National Bank where, coincidentally, both you and he are account holders. Whoever robbed First National Bank was able to bypass the alarm system and break in after hours—there were no witnesses. Unfortunately, Nigel has been arrested and released on technicalities for three other bank robberies, so police immediately rounded him up.

The prosecution's case hinges on DNA analysis of hair samples found both in the carpet outside the bank's main entrance and in front of one of the teller windows. You're sure Nigel is innocent. Think of at least three ways you can convince a jury that you're right.

Notes for the Teacher:

Answers:

2a. A drop of blood, piece of skin, or strand of hair.

2b. Answer not given.

2c. They observe that sequences occur in different places along the DNA in each individual. The sequences may also be part of either a large or a small fragment in each person's DNA.

2d. If the sample comes from the same person, it will have the same DNA structure whether it comes from skin or blood. If the blood is from one person and the skin from another, then the DNA will be different.

2e. The article asserts that the odds are 13.5 million to one against.

2f. Answer not given. This is one of the arguments lawyers for O.J. Simpson made against DNA evidence—that is, that DNA analysis has not been used long enough to determine accurately the odds against a match. The argument is overstated: though exact odds may vary, their order of magnitude is certain.

3a. The case depends on two main factors: (a) Was Donald Hockstraw aboard his boat the day of the murder, and (b) does the absence of DNA evidence at the crime scene prove his innocence? Clearly, the blood and hair aboard Insider Trader doesn't prove when Donald was there. It could be from any time or even planted by a third party. Nor does the absence of DNA evidence prove Donald wasn't at the crime scene, though it does make it seem unlikely. Perhaps he vacuumed the room, or police were simply unable to turn up any evidence. Without placing Donald at the crime scene, even though his alibi is weak, Donald couldn't be convicted by any responsible judge or jury—the evidence against him (the motive of the insurance policy) is only circumstantial. Police should look for the gun and for a third party (someone either drove the boat or murdered Susie).

3b. Nigel should definitely get off. (a) The attorney should show that Nigel has been at the door and the teller window of First National many times as a customer, at which times he might have left the DNA samples. (b) The attorney should have a secondary expert demonstrate all the other DNA samples found at the scene—workers, other customers, and so forth. (c) The attorney should suggest that the police want to entrap Nigel (as a former felon) and that they might have planted the evidence. (d) The attorney might also mention the possibility of a faulty match and get his expert to show how that might happen. Police should be able to find evidence of the money itself in Nigel's possession if he really committed the crime.

Genetics:
Send in the Clones

Purpose:

- To learn about bioethics and biotechnology
- To understand what biologists are doing today

Method:

The biotechnology industry has already had an enormous impact on medical diagnostics and treatment. Ethical questions around new treatment methodologies and accessibility will continue to arise. Environmental and agricultural changes due to biotechnology applications may well be decided by public referendum. Informed decision making requires an understanding of the issues and outcomes related to the technology in question.

Read and think about the following hypothetical situations (they might come true in the future!). Answer the questions and provide several reasons for your answer.

Prometheus University has a strong biochemistry department. After years of hard work, scientists at P.U. have developed a process that they believe will allow them to clone (create an exact duplicate of) an entire human being by using the genetic information contained in a single cell.

As soon as this breakthrough is made public, P.U. is flooded with applications from people who want to be cloned for various reasons.

You have been hired by the biochemistry department to screen the applications and decide who should and should not be allowed to participate. What would be your response to the following applicants and why?

1. Bob and Ethyl have tried to have a baby for 9 years without success. Ethyl finally became pregnant 6 months ago and recently gave birth to a premature infant. The baby had no genetic abnormalities but developed respiratory problems and died a week later. Bob and Ethyl arranged for skin cells from their baby to be kept alive in cell culture. They are both getting older and are afraid they won't be able to have a healthy baby the regular way.

Should P.U. clone them a baby from the cells they have saved?

2. Fred and Rachel have a healthy newborn baby. Both Fred and Rachel have histories of severe heart disease in their families, and they are afraid their baby may grow up to face heart disorders, too. They want to clone a copy of their baby and keep it in storage (under sedation) so that if their baby grows up and needs a heart transplant, they'll be sure to have a compatible donor ready. (Fred is very wealthy, so money is no problem.)

Should P.U. clone them a baby?

3. Lavinia is a brilliant 90-year-old scientist who is working on a cure for cancer. She is still years away from perfecting the cure, but her results are very promising. Recently, Lavinia was diagnosed as having a rare blood disease and has only a few months to live. Lavinia wants to clone herself to keep her genes on earth; her hope is that her clone will grow up and resume her work where she left off.

Should P.U. clone Lavinia?

4. Mohammad and Safora have just had a baby. Safora herself was a twin and wants her baby to have the chance to grow up with a constant identical best friend as she did.

Should P.U. clone them another baby?

5. George is President of the United States. He has found a young man named Joe and a young woman named Jane. Both are in excellent health, with good eyesight, quick reflexes, strong muscles, and the ability to follow directions. George is requesting that P.U. clone several million copies of Jane and Joe, which will be turned over to the army when they grow up. These Joes and Janes will replace the current army so nobody would ever have to be drafted again.

Should P.U. clone an army for George?

Issues to Explore Further:

1. Should the clone have the same legal rights as the original?
2. Should the clone have the right to terminate its own existence if it wants to?
3. Should a clone have the right to request further clones to be made of itself?

SOURCE: Goldberg and Moulton (1992). Used with permission.

Genetics:
Your Baby Adoption

Purpose:

- To learn about the responsibilities of child rearing
- To research a genetic disorder and how to care for an infant who suffers from it
- To demonstrate that you can synthesize material we have learned into learning aids for children

Materials:

One 5-lb bag of flour per student
Two white plastic bags per student
Art supplies:
    Felt markers
    Cloth pipe-cleaners
    Colored tape
    Yarn
    Glitter
    Glue
    Cotton balls, and so forth

Method:

1. Adopting a baby

   Because of overpopulation and your love of children, you have decided to adopt a newborn baby. . . . Fortunately, you have studied evolution and animal behavior! Adopting a baby will be a big responsibility but a lot of fun, too.

   a. Get 2 plastic bags and one bag of flour from the adoption agency.
   b. Open the flour, and pour it into one of the plastic bags. Then, seal the bag by rolling and stapling it, or close it with a twist-tie. Now, place it inside the second plastic bag, and seal it, too.
   c. Decorate your baby using the art supplies.
   d. Make "official" adoption papers.

2. Research

   Unfortunately, your baby is afflicted with a genetic disorder. Take it to the hospital (teacher's desk, where you will draw a slip of paper from a hat) to find out what disorder it has.

   You'd better do some library research to find out what you need to do to provide your new child with nourishment and support. Read up on caring for infants and about the genetic disorder from which your child suffers.

3. Care

   a. Based on your research, make a list of daily responsibilities for the proper care of your baby.
   b. Choose at least two things from the following list of activities to ensure proper care and development of your baby:

      - Write a book or story about animal behavior, especially learning and reading. You'll want your baby to be reading by 4 years of age.
      - To teach your baby about human evolution, draw and describe the stages, changes, and adaptations.
      - Based on your systems chapter, make a coloring book.
      - Read and summarize a child development article on the acquisition of language.
      - Create your own activity!

Note for the Teacher:

Any genetic anomaly is fine, but some suggestions are color blindness, hemophilia, sickle-cell anemia, phenylketonuria, Tay-Sachs disease, cystic fibrosis, brachydactyly, Down's syndrome, cleft palate, spina bifida, or hypothyroidism.

Gender Awareness: Mother of the Year Contest

Teaches Gender Awareness
Fosters Collaboration
Is Interdisciplinary

Purpose:

- To stimulate discussion of traditional attitudes about child rearing and the new awareness of men's and women's roles
- To learn to present conflicting opinions in a group setting and to argue effectively to advance your case

Method:

1. Read the following passage about the Mother of the Year Contest:

You have been selected to serve on the National Selection Committee (composed of several subcommittees of 6 persons each) for the Outstanding Mother of the Year Contest. Your mission is to pick one from the six regional winners whose qualifications are described in the following section. The selection must be the unanimous decision of the group.

A spokesperson for your committee will be asked to give the reasons each candidate was selected or rejected.

Candidates:

Ms. Ann Semmler, San Francisco, California
Sponsor: Association for Volunteer Sterilization

Age 29—husband is sales representative for IBM—won court case establishing the right to be sterilized, regardless of number of children—adopted her two children, a boy 4 and a girl 2—graduated Phi Beta Kappa from Vassar—teaches a course on women's rights at the University of California, Berkeley—president of local chapter of National Organization for Women (NOW)—member of Zero Population Growth and Sierra Club—hobby: gourmet cooking

Mrs. June Hunter, Boise, Idaho
Sponsor: American Association of University Women, Greater Boise Branch

Age 37—husband manages Montgomery Ward store in Boise—mother of three boys, all honor students in high school and junior high—BS, Idaho State University; MS, University of Idaho—elementary school teacher, 10 years

of experience—past president of Idaho Education Association—presently programming a new math series for slow learners—led push for equal pay for equal work for women teachers and state employees—Democratic candidate for Idaho House, 1974

Mrs. Jean Fixon, Cedar Bluffs, Nebraska
Sponsors: Lincoln Kiwanis Club and Daughters of the Pioneers, Nebraska Chapter

Age 72—mother of 11, grandmother of 73, great-grandmother of 29—resides on farm, built 160-acre homestead into 2,000-acre dairy and fruit farm—one of the original homesteaders in Nebraska, she and her late husband built sod hut as their first home—Nebraskan "Mother of the Year" in 1954 and again in 1969—stated in recent newspaper interview, "Children are the spice of life and the salt of the earth."

Ms. Joann Green, Chicago, Illinois
Sponsor: Cook County Zero Population Growth

Age 32—unmarried—one son, 4 years old—lives with environmental lawyer, past 3 years—MA from the University of Chicago in Sociology, Magna Cum Laude—organized Chicago chapter of NOW—presently writing book, "The Future of Women in Eliciting Corporate Responsibility"—refused honorary doctorate from Antioch College as irrelevant—organized a day care center that involves both men and women and provides familylike relationships for the children.

Mrs. Betty Baker, Syracuse, New York
Sponsor: Syracuse Chamber of Commerce

Age 49—immigrated from England at 18 years old—husband is prominent corporation lawyer—mother of 5 girls and 3 boys; 5 are graduates of City College of New York, three in high school; one son has doctorate in nuclear physics from MIT, one is in cancer research—graduated from high school at age 40—same class as second daughter—Girl Scout leader since her mid-20s—Matron of Eastern Star—Republican precinct worker—Ruling Elder, Episcopal Church—winner of Syracuse Women's Club's Outstanding Woman of the Year, 1989

Mrs. Jayne Watson, Atlanta, Georgia
Sponsor: Retail Clerks Union, AFL-CIO

Age 52—migrated from Montford, Alabama, after husband died, 5 years ago—mother of five plus two adopted children—three sons have been killed in the service—last death in Vietnam War—employed as a clerk in chain supermarket—does considerable volunteer work at Community Action Center—member of NAACP for 15 years—not in leadership role—winner of Montford County Fair Cooking Contest in 5 of 8 years she entered.

2. In your group, select one member to write down your responses; then, decide on the following:

   a. Select your winner.

   b. What qualities do you consider most important in your selection? Which did you consider weaknesses? Why?

   c. Would your selection be the same if you were asked to choose one of these women to be your own mother? your own role in life?

   d. What trends and issues influenced your selection? Would your choice be the same if you were older or younger?

   e. What is the ideal family size? Take a poll of your classroom, and figure the average number of children per family needed, in view of the current U.S. population's age distribution and immigration policy, to achieve zero population growth.

   f. What attitudes and trends in our society encourage continued population growth? Do these attitudes have any other effects?

SOURCE: Developed by participants of the 1971 NSF Summer Institute, University of Cincinnati.

Drugs and Human Systems:
Orphan Drugs: Are They Fair?

Relates to Real World
Fosters Social Activism
Fosters Critical Thinking
Incorporates Alternative Assessment
Is Interdisciplinary

Purpose:

- To learn about orphan drugs
- To learn how science and ethical issues interrelate
- To demonstrate the ability to think critically and analytically about scientific issues

Method:

As of 1989, *human growth hormone* was classified as an *orphan drug*. Sometimes, researchers discover new drugs that will be useful only to small numbers of people. Therefore, the drug company that discovered the drug probably will not make a big profit and may even lose money by manufacturing the drug.

To encourage drug companies to produce drugs that have little profit value but will be of great benefit to small numbers of people, Congress has enacted the Orphan Drug Law. The Orphan Drug Law prevents companies other than the one that first discovered the new drug (to the point of getting use approved) from producing the drug for 7 years. Without competition, the company making the orphan drug can charge more money and thus will be more likely to make a profit. To make a profit, a drug company must pay for the expenses involved in manufacturing the drug as well as the initial costs incurred in the discovery and development of the drug.

Only two companies have been allowed to sell human growth hormone in the United States because of its orphan drug status. Some people argue that it should not be classified an orphan drug. They claim that the two companies that sell the hormone are making sizable profits from its sales. They also claim that if more companies were selling it, prices would go down and the drug would be available to more people.

1. Think for a moment about the reasons for each side of the argument. Read some articles about the benefits and dangers of human growth hormone. In one column, list the advantages of keeping human growth hormone an orphan drug. Beside it, list the disadvantages. What do you think should be done?
2. Think of some other drugs that are very beneficial but only to a small number of people. Do the same ethical issues apply?
3. Write a letter to your Congressman about the Orphan Drug Law. Your letter should request that he or she send you a position statement (his or her opinion) on the Orphan Drug Law. Your letter should also present your opinion, with well-reasoned arguments, and advise the Congressman of what you think he or she should do.

Disease:
Investigating the Ebola Virus

**Teaches Scientific Method
Relates to Real Life
Fosters Collaboration**

Purpose:

- To learn how scientists use the scientific method to solve medical mysteries
- To understand the basic principles of epidemiology
- To learn to think critically about the way scientific issues are presented in the media

Materials:

Excerpt from a newspaper article describing early incidences of the Ebola virus.
VCR, television, and movie *Outbreak*
Excerpts from scientific journal articles describing incidences of the Ebola virus.

Method:

Scientists who study diseases often have to work like detectives, gathering clues about the cause of the disease and the way it is transmitted. In this activity, you will gather "data" from three different types of sources and then develop a hypothesis for the beginning and spread of the Ebola virus. See Figure 12.1 for general information about viruses.

1. Your teacher will show you a short clip from a movie. Remember, Hollywood often takes liberties with the truth—what you see might not accurately represent what actually happened.
2. Read the two excerpts from articles. As you read, underline important facts and information you think may be a clue to the source and spread of the disease.
3. On a separate sheet of paper, answer the following questions:
   a. Discuss environmental factors that could contribute to the spread of *Ebola*.
   b. When Ebola first manifested, doctors who tried to treat it and others who helped the victims immediately contracted the disease. Those who avoided contact with the afflicted did not. Formulate a hypothesis to account for this occurrence.

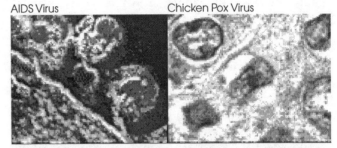

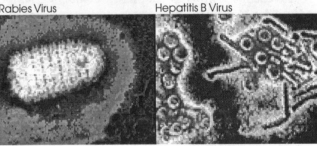

Figure 12.1. *Viruses*
Viruses are abligate intercellular parasites, particles composed of genetic material (DNA or RNA, but not both) surrounded by a protective protein coat. Outside a host cell, they are inert; inside, they enter a dynamic phase in which they replicate, pirating the host cell's enzymes, nucleic and amino acids, and machinery to accomplish what they are not equipped to do alone. SOURCE: Microsoft Illustration: "Viruses," Microsoft® *Encarta® 96 Encyclopedia.* (c) 1993–1995 Microsoft Corporation. All rights reserved.

   c. Without knowing the cause of the Ebola virus or how to cure it, what are some ways we can help to control it?
   d. What is a virus? List some viruses and the ways they can be transmitted.
   e. Was the Ebola outbreak presented accurately in the news? Why or why not?
   f. Did you notice differences between the way Ebola was presented in the three sources (video, article 1, article 2) that you examined? Which presentation was most accurate? Why?

Investigating the Ebola Virus:
Suggested Article #1

**"The Deadly Virus in Zaire:
Sifting the Many Mysteries"**

Lawrence K. Altman

Atlanta (May 12, 1995)—The Ebola virus that is causing an epidemic in Zaire is one of the deadliest infectious agents, and no one knows why.

Scientists can only guess why the thread-shaped virus has suddenly erupted to cause its third major outbreak in central Africa since 1976, when it was discovered in Zaire. Scientists do not know where the virus usually exists in nature or where it has hidden since it caused its last major outbreak, in southern Sudan in 1979.

But they do know ways the epidemic may be stopped, and that is why the World Health Organization, a United Nations agency in Geneva, has sent scientists to Zaire to control a further spread of the virus, which has killed 48 people by the W.H.O.'s count.

Most of the 65 cases of suspected infection that the team has identified have occurred among health workers who lacked adequate medical supplies. By applying simple hygiene and infection-control measures in caring for the victims, the W.H.O. expects to stop the outbreak.

That confidence is based on experience from the two previous known epidemics: simple isolation procedures like masks, gloves and gowns stopped those outbreaks cold.

Investigating the Ebola Virus: Suggested Article # 2

"Back in the Hot Zone"

Richard Preston

. . . The city was in a panic. The Army had sealed off roads and wasn't allowing anyone to leave. The unknown infectious agent was causing people to die with hemorrhages flooding from the natural orifices of the body. That is, victims were bleeding out. The local people were calling it "the red diarrhea."

. . . In the initial report received at the W.H.O., the agent was said to have infected 72 people and killed 56. There were rumors that a medical technician had become sick, had been taken into surgery, and had virtually exploded in the O.R.—had bled all over the place. A number of people on the surgical team, it was said, had later died. Whatever was happening, it seemed that the Kikwit agent had zeroed in on the city's medical personnel and was taking them out.

When this scary news in its unreliable shapes reached the W.H.O., it happened that a W.H.O. scientific team was preparing to fly to the Ivory Coast, in West Africa, to investigate a confirmed case of a new strain of Ebola virus there. . . . One of the South African doctors is a gigantic figure in the history of infectious-disease outbreaks, named Margaretha Isaacson. She is a grandmotherly woman who retired a couple of years ago from the South African Institute for Medical Research and went to live in a retirement community outside Johannesburg. Last week, she left a message on her home answering machine that went, "Dr. Isaacson is not available," and she came out of retirement and flew to Zaire, and joined the team. . . .

Investigating the Ebola Virus: Suggested Article #3

Ebola Tamed—for Now

Mark Caldwell

Last spring's plague movie, *Outbreak,* had to compete with a real-life cliff-hanger: an appearance, in Zaire, of the dread Ebola virus. . . . In its worst previous human visitation (also in Zaire, in 1976), Ebola virus achieved a death rate near 90 percent. There's no vaccine, no cure. . . .

On August 24 the World Health Organization announced the apparent end of the 1995 epidemic, noting that two full 3-week incubation periods had passed without the appearance of a new case. There'd been 315 known victims, of whom 244 (or 77 percent) had died. A horrendous toll, surely, but far short of the uncontrolled worldwide spread some pessimists feared. (In the 1918 influenza epidemic, for instance, 20 million people died and more than a billion were sick). Luckily, the Zaire strain of Ebola virus, while devastating to those it attacks, is fairly easy to contain. The incubation period is short, the symptoms too catastrophic to be ignored, and the virus itself is hard to transmit, apparently requiring either exposure to infected blood products or very close contact with a sick individual.

Note for the Teacher:

Use your judgment to decide how many "clues" the articles should include. A general description of viruses from the textbook is also helpful.

Watch the video *Outbreak* at home, and decide which scene(s) you want to show the class (manifestation of symptoms, for instance).

Disease:
The Mystery of the Alpine Slide

Teaches Scientific Method
Relates to "Real Life"
Is Interdisciplinary

Introduction:

During the 2-week period from 22 July to 8 August, 1982, five young men vacationing in Vermont experienced severe allergic reactions. Certain areas of their skin displayed slightly raised patches that were inflamed and produced rather severe itching. They had hay-fever-like symptoms in the nose and eyes. They had some difficulty breathing and their blood pressures were in the low range.

The doctors who treated the five recognized from their symptoms that they were reacting in a highly sensitive manner to the presence of some foreign substance in their bodies. They were quickly treated with injections of antihistamines and epinephrine, drugs that prevent the production of the agents that cause the reactions. All five men recovered.

The doctors were puzzled by these medical events. In checking out their patients, they found all five shared a common experience. All their allergic reactions occurred within a 3-minute to 20-minute period after each one of the five had sustained some skin abrasion injuries while riding on an amusement device called an alpine slide. These slides are common in ski areas, where they are built on the ski runs. They generate income for the ski areas during the spring, summer, and fall.

The slide consists of a free-running sled that glides down a mountainside on an asbestos-cement track. The abrasion injuries occurred as a result of falling off sleds that were running the alpine slide course.

A check of 27 similar alpine slides in the United States revealed 24 similar cases of severe allergic reactions, 22 of which followed skin abrasions. So evidence seemed to indicate a relationship between allergic reactions and skin abrasions while riding on alpine slides.

The doctors knew that skin abrasions by themselves do not bring about severe allergic reaction. Something more must be involved. Put yourself in the place of the medical team investigating this problem. Think about the environment of the alpine slide. What factors might play a role in the apparent interaction between skin abrasion and severe allergic reactions? Discuss the possible environmental factors with your teacher and the rest of the class. Your teacher will then pose some additional questions.

Purpose:

- To use data to formulate hypotheses
- To use information from earlier activities to explain and observe an allergic reaction

Materials:

None

Method:

1. List possible factors connecting skin abrasion and severe allergic reactions:
   Time of year
   Plant life surrounding the slide
   Animal life surrounding the slide
   Altitude
   Time of day
   Presence or absence of rainfall
   Temperature at time of skin abrasion
   The asbestos on the slide
   Fear induced by the ride
   Clothing worn by the riders

2. Consider additional information:
   a. Data from the alpine slide in Vermont:
      - Riders per day: approximately 1,400
      - Rate of injury: 1% to 2% (14-18) per day [abrasions alone do not cause severe allergic reactions]
   b. Historical data (1976-1981) on the severe allergic reactions, regarding time of year:
      - 23 May to 27 June: 0 cases
      - 28 June to 4 August: 1.71 cases/10^5 rides
      - 5 August to 6 November: 0 cases

[Other alpine slide operators across the United States reported 24 cases of severe allergic reactions; 22 occurred in the period from late June to early August.]

3. Begin by eliminating those proposed causes that do not vary with the calendar. Can you think of a plant process

that could play a role in causing severe allergic reactions?

Results:

The occurrence of severe allergic reactions, according to the data, coincides with the grass pollination season in the mountains. Two major factors were demonstrated: (a) the presence of pollen grains in the area of the slide and (b) sensitivity to pollen of that type on the part of the five patients. Factor b was determined by skin tests. Of the four patients tested, all were positive on the tests for grass and ragweed pollen. To investigate Factor a, researchers used glass slides coated with silicone grease and affixed to the front and rear of five sleds to collect pollen grains. More pollen grains were found on the rear slides than on the front slides. The range was from 4 grains (front of sled, slow speed) to 1,600 grains (rear of sled, high speed).

Based on the evidence presented, the most likely hypothesis is that severe allergic reactions were caused by pollen grains that were introduced into persons who are allergic to grass pollen. This occurred through breaks in the skin as a result of abrasions sustained while riding the amusement slides. The evidence is strong but is still not conclusive. All other variables have not been controlled.

Questions for Review:

1. Consider the symptoms listed in the activity describing severe allergic reactions: itching and inflamed skin, watery and reddened nose and eyes, difficulty in breathing. Can you think of any other human afflictions that result from allergic reactions?
2. If you were the operator of an alpine slide and knew that skin abrasions during the grass pollination season could lead to severe allergic reactions, what steps could you take to protect your customers?

13

Laboratory Experiments

The 23 experiments to be found in this chapter cover 13 topics of study. They are designed to involve the imaginations and, sometimes, the senses of humor of the students and to engage them in ways that will ensure that the knowledge they gain will be usable and there to stay.

Here follows the break-down of topics and the corresponding experiments:

Scientific Method: Puzzle Piece Investigation

Teaches Scientific Method
Fosters Collaboration

Introduction:

The scientific method is a natural tool for problem solving, which humans have used from time immemorial. It is based on a single basic principle: objectivity. What does that mean? An objective observer bases his or her opinion not on some preconceived notion or belief but only on what he or she can actually observe.

An objective statement: Every day, I see the sun rise in the east and set in the west.

A subjective statement (prejudiced by belief in a particular system): God made the earth the center of the Universe.

The first step in the scientific method, therefore, is to observe objectively the phenomenon you want to explain. (In this case, whether the sun revolves around the earth or vice versa). The second step in the scientific method is to form a tentative conclusion based on your observations. This informed guess is called a *hypothesis*. Sometimes, objective observation can lead one to the same hypothesis as subjective prejudice:

The sun rises in the east and sets in the west; therefore, the sun revolves around the earth.

God made the earth the center of the Universe; therefore, the sun revolves around the earth.

Note that just because prejudice and observation can lead you to the same conclusion doesn't mean that that conclusion is correct.

The third, and perhaps most important, step in the scientific method is experimentation. Experimentation is how you test whether the hypothesis you formed is accurate. Thus, if you observed that your mother, who eats 2 pounds of popcorn a day, is not overweight and hypothesized that, therefore, popcorn consumption must stimulate weight loss, you'd have to test this theory before you launched your advertising campaign! How would you test your hypothesis?

You'd need to find test subjects (people or animals) to supplement their diets with popcorn without otherwise changing the amounts or the kinds of food they ate. You'd

also need a control group to test whether another factor (not the popcorn) was causing the weight loss. For instance, you might have several control groups each eat substantial quantities of other foods (e.g., the bean group, the brussels sprouts group, etc.). That would help you find out whether it was popcorn in particular that stimulated weight loss or just eating a large amount of the same type of food on a regular basis.

After you performed your test, you'd have to look at your results and evaluate whether they proved or disproved your hypothesis. That's the fourth step in the scientific method: evaluating your hypothesis. Usually, one experiment isn't enough to prove a hypothesis right, so you'll need to retest. If your hypothesis is proven wrong, you'll need to observe the results of your experiment, form a second hypothesis, test it through experimentation, and evaluate it.

In this exercise, you'll practice using the scientific method to solve problems.

Purpose:

1. To learn to work together as a group
2. To learn about the principles of the scientific method

Materials:

A jigsaw puzzle, with approximately one puzzle piece per student or one piece per lab group.

Method:

1. Your teacher will distribute puzzle pieces to each student or group.
2. Examine your puzzle piece and describe it. In this step, don't make any conclusions about what the overall picture might be (that is, don't say: "It's part of a banana"). Instead, describe only what you can actually see on your single piece. For example, you might say, "The piece is yellow in color with small, brown spots." Write down as specific a description of your puzzle piece as you can.

3. Based on your observations of your piece, develop a hypothesis (an informed guess) about what the overall picture might be. Write down your hypothesis and your reasons for it.

4. When everyone has completed his or her hypotheses, the teacher will instruct each student or group to write them on the board.

5. Now, with the aid of the other students' hypotheses, are you able to guess what the picture might be? Write down your new hypothesis.

6. Working together as a class, come to agreement about what you think the puzzle is.

7. Collect the pieces and put together the puzzle.

Scientific Method: Black Box Investigation

Teaches Scientific Method
Fosters Collaboration

Introduction:

Whether we realize it or not, whenever we are faced with a problem, we use the same method scientists use to solve it. After determining exactly what the problem is, you suggest an explanation or make an informed guess about the solution. The scientist calls this a hypothesis.

Next, you figure out how you can test this explanation. You make a prediction about what the outcome will be. This is usually stated like this: If . . . then . . . . Next, you go about testing your explanation; that is, you perform an experiment, observe what happens, and interpret those results. Last, you draw conclusions about your original hypothesis. Either your hypothesis was correct, or you must form a new hypothesis and start again. Sometimes, when you form a hypothesis, you take certain ideas for granted. These ideas are called *assumptions.*

Purpose:

1. To practice the scientific method
2. To learn to work together in groups

Materials:

Black box
Paper clips
Marbles
Staples
Magnets
Triple Beam Balance

Method:

In this lab, you will be given a sealed box. Each box contains an item from the collection of items on display on the overhead projector. By applying the steps described earlier, you will attempt to determine what is in the boxes. *Do not open the box.*

For example, you might guess that the object in the box is a glass bead. You predict it will roll as you tilt the box. You experiment by tilting the box and listening. You then interpret what you hear and draw conclusions about your original guess. Of course, you have assumed that the bead will roll. You did not first test to see if the bead would roll. You also assumed that the item in the box was one of those shown.

Such an hypothesis is called a *black box* hypothesis because the guess cannot be tested directly. You may use any of the instruments your teacher has placed on the materials table for your experiment (magnets, balances, etc.).

Use the following format to write up your experiment:

Box number:
Hypothesis:
Experiment:
Results (observations):
Conclusions:
    I CAN DO SCIENCE!

Scientific Method: The Scissors Game

Teaches Scientific Method
Fosters Collaboration
Is User-Friendly

Introduction:

Whether we realize it or not, whenever we are faced with a problem, we use the same method scientists use to solve it. After determining exactly what the problem is, you suggest an explanation or make an informed guess about the solution. The scientist calls this a hypothesis.

Next, you figure out how you can test this explanation. You make a prediction about what the outcome will be. This is usually stated like this: If . . . then . . . . Next, you go about testing your explanation; that is, you perform an experiment, observe what happens, and interpret those results. Last, you draw conclusions about your original hypothesis. Either your hypothesis was correct, or you must form a new hypothesis and start again. Sometimes, when you form a hypothesis, you take certain ideas for granted. These ideas are called *assumptions.*

In this exercise, we will observe the scientific method at work in a simple game.

Purpose:

To practice the scientific method: observation, hypothesis, and experimentation

Materials:

1 pair of scissors

Method:

Move your chairs into a circle. Your teacher will begin passing a pair of scissors around the room. Each time the scissors pass to a new participant, that person will guess either "crossed," or "uncrossed." Observe carefully which students the teacher says are right, and try to figure out the secret.

Note for the Teacher:

When you pass the scissors, open and close them—this is a red herring but useful for the exercise. The real secret is whether your legs are crossed or not, so sit somewhere that students can observe them. If your legs are crossed, say, "Crossed," and pass the scissors to the student next to you. If your legs are uncrossed, say, "Uncrossed."

Use as minimal an explanation as possible. You'll find that students exercise the scientific method not only to discover the secret of the game but also to work out its playing procedures.

Sometimes, it's a good idea to let one or two students in on the secret prior to the game's beginning—that gives the remaining students more reliable cues. Don't reveal who knows the secret!

Cells: Cell Models

Demonstrates Abstract Concept
Is Interdisciplinary
Uses Hands-On Activity

Introduction:

The word *cell* refers to entire organisms, such as paramecia, dinoflagellates, and diatoms; disease organisms, such as spirochetes; and the specialized parts of higher multicellular organisms, such as lymphocytes, erythrocytes, muscle cells, nerve cells, cardiac muscle, and chloroplasts. Regardless of size or whether the cell is a complete organism or just part of an organism, all cells have certain structural components in common. All cells have some type of outer cell boundary that is semipermeable, and cell interiors are composed of a water-rich, fluid material called *cytoplasm*, which contains hereditary material in the form of DNA (deoxyribonucleic acid).

In this exercise, you will construct a model of a cell of your own choosing.

Purpose:

To learn about cell structures

Materials:

Whatever you choose

Method:

Preparing the model:

1. You should make a model of *either* an animal cell or a plant cell.
2. Submit a preliminary proposal to your teacher.
3. You may construct your cell model out of any available materials; however, it must be three-dimensional (i.e., a box, a cake, or other three-dimensional structure).
4. Your model should be prepared in the shape of the structure being depicted (for example, the structure should not just be an icing outline on the surface of a cake).
5. The cell model itself should not be labeled with the names of the organelles. You should, however, number the organelles on your model and construct a separate key on which you *list* and *define* the cell parts.
6. You must think of creative ways of including the following organelles and parts: cell membrane, cell wall (if present), lysosomes, vacuoles, centrioles, DNA, nucleolus, chloroplasts (if present), Golgi complex, cytoplasm, ribosomes, mitochondria, endoplasmic reticulum, nucleus.

Presenting the model:

1. Your teacher will take a picture of your cell model, and all the pictures will be displayed on the classroom bulletin board.
2. You must prepare a 2-minute presentation to the class during which you will display and explain your cell model.
3. If your cell model is edible, you may cut and serve it to the class!!

Classical Genetics: Mitosis and Meiosis

Introduction:

A variety of active learning techniques permits students to experience and live what they are learning. The following four can be integrated into the lecture or used as laboratory exercises. The first experiment teaches mitosis and meiosis with playing cards. The second uses movable, transparent chromosomes on an overhead projector. The third lesson involves students carrying giant paper chromosomes in role-playing mitosis and meiosis. The last is for small groups or individuals to practice mitosis and meiosis using colored pipe cleaners and Cheerios.

Playing Cards

Materials:

Two decks of the same playing cards
Paper clips
Different yarn colors

Method:

Mitosis

1. Make a large circle with one color of yarn. In it, put the 2, 3, 4, and 5 of hearts and the 2, 3, 4, and 5 of clubs. What do these represent? Why different suits? What is the diploid number?

2. Make a spindle with another color of yarn. What are these? What stage is this? What happens now? Chromosomes shorten and thicken.

3. Line up replicated chromosomes at the equator. What happens now?

4. Split the centromeres and migrate towards the poles. What stage is this?

5. Chromosomes reach the poles. What stage is this?

Cytokinesis

What is the result? Two cells with the exact same chromosomes. Why does this happen? Growth, repair, replacement (reproduction).

Meiosis

Same start, but at Metaphase I, tetrads line up and the centromeres do not split at anaphase. After cytokinesis, follow the chromosomes through meiosis II. In what ways are mitosis and meiosis different?

Transparent Chromosomes

Materials:

Overhead projector
Blank transparency sheets
Colored transparency pens

Method:

Blank transparency sheets can be colored with transparency pens to form chromosomes: red for maternals and blue for paternals. These can be made of different lengths, indicating chromosome pairs 1, 2, and 3 of the 23 human chromosome pairs.

Following a very brief description of mitosis, these transparent chromosomes are brought into action at the overhead projector. These can demonstrate steps of mitosis in an animated manner—much like a film or film loop—except that these chromosomes can be handled and regrouped to answer class questions.

These are used initially by the instructor. Later, students can volunteer to come up to the overhead and show the process. After describing mitosis with the help of these chromosomes, what next? Compare meiosis to mitosis using movable transparent chromosomes. When genetics is studied, these same chromosomes can be marked (with green or black letters) to represent genes for different traits. Then, the relationship of Mendel's laws to meiosis can be readily demonstrated.

Role-Playing Mitosis and Meiosis

Method:

Each student plays the role of a chromosome. Each carries a large paper cut in the shape of a chromosome. Usually, 12 students participate, although 8 or 16 may be used. The 12 chromosomes are colored red (maternal = M) or blue (paternal = P), and each colored set is numbered.

1. Fertilization

Single maternal chromosomes #1, 2, and 3 sit huddled together in the middle of the classroom floor. They represent the 23 maternals in the ovum. Meanwhile, milling around out in the hall are the three homologous paternals. These enter the room and mingle with maternals. (Students have witnessed fertilization.) Point out that although homologous partners are present, they do not pair up yet.

2. Mitosis

This diploid cell (zygote) will now undergo its first mitotic division ever. Ask students what they should do first. Remind them that the original six chromosomes must first replicate. Because this is not feasible, each can imagine that she replicates: Just call from sidelines of the room a "duplicate self." They (such as two maternal #1s) link arm in arm to indicate where they are held together at centromere. (At anaphase, they unlink arms as the centromere splits.) You call out phases much like a square dance: "Interphase, prophase, metaphase . . . ," and they act it out. You mention that this process, from that very first division (of the zygote), goes on throughout life, in all body parts, producing billions of cells. Even cells of ovaries and testes result from meiosis.

3. Meiosis

But then, some cells of the gonads undergo the "meiotic dance", a variation of mitosis. First, the students will need to determine that again, chromosomes must replicate as the process begins, so 12 students will be on the "dance floor" once again. These should be linked at centromere (elbow). But now homologous partners must find each other. The red arm-linked #1s must locate the blue arm-linked #1s; these form a line of four (a tetrad) as synapsis occurs. They can cross over ankles and wrists between the inner red and inner blue in each tetrad. Show possibilities for random assortment (at Metaphase I): Have tetrads line up on the equator, reds on one side, blues on the other. Each tetrad decides, then, if—at the count of three—their group wishes to assort differently (switch blues with reds). Finish phases. Contrast oogenesis to spermatogenesis: In oogenesis, one group takes up more of the room (cytoplasm). Later, discuss traits (drawn on each chromosome) for genetics study.

Pipe Cleaner Chromosomes

Materials

Red and blue pipe cleaners (three lengths of each color)
Cheerios

Method:

Students work on their own or in groups, using red and blue pipe cleaners cut in three lengths (6" or approximately 15 cm for #1, 4" or APA. 10 cm for #2, 2" or approximately 5 cm for #3). Work on white lab trays or on paper or just on the floor. If desired, run races: See who can "break 11 seconds" for meiosis. Cheerios are centromeres; they can be broken apart when centromeres split (e.g., in Anaphase II, not I, of meiosis).

Classical Genetics: Human Inheritance Lab

Is a Nontraditional Laboratory
Fosters Collaborative Activity
Relates to Real Life

Purpose:

1. To learn how inherited characteristics are transmitted
2. To study the transmission of dominant and recessive traits in a sample population

Method:

A number of genes are involved in the production of most human characteristics, but quite often, the variation of only one inherited gene determines whether a person will have a certain characteristic or not. Some characteristics determined by a single gene are listed following the next paragraph.

Try to determine your genotype and phenotype for these characteristics. When you show a dominant characteristic, it is impossible to determine whether you carry two genes for it (homozygous) or one dominant and one recessive gene (heterozygous). In this case, we use a dash (-) to represent the unknown second gene when we write the genotype. For instance, albinism is a recessive trait, so it only results when a person has two recessive genes (aa). If you are not an albino, you may have genotype Aa or AA. Because we can't be sure, we express your genotype as A-, which indicates that the second gene is unknown.

Inherited Traits

Attached Ear Lobes

In most people, the ear lobe hangs free, but when a person is homozygous for a certain recessive gene (e), the ear lobes are attached directly to the head so that no lobe hangs free. With a mirror or by asking a classmate, determine your phenotype for this characteristic and write it in your data table. As you observe your classmates' ears, you will find considerable variations in the size and appearance of ear lobes. These variations are caused by other genes, so you should concentrate only on the presence or absence of ear lobes for this study.

Widow's Peak

Some people's hairlines drop downward to form a distinct point in the center of their foreheads, known as the widow's peak. The widow's peak is caused by the dominant gene (W). Determine your phenotype by examining your hair line, and note phenotype in the data table.

Tongue Rolling

A dominant gene (R) gives some people the ability to roll the tongue into a distinct U shape when the tongue is extended from the mouth. Others who do not possess this gene can do no more than a slight downward curve of the tongue when it is extended. Try rolling your tongue, and write down your phenotype.

Bent Little Finger

A dominant gene (B) causes the last joint of the little finger to bend inward toward the fourth finger. Lay both hands flat on the table, relax the muscles, and note whether you have a bent or straight little finger.

Long Palmar Muscle

When a person is homozygous for a certain recessive gene (l), he or she has a long palmar muscle, which can be detected by examining the tendons that run over the inside of your wrists. Clench your fist tightly and flex your hand. Now feel the tendons. If there are three, you have the long palmar muscle. If there are only two, you do not have this muscle. Examine both wrists, because the long palmar muscle sometimes appears in one wrist and not the other due to variations in the expression of the genes. If you find it in one or both wrists, you have the two recessive genes. If it is not present in either wrist, you have the dominant gene (L).

Pigmented Iris

When a person is homozygous for a certain recessive gene (p), there is no pigment in the front part of the eyes, and a blue layer at the back of the iris shows through. This gives blue eyes. A dominant allele of the gene (P) causes pigment to appear in the front layer of the iris and mask the blue to varying degrees. Other genes determine the exact nature and density of this pigment, thus creating brown, hazel, green, and other eye colors. We will concern ourselves here, however, only with the presence or absence of pigment. Determine your phenotype for pigmented or unpigmented irises. (Note: Sometimes, the layer at the back of the iris is gray, so gray eyes should also be considered unpigmented.)

PTC Tasting

Some people can taste a chemical known as PTC (phenyl thiocarbamide), whereas others detect no taste at all. This chemical is entirely harmless to humans. Place a piece of filter paper impregnated with this chemical on your tongue. If you detect no taste, chew the paper. If you still detect no taste (other than the paper itself), you are a nontaster and are homozygous for the recessive gene (t). The tasting ability for this chemical indicates the presence of the dominant gene (T). Do not report a taste if you are doubtful of it. If you are a taster, the flavor will be very distinct.

Mid-Digital Hair

Some people have hair on the second and middle joints of the fingers, whereas others don't. The complete absence of hair is due to a recessive gene (m) and its presence due to the dominant allele (M). There seems to be a number of these alleles, which determine whether the hair will grow on one, two, three, or four fingers. This hair may be very fine. You should use a hand lens and look very carefully at all your fingers before you decide whether you do or do not have mid-digital hair. Tabulate your results.

Blood Groups

Blood type is an inherited trait. Three genes determine your blood type. Gene A produces the A-antigen, gene B produces the B-antigen, and gene O does not produce either A or B antigens. The A and B genes are intermediate when present together, but are both dominant over the O gene. A person carrying a gene for the A-antigen and a gene for the B-antigen has type AB blood because both genes are expressed. A person with the gene for the A-antigen and the O gene has "type A" blood. Only the persons homozygous for the gene for O have "type O" blood. Tabulate your phenotype and genotype for this blood characteristic.

Second Finger Shorter Than the Fourth

Hold your fingers together, and place your hands down on a sheet of paper so that the fingers are perpendicular to the horizontal lines. Now, move your hand up or down until the tip of the fourth finger barely touches one of the lines. Look at your second finger to see if it reaches the line. If it doesn't, your second finger is shorter than your fourth. Some scientists suspect that this short second fin-

ger results from a gene that is influenced by the sex of the individual: the gene is dominant in males and recessive in females. Use the symbol Ss for the gene for the short second finger and the symbol Sl for the gene for the longer second finger. Tabulate your results according to sex as well as second finger length.

Genetic Individuality in Humankind

Given all the people on earth, you might think that people with the same exact gene combination must be born sometimes. Remarkably, that doesn't happen except in the case of identical twins, who start life as a single cell that divides (asexual reproduction) to form two people. There is no one on earth with the same genetic structure you have, unless you have an identical twin. In this exercise, we will try to use our results from the preceding questions to show the extent of the variations among inherited traits.

Your instructor will call on several persons to read out their characteristics one at a time. When a person reads his or her first characteristic, all those who have this characteristic should raise their hands and keep them up. Then, he or she will read the second characteristic. Those with their hands up who *also* have this characteristic should keep their hands up. Those who don't can put their hands down. Continue reading characteristics until all hands are down. How many characteristics were necessary to make this person stand out as genetically different from every other person in the class?

When we consider the many thousands of genes in humans and the numerous combinations and variations of each gene, it is easy to understand why no two persons will get the same combination of genes, not even brothers and sisters, unless they happen to be identical twins. After about five persons in the class have read their genetic characteristics, determine how many characteristics on the average are required to demonstrate genetic individuality.

Probability in Human Inheritance

We will first show how the laws of probability can be used to predict the chances of two independent events happening simultaneously. This can be determined by multiplying the chances of each event happening separately. For example, suppose there are 10 persons in a class of 30 who have attached ear lobes. Because 10 is one third of 30, we say that the chances that a person in the class will have attached ear lobes is one out of 3 or $\frac{1}{3}$. Now, suppose that 15 in the class can roll their tongues. The chances that a person chosen at random can roll his or her tongue is 15 out of 30 or 1 out of 2 or $\frac{1}{2}$. To determine the odds of a person having both these characteristics at the same time, we multiply the fractions ($\frac{1}{3} \times \frac{1}{2} = \frac{1}{6}$). This means that about five persons in the class should have both characteristics, *if* these are truly independent events. Choose two of the characteristics of the 10 that you have studied, and determine the chances of each event happening separately and the chances that they will both occur together. Now, count the number of people who show both these characteristics and compare that number to the figure you determined mathematically. In a large sample, if the figure obtained by actual count differs from that which has been calculated, we may assume that something besides chance is operating. In other words, the two events are not truly independent.

Human Inheritance

Tabulate the results of your studies of inherited human characteristics. Check your phenotype, give possible genotype, and give the total number of students in the class that show each of the characteristics.

Number of fingers with mid-digital hair: 1. ___

                                          2. ___

                                          3. ___

                                          4. ___

Choose one of the characteristics from this group for which you know the phenotype of your parents, and draw a diagram showing how the genes from your parents could have been passed to you to give you your phenotype. If you do not know the phenotype of your parents for any of these, make up two hypothetical phenotypes that could have produced your phenotype.

Tabulate the number of persons in the class whose hands remain up after each characteristic is called. Do this for five persons.

What is the average number of characteristics that must be considered before all hands go down? Explain.

Probability in Human Inheritance

List two characteristics, and determine the chance of each showing in any person in the class picked at random.

Characteristic #1 _____

Number in the class who show this characteristic: _____

Total number of persons in the class: _____

Chance of any one person showing this characteristic: _____

Characteristic #2 _____

Number in the class who show this characteristic: _____

Total number of persons in the class: _____

Chance of any one person showing this characteristic: _____

Now, figure the chance of any one person showing both of these characteristics. Show how you get your results.

How many in the class would be expected to show both characteristics, according to this figure? Show your work.

How many in the class actually show these two characteristics?

What is the percentage deviation of the actual result from the expected result?

Considering that there aren't many people in the class, do you think that this deviation is great enough to indicate that something other than chance is operating? If so, tell what it might be.

Suppose you made a study of an equal number of people at a family reunion. Would you expect it to more or fewer characteristics before all hands went down? Explain.

Classical Genetics:
The Case of the Double-Stranded Strangler

Relates to Real Life
Teaches Scientific Method
Fosters Collaboration

Purpose:

1. To reinforce some selected principles in Mendelian and molecular genetics and apply current techniques and problem-solving skills in a forensic setting
2. To practice critical-thinking skills and data analysis and creative writing

Method:

1. Divide the class in half. Each half will work together to create the following:

   a. Crime scene scenario
   b. Victim and suspect descriptions, including individuals' ages, occupations, physical descriptions, and some facts about their homes, childhoods, personal lives, and reasons for being a suspect or victim
   c. "Evidence bags:" Four suspect packs and one victim pack (which must match one of the suspects), each containing the following:

      Electrophoresis gel results
      ABO blood typing
      Analysis of fingerprinting
      Handprints
      Fabric samples
      Hair samples

      (Teacher should check to make sure that only one of the suspect packs matches the victim pack.)

2. The two groups exchange "crimes." Each must solve the crime by determining the identity of the "criminal" based on the evidence provided! Collaborative and cooperative group effort is encouraged for better results.

Results:

1. Collect evidence and tabulate in a legible format.
2. Show all work.

Conclusion:

Write out your solution to the crime, interpreting the evidence you tabulated in your results section.

Note for the Teacher:

Time Requirement: This assignment is intended to be carried out over a 2-week period using in-class and out-of-class time. This will be used by students to research and collect the information for the suspect packs.

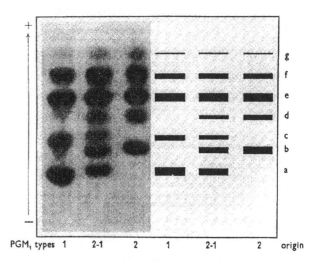

Figure 13.1. *Enzyme Electrophoresis*
SOURCE: Saferstein, Richard, *Criminalistics: An Introduction to Forensic Science*, 5/e, © 1995. Reprinted by permission of Prentice Hall, Inc., Upper Saddle River, NJ.
NOTE: Photograph and diagram of the separation of PGM isoenzymes accomplished by electrophoresis. PGM can be grouped into one of three types: 1, 2-1, and 2 according to band patterns.

Figure 13.2a. *Microscopic View of Normal Red Blood Cells (225x)*
SOURCE: Saferstein, Richard, *Criminalistics: An Introduction to Forensic Science*, 5/e, © 1995. Reprinted by permission of Prentice Hall, Inc., Upper Saddle River, NJ.

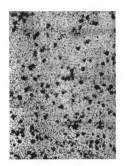

Figure 13.2b. *Microscopic View of Agglutinated Red Blood Cells (225x)*
SOURCE: Saferstein, Richard, *Criminalistics: An Introduction to Forensic Science*, 5/e, © 1995. Reprinted by permission of Prentice Hall, Inc., Upper Saddle River, NJ.

Forensic Criteria

Enzyme Electrophoresis

Using refined electrophoretic techniques, scientists can now identify 10 common PGM variants (see Figure 13.1). This discovery has allowed forensic analysts to narrow the possible sources of a bloodstain even further than before. For example, where PGM 2–1 is present in 36% of the population, its subtypes PGM 2+1, 2+1–, 2–1+, and 2–1– are found in approximately 25%, 5%, 4%, and 2%, respectively, of the population.

Apparently, there are numerous polymorphic enzymes in red blood cells that offer themselves as potential markers for determining blood origin. Also, a number of polymorphic proteins have been found to exist in blood serum. However, from a practical point of view, only those enzymes and proteins that are capable of surviving the drying and aging processes are of any value to the forensic serologist. (See Figure 13.2a and b for microscopic views of normal and agglutinated red blood cells.)

Dried Blood Typing

The absorption-elution technique is the current method of choice for the indirect typing of bloodstains. The procedure consists of the following illustrated four steps:

Step 1: The antiserum is placed on the bloodstained material, with sufficient time allowed for the antibodies to combine with their specific antigens.

Figure 13.3. *Step 1: Treatment with antiserum— Antibody binds to its specific antigen.*
SOURCE: Saferstein, Richard, *Criminalistics: An Introduction to Forensic Science*, 5/e, © 1995. Reprinted by permission of Prentice Hall, Inc., Upper Saddle River, NJ.

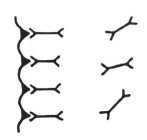

Step 2: The unreacted serum is removed by being washed off the bloodstained material.

Figure 13.4. *Step 2: Excess antibodies are removed by washing.*
SOURCE: Saferstein, Richard, *Criminalistics: An Introduction to Forensic Science*, 5/e, © 1995. Reprinted by permission of Prentice Hall, Inc., Upper Saddle River, NJ.

Step 3: Once an antibody combines with an antigen, it is possible to break the complex apart by a process known as *elution*. To do this, the stained material must be heated to 56° C. This allows the antibody-antigen bond to break, freeing both antibody and antigen.

Figure 13.5. *Step 3: Antibodies and antigens are eluted or freed from one another by heating the stained material.*
SOURCE: Saferstein, Richard, *Criminalistics: An Introduction to Forensic Science*, 5/e, ©

Step 4: When the eluted antibodies are combined with known red blood cells so that the presence or absence of agglutination can be observed, they can be identified.

The identification of A-B-O type by the absorption-elution technique is summarized in Table 13.1.

Figure 13.6. *Step 4: After known red blood cells are added, agglutination occurs if antigens present on the added blood cells were originally on the stained material as well.* SOURCE: Saferstein, Richard, *Criminalistics: An Introduction to Forensic Science,* 5/e, © 1995. Reprinted by permission of Prentice Hall, Inc., Upper Saddle River, NJ.

Figure 13.7. *The Three Basic Fingerprint Patterns* SOURCE: Abouse (1987). The Fingerprint Patterns were reprinted from the Great Explorations in Math and Science (GEMS) teacher's guide titled *Fingerprinting,* copyright by The Regents of the University of California, and used with permission. The GEMS series includes more that 60 teacher's guides and handbooks for preschool through 10th grade, available from LHS GEMS, Lawrence Hall of Science, University of California, Berkeley, CA 94720-5200. (510) 642-7771.

TABLE 13.1 Identification of Blood Types by the Absorption-Elution Technique

Bloodstains tested with

Antigen A + A Cells	Antigen B + B Cells	Antigen Present on Stain	Blood Type
+	–	A	A
–	+	B	B
+	+	Both A and B	AB
–	–	Neither A nor B	O

SOURCE: Saferstein, Richard, *Criminalistics: An Introduction to Forensic Science,* 5/e, © 1995. Reprinted by permission of Prentice Hall, Inc., Upper Saddle River, NJ.
NOTE:
+ shows agglutination
– shows absence of agglutination

Fingerprint Patterns

Every person in the world has a unique set of fingerprints, unlike those of any other person who ever lived.

Even though everyone's fingerprints are unique, there are basic patterns that are always found. These patterns help criminalists classify fingerprints.

The three basic patterns are *whorl, arch,* and *loop,* as illustrated in Figure 13.7.

Whorl patterns have lots of circles that do not leave either side of the print. Arch patterns have lines that start on one side of the print, rise toward the center, and leave on the other side of the print. Loop patterns have lines that start on one side of the print, rise toward the center,

turn back, and leave on the same side from which they started.

Hand Patterns

The shapes and characteristics of people's hands are also genetically determined. The condition known as brachydactilism (short fingers) is caused by a dominant allele. Another dominant gene causes the last joint of the little finger to bend inward toward the fourth finger.

Hair Analysis

In comparing hair, the criminalist is particularly interested in matching the color, length, and diameter. Other important features are the presence or absence of a medulla and the distribution, shape, and color intensity of the pigment granules present in the cortex. A microscopic examination may also be able to distinguish dyed or bleached hair from natural hair. A dyed color will often be present in the cuticle as well as throughout the cortex. Bleaching, on the other hand, tends to remove pigment from the hair and to give it a yellowish tint. If there has been a growth of hair since it was last bleached or dyed, the natural-end portion will be quite distinct in color. An estimate of the time since dying or bleaching can be made because the hair is known to grow at a rate of approximately one centimeter per month. Other significant but less frequent features may be observed in hair. For example, morphological abnormalities may be present due to certain diseases or deficiencies. Also, the presence of fungal and nit infections can serve to further link a hair specimen to a particular individual.

See Figure 13.8 for a comparison of six species' hair patterns as seen through a microscope.

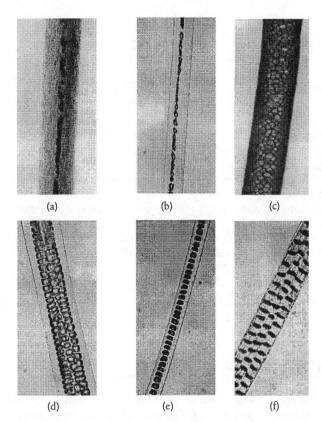

Figure 13.8. Comparison of Hair From Six Species
SOURCE: Saferstein, Richard, *Criminalistics: An Introduction to Forensic Science*, 5/e, © 1995. Reprinted by permission of Pren-

Suggested Reading:

Abouse, J. J. (1987). *Fingerprinting* (p. 21). Berkeley: University of California, Lawrence Hall of Science.
Curtis, H., & Barnes, N. S.. (1989). *Biology* (p. 979). New York: Worth.
Saferstein, R. (1987). *Criminalistics: An introduction to forensic science.* Englewood Cliffs, NJ: Prentice Hall.

SOURCE: Written in collaboration with Linda J. McIntosh.

Classical Genetics:
Your Genetic Family Tree

Is a User-Friendly Lab
Relates to Real Life

Introduction:

As you have learned in your study of genetics, the reason that children share certain characteristics with one or both of their parents is that these traits are encoded in genes, which tell the human body how to develop. Not all characteristics can be inherited, however. Some of the characteristics children share with their parents can be caused by nurture rather than nature. That is, the child may walk like his or her mother, for instance, because he or she has learned to mimic her behavior, not because it's a genetically inherited trait.

Some of the most obvious inherited traits include eye color, hair color, height, facial features, and even tendency toward heart disease and other ailments. Think for a moment about the similarities between yourself and a family member who's biologically related to you. Which of these similarities do you think are genetically inherited?

In this activity, you will learn more about your genetic family tree by interviewing and obtaining information about as many of your relatives as you can. You should take note not only of their physical characteristics but also any other interesting similarities among them. Later, you can decide whether you think these similarities are genetic or learned. After you have conducted your interviews, you will present it in a family tree that will provide a historical record of your family.

Purpose:

1. To learn how genetics influences your family
2. To practice scientific survey investigation techniques
3. To investigate recessive and dominant traits

Materials:

A genetically related family
Paper
Magic markers

Method:

1. Conduct interviews with as many family members as you can.

   a. Who to ask or ask about?
      You
      Brothers
      Sisters
      Mother
      Father
      Grandparents
      Great grandparents
      Other family members

   b. What to ask?
      Full name
      Date of birth and location
      Date of death and location
      Occupations
      Inherited traits and diseases (eye color, heart disease, etc.)
      Other interesting facts or characteristics
      Other ideas you may have

2. Draw your own family tree.

Enjoy this opportunity to learn about your heritage! Be flexible! Ask as many questions as you can. Write everything down.

Classical Genetics: Jelly Genes

Is a User-Friendly Lab
Demonstrates Abstract Concept
Fosters Collaboration

Introduction:

The class mission is to construct peanut butter sandwiches, using three different sets of instructions. One set is normal, and the other two have been altered in small ways. Select one student as the narrator. It is this student's job to read the list of instructions. Have the remaining students line up. As the narrator reads each numbered instruction from the list, a student in line should come to the table, perform the function exactly as read (no more, no less) and return to the end of the line. The results represent the assembly of a strand of DNA, which may be normal or with a deletion or mutation.

Purpose:

1. To illustrate the importance of accurate information transfer, as in DNA replication, transcription, and translation

Materials:

Jar of peanut butter
Jar of jelly
Loaf of bread
Table knife
Napkins

Method:

1. Have the narrator read the list labeled "Normal." The result will be a fairly normal sandwich. This represents information on a normal strand of DNA.
2. Next, have the narrator read the list labeled "Deletion." In this list, two steps are missing. If there is no step telling the students to pick up a knife, then they have to make do . . . with, say, their *fingers!* The resulting sandwich will look like a normal sandwich, but students should (hopefully) be more reluctant to eat it. This represents a DNA strand that is missing key information.
3. Last, have the narrator read from the list labeled "Mutation." In this list, the information in Step 6 has been

altered. (The student who does Step 6 should stay at the table.) The resulting sandwich should be very different in appearance from the other two! This represents a DNA strand in which *new* information has been substituted for original information.
4. Students can generate their own lists of procedures (fixing a flat tire, baking a cake, wrapping a present, etc.) and then delete or mutate key steps to produce bizarre results.

Normal

1. Open up the bag of bread.
2. Remove two slices of bread.
3. Close the bread bag.
4. Open the jar of jelly.
5. Pick up a knife to use as a spreader.
6. Spread jelly on the bread.
7. Wipe your spreader with a napkin.
8. Put your spreader down.
9. Close the jelly jar.
10. Open up the jar of peanut butter.
11. Pick up a knife to use as a spreader.
12. Spread peanut butter over the jelly you just spread.
13. Wipe your spreader with a napkin.
14. Put your spreader down.
15. Close the peanut butter jar.
16. Pick up the clean slice of bread.
17. Put it on the peanut butter.
18. Eat your sandwich.

Deletion

1. Open up the bag of bread.
2. Remove two slices of bread.
3. Close the bread bag.
4. Open the jar of jelly.
5.
6. Spread jelly on bread.
7. Wipe your spreader with a napkin.
8. Put your spreader down.
9. Close the jelly jar.

10. Open up the jar of peanut butter.
11.
12. Spread peanut butter over the jelly you just spread.
13. Wipe your spreader with a napkin.
14. Put your spreader down.
15. Close the peanut butter jar.
16. Pick up the clean slice of bread.
17. Put it on the peanut butter.
18. Eat your sandwich.

Mutation

1. Open up the bag of bread.
2. Remove two slices of bread.
3. Close the bread bag.

4. Open the jar of jelly.
5. Pick up a knife to use as a spreader.
6. Spread jelly on your hand.
7. Wipe your spreader with a napkin.
8. Put your spreader down.
9. Close the jelly jar.
10. Open up the jar of peanut butter.
11. Pick up a knife to use as a spreader.
12. Spread peanut butter over the jelly you just spread.
13. Wipe your spreader with a napkin.
14. Put your spreader down.
15. Close the peanut butter jar.
16. Pick up the clean slice of bread.
17. Put it on the peanut butter.
18. Eat your sandwich.

Reproduction: Pregnancy Testing

Relates to Real Life
Uses Current Science
Uses Hands-On Activity

Purpose:

■ To determine how a home pregnancy test kit really works

Materials:

1 home pregnancy test kit per student
1 test tube containing "body fluids" per student

Note for the Teacher:

Use distilled water colored yellow as the base for the fluids. So that different results will be achieved, add varying amounts of glucose to a number of them.

Method:

1. Open the pregnancy test kit and take out the directions.
2. The fluid in the test tube will be used for the test, not your body fluids.
3. Follow the step-by-step directions, writing down each step with an explanatory note.

Results:

Record the results of your test.

Questions:

1. What does it indicate if the results were positive? Negative?
2. What causes the color change?
3. How have new biotechnology techniques been used to produce this pregnancy test kit?
4. What is a false positive result? A false negative?
5. What body fluid is used for an actual test?
6. What substance in the fluid is actually being measured?
7. Explain how this pregnancy test really works.

Further Study:

Compare several brands of home pregnancy test kits for accuracy and ease of use. Compare home pregnancy testing to medical laboratory testing under the supervision of a doctor.

Biotechnology: Tide Eats Jell-O

Relates to Real Life
Is User-Friendly
Uses Current Science

Introduction:

This experiment introduces students to biotechnology and how it functions in their everyday lives. Students investigate proteases found in laundry detergents. Each detergent is assayed to determine which ones contain the enzyme *protease* and which contains the most protease activity. Each detergent is tested on a Jell-O substrate.

Purpose:

1. To demonstrate protease activity in laundry detergents
2. To observe Jell-O in assaying for protease
3. To test many laundry detergents and determine which has the most protease activity
4. To compare the results of the protease test with each detergent's label

Research:

Look up the following terms:

Enzyme
Protease
Collagen
Names of other enzymes
Gelatin
Detergent
Proteolysis
pH of wash water with detergent added

Materials:

Test tubes and test tube rack
Jell-O gelatin
Distilled water
Wax pencil or tape
Washing soda ($NA_2 CO_3$)
Droppers or pipettes
Graduated cylinder
Detergent solutions (prepared)
Metric ruler
pH paper

Method:

Day 1:

1. Prepare Jell-O as directed on the package.
2. Weigh out 0.7 g of washing soda. This will help raise the pH of the Jell-O to match the pH of a washing machine (pH 8).
3. Add the washing soda to the dissolved Jell-O, stirring slowly.
4. Pour about 5 ml of liquid Jell-O into six test tubes. Try to make the amount of Jell-O in each tube the same, and try to remove the bubbles.
5. Cover tubes with cellophane or tape. Refrigerate Jell-O tubes overnight.

Day 2:

1. Remove Jell-O tubes from the refrigerator and *mark* the surface level on each test tube.
2. Place 10 ml of distilled water into a clean test tube.
3. Measure out 1 g or 1 ml of a detergent.
4. Add the measured detergent to the test tube containing the 10 ml of distilled water. Stir slowly. (If the detergent is a powder, filter out any insoluble particles).
5. Pipette one ml of detergent solution onto the surface of one of your Jell-O tubes. Label the tube with the detergent's name.
6. Repeat steps 2 to 5 with another detergent.
7. Continue repeating until all 5 detergents have been used in the test.
8. In test tube #6, place one ml of distilled water.
9. Seal all Jell-O tubes with cellophane or tape. Let stand at room temperature (away from direct heat) for 24 hours.

Day 3:

1. Pick up your Jell-O tubes for observation.
2. Look for evidence of proteolysis.
3. Use a metric ruler and measure any change in the level of the interface between the Jell-O and the test solution.
4. Record your results in a table.
5. Examine the detergent's package. Is the enzyme listed on the label?

6. Record your results in your table.
7. Record your group data on the chart provided by your instructor at the front of the room.
8. Copy the class chart, when it is completed, and *compute* the *average* for each detergent.
9. The coloring agent is locked into the protein matrix of the Jell-O. If the protein matrix is disturbed, the color can diffuse into the clear solution. Write a description of the extent of the diffusion for each detergent tested.
10. Make a labeled bar graph of your data and the class data.

Biotechnology:
"Quick" Lima Bean Bacteria DNA Extraction

**Demonstrates Abstract Concept
Uses Hands-On Activity
Is Interdisciplinary**

Purpose:

1. To demonstrate knowledge of chemical reactions
2. To practice communicating information with chemical equations

Materials:

15-ml culture tube with cap or test tube with stopper
Palmolive detergent
10-ml graduated cylinder
Ice cold 95% ethanol
Glass stirring rod
Test tube rack or 250-ml beaker
Lima bean bacteria suspension
Dried lima beans
Tap water

Preparation of Bacteria Suspension:

Place 1 to 2 handfuls of dry lima beans in a large jar and fill halfway to the top with tap water. Cover and let sit in a warm room for 3 to 4 days. The suspension should be cloudy and smelly when ready. Pour through a strainer, and keep the liquid for the extractions.

Method:

Laboratory Experiment

1. Add 6 ml of lima bean bacteria suspension to a culture tube.
2. Add 1 ml of Palmolive detergent to the tube.
3. Cap and shake for 10 to 15 minutes.
4. Carefully pour 6 to 7 ml of ice cold ethanol down the side of the tube to form a layer.
5. Let the mixture sit undisturbed for 2 to 3 minutes, until the bubbling stops.
6. You will see a precipitate in the alcohol. Swirl a glass stirring rod at the interface of the two layers. The precipitate is DNA.

Laboratory Write-Up

For this lab report, you will write a "cookbook" translation. That means, instead of writing down the steps of the lab and the laboratory results in sentence form, you will write them in chemical notation.

The rules:
1. Use no words.
2. Chemical symbols and numbers are allowed.
3. Number each procedure as it appears in the lab.

Cookbook Translation

METHOD:

Define the following:
1. The control:
2. The independent variable:
3. The dependent variable:
4. The constants:

Did the experiment work as expected?

Explain here:

Please summarize your results here. If a graph or table is needed, please add it.

Body Heat:
Living Thermostats

**Relates to Real World
Uses User-Friendly Materials
Fosters Collaboration**

Purpose:

1. To demonstrate how environmental conditions affect the temperature of warm-blooded animals
2. To learn to measure accurately
3. To learn to conduct controlled experiments

Introduction:

Our normal body temperature stays at about 98.6° F (37° C). This fact is remarkable. Somehow, the bodies of mammals and birds keep within a very small temperature range. The cold-blooded animals, however, do not maintain a certain temperature. Their bodies become hot or cold with the temperature outside.

What happens to your body temperature when your skin is chilled or warmed? And again, what happens to the body temperature after you exercise? You know you give off heat when you exercise. But does your temperature go up very much? If not, why not?

Problem:

Is the internal temperature of the body changed very much by the environment?

Method:

1. Your teacher will divide the class into groups of five students. One student will serve as the subject for the hot-water test, another for the cold-water test, and a third for the exercising test. The other two members of the group will record data and take oral temperatures.
2. Two additional students will be needed for the class as a whole. One will maintain the temperature of the water baths. The second will be the sole person to operate the delicate thermistorized thermometer.
3. Specific responsibilities are assigned to each student. Follow the procedure for your task as it is described below.

   a. *Oral temperature takers:* Familiarize yourself with the clinical, or fever, thermometer. This thermometer must be thoroughly sterilized before and after each use.

   Practice taking oral temperatures and reading the graduated scale on the thermometer. If the mercury level is between two markings, use the lower of the two readings.

   Take the oral temperatures of the three subjects in your group as they are exposed to cold water, warm water, or exercise.

   b. *Thermistorized thermometer operator:* You will be working with a very sensitive instrument. It quickly records temperatures electronically. Examine the thermometer, and familiarize yourself with the calibration methods and the scales.

   You are to take the skin temperatures for all groups. Temperatures are to be taken immediately before and after each of the tests. Announce the temperature readings to the recorder of each group.

   c. *Hot-water subject:* Have your oral and skin temperatures taken before you begin the first test. Then, immerse your two arms in 45° C water for 3 minutes, and have both temperatures taken again.

   After a 2-minute interval, have your temperatures taken, and repeat the test. The tests will determine how much variation there is between skin and oral temperatures.

   d. *Cold-water subject:* Have your oral and skin temperatures taken before you begin the first test. Then immerse your two arms in 10° C water for 3 minutes. The water will be very cold but not cold enough to endanger your health. Have both temperatures taken immediately.

   After a 2-minute interval, have your temperatures taken. Then, immerse your arms in the cold water for the second time. Immediately after the second immersion, have your oral and skin temperatures taken.

   e. *Exercising subject:* You will perform a standardized exercise given to you by your instructor. It is important that you do the exercise exactly as given to you. If one person works twice as hard as the next, the data may be worthless. Have your skin and oral temperatures taken before and immediately after the period of exercise.

You will be given a 2-minute rest. And again, your skin and oral temperatures will be taken before and immediately after exercising.

f. *Data recorders:* You are responsible for taking down the data on each subject in your group. Study the table in your Record Book carefully. Place the name of each subject in the appropriate place. Temperatures will be given to you in degrees Celsius, or in the case of oral temperatures, in degrees Fahrenheit. Stand to one side of the testing area to not be in the way. You will have to notify the thermistorized thermometer operator when you are ready for her or his services. Students who are acting as temperature takers must give you all the information you need about each subject.

After all tests are completed, make your Record Book available to the other members of the group.

g. *Systems manager:* It is your responsibility to maintain temperatures in all the water baths. Make certain that adequate supplies of ice and hot water are available. Stir all water periodically to ensure even temperatures throughout the bath. If the temperature varies more than 1° C from the required temperature, stir in more hot water or ice. Do not rest the thermometers on the bottom of the bath; it is the temperature of the water that is to be taken.

Results:

Each student in the group should examine the Record Table.

Examine the data for fluctuations. How many degrees did internal (oral) temperatures vary from skin temperatures?

Conclusions:

1. Formulate a hypothesis for why the data did or did not fluctuate. Do you think your results stem from an error in the experimental procedure or do they represent accurate information about how the human body works? How could you find out in further experiments?
2. What body system do you think operates to warm the body internally? Try to write an explanation of how the body warms itself.
3. What body systems do you think are called into play in cooling the body?

Support: Skulls and Bones: The Inside Story

Relates to Real Life
Fosters Collaboration
Employs Hands-On Learning

Purpose:

1. To practice basic dissection techniques
2. To learn about skeletal structures from actual skeletons

Materials:

Boiled mammal skulls (1 per group). Mammal skulls can be obtained from local trappers (in rural areas) or from conservation officers. Teachers should boil the skulls until all the flesh and much of the soft tissue has been removed.

Lab probes (1 per student)

Cheesecloth (sufficient quantity to make improvised bags for each skull)

Ammonium hydroxide for soaking skulls

Essentials of Human Anatomy and Physiology (4th ed.) by Elaine N. Marieb, 1994.

Method:

Preparing Your Mammal Skull

1. Obtain a boiled mammal skull from your teacher. Using the lab probes, remove as much soft tissue from the skull as possible. Some of the bones of the face, such as the zygomatic bone, are fragile, so take care not to be too rough. Some of the teeth may be loose enough to fall out; don't lose them!
2. Insert a probe into the foramen magnum, and break up the brain. Use a flow of water to flush this tissue out.
3. When you have removed as much tissue as possible, wrap your skull and any loose teeth in the cheesecloth, and staple it shut. Label the bag you have made, and place it into the bucket of ammonium hydroxide, where it will soak for 3 or 4 days. We will return to the skulls at the end of the week to finish the lab.

Skeletons and Skulls, Up Close and In Person

Your skeleton serves many purposes, from producing your blood to providing a place of attachment for your muscles. Unless you fracture one, you seldom think of your bones. Seldom, if ever, do you see them. In this lab,

you are to work in groups and move from station to station examining human bones and the skeletons of other animals. It is not necessary to do the stations in any special order. Just be sure to do them all and answer all questions.

Station #1: The Human Skull

Be *very careful* with the skulls. They contain many thin bones that are easy to break.

The human skull is composed of the *cranium*, which contains the brain, and the bones that make up the irregularities of the face. Unlike most of the bones of the skeleton, skull bones are immovably joined together by *sutures*, immovable joints that look like the joints in a jigsaw puzzle.

Examine the top of the skull. The two large bones that make up the top and the sides of the skull are the *parietal bones*.

1. What is the line between these bones called?

2. The top of this skull is hard; at what stage of life is the top of the skull soft? Why is it soft at this time?

On the back of the skull, there is a large bump, called the *occipital protuberance*. Find this "bump" on the skull and then find it on the back of your own head. Turn the skull over; the large hole on the bottom is called the *foramen magnum*.

3. What passes through the foramen magnum?

4. Why is there no "ear" on the skull?

Linda S. Samuels, *Girls Can Succeed in Science!* Copyright © 1999 by Corwin Press, Inc.

Examine the face of the skull. The cheek bone that protrudes outward is the *zygomatic bone.* The nose is composed of two nasal bones.

5. Why is there no "tip" of the nose on the skull?

The maxillary bone forms the top of the mouth. It contains sockets, called the *alveolar process,* which hold the teeth.

6. How many teeth are there in the upper jaw?

The *mandible* is the "jaw bone" and the only movable facial bone. It also has an alveolar process that consists of sockets that hold the teeth.

7. How many teeth are there in the lower jaw?

A rounded thickening in the middle of the mandible is the *mental protuberance.* Find it on the skull, then find it on your own mandible. There are openings on each side of it called the *mental foramens,* which allow blood vessels and nerves to enter the bone. Find these on the mandible.

8. Can you locate any other foramens on the skull? Where are these located?

Another bone of the skull is the *sphenoid bone,* which makes up the inside of the eye socket and part of the inner part of the cranium. Locate the opening at the back of the eye socket, which is the *optic foramen.* This opening is located in the sphenoid bone.

9. What passes through the optic foramen? Where does it run to?

Station #2: Other Mammal Skulls

Located at this station are other mammal skulls, which you will compare and contrast to the human skull. Again, you need to be cautious handling these skulls.

Raccoon Skull

Examine the skull of this mammal.

10. What is the name of bone "A"?

11. What is the name of bone "B"?

Describe the type of teeth this animal has. How are these teeth related to its diet?

Deer Skull

Examine the skull of this mammal.

12. What is the name of bone "C"?

13. What is the name of bone "D"?

Describe the type of teeth this animal has. How are these teeth related to its diet?

Fox Skull

Examine the skull of this mammal.

14. What is the name of bone "E"?

15. What is the name of bone "F"?

Describe the type of teeth this animal has. How are these teeth related to its diet?

Mammal Skulls: Compare and Contrast

In what ways are the five mammal skulls at this station the same?

Beaver Skull

Examine the skull of this mammal.

16. What is the name of bone "G"?

What do those similarities imply?

17. What is the name of bone "H"?

Describe the type of teeth this animal has. How are these teeth related to its diet?

In which ways are these five mammal skulls different?

Why do these animals have these differences?

SOURCE: *Skulls and Bones: The Inside Story.* Printed with permission from Gary Fadden.

Neuroscience: Stress and the Nervous System

Introduction

In this lab, you will examine the *stress response* and the roles of the nervous and endocrine systems in the response. You will analyze data collected from "stressful" activities, then design experiments to study how different factors influence stress.

The nervous system regulates the homeostasis of the body, either directly, by sending messages to various parts of the body, or indirectly, by relaying them via the hypothalamus, the pituitary gland, and other endocrine organs. Reaction to stress is particularly complex and affects many physiological mechanisms. Selye (1974), the researcher who first used the term, called stress the "non-specific response of the body to any demand." The stress reaction helps the body deal with stimuli perceived as a threat, or it can contribute to peak performance during an athletic or intellectual task. This response to stress requires that large amounts of stored energy be released quickly. Overall, this response is an inefficient use of the body's energy, as the body must use energy to regain a homeostatic state and replenish the depleted stores of energy. Even with ample supplies of energy, the ability to resist chronic or prolonged stress will diminish until a state of exhaustion occurs.

Stimuli come from two general areas—peripheral nerves and the brain—to activate the stress response system of the body. Environmental stimuli that cause pain, an allergic reaction, or an internal stimulus caused by a drastic fall in blood pressure send messages over peripheral sensory nerves to the midbrain. From the midbrain, the messages pass to the thalamus located deep within the brain's core. The thalamus relays sensory information to the hypothalamus located below it and to the cortex of the brain, as shown in Figure 13.10.

The second source of stimuli is from the brain. Fear or anxiety may occur when one perceives situations similar to previous unpleasant experiences. The prospect of a pop quiz is an example that is incorporated into this activity. In this case, anxiety stimulates messages to be sent from the cerebral cortex (see Figure 13.11) and limbic system to the hypothalamus. The response to stress varies with the individual's age, gender, and genetic makeup. Environmental factors, such as diet, drugs, and temperature extremes, also influence the response to stress.

The hypothalamus is powerful because it is the meeting place for the body's two control networks: the nervous system, which exerts control via electrical messages through the nerves to release chemical neurotransmitters,

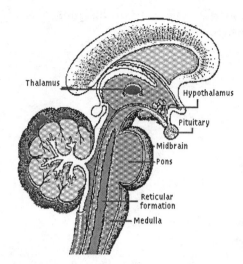

Figure 13.10. *Structure of the Brain Stem*
The brain stem, shown here in cross section, is the lowest part of the brain. It serves as the path for messages traveling between the upper brain and spinal cord but is also the seat of basic and vital functions, such as breathing, blood pressure, and heart rate, as well as reflexes like eye movement and vomiting. The brain stem has three main parts: the medulla, pons, and midbrain. A canal runs longitudinally through these structures carrying cerebrospinal fluid. Also distributed along its length is a network of cells, referred to as the reticular formation, that governs the state of alertness.
SOURCE: Microsoft (1996).

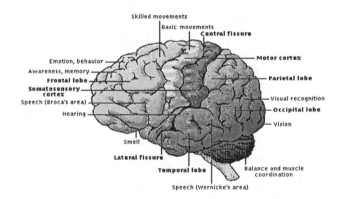

Figure 13.11. *Functions of the Cerebral Cortex*
Many motor and sensory functions have been "mapped" to specific areas of the cerebral cortex, some of which are indicated here. In general, these areas exist in both hemispheres of the cerebrum, each serving the opposite side of the body. Less well defined are the areas of association, located mainly in the frontal cortex, operative in functions of thought and emotion and responsible for linking input from different senses. The areas of language are exceptions: both Wernicke's area, concerned with the comprehension of spoken language, and Broca's area, governing the production of speech, have been pinpointed on the cortex.
SOURCE: Reprinted with permission by the National Association of Biology Teachers and Microsoft (1996).

TABLE 13.2 Response of the Two Parts of the Autonomic Nervous System

Sympathetic Nervous System Stimulation Response Includes:	Parasympathetic Nervous System Stimulation Response Includes:
Increase in heart rate and blood pressure	Decrease in heart rate and blood pressure
Sweating	No sweating
Glycogen released form the liver to handle increased energy demands	Slight glycogen synthesis
Increase in skeletal muscle strength	No increase in skeletal muscle strength
Decrease in blood flow to the skin, kidneys, and digestive tract	No decrease
Dilation of lung bronchi and constriction of blood vessels	Constriction of lung bronchi and dilation of blood vessels
Dilation of pupils	Constriction of pupils
Increase in mental alertness	No increase in mental alertnes

SOURCE: Adapted from Asterita (1985), pp. 22-26.

and the endocrine system, which sends chemical messengers called hormones through the blood to act on organs directly (McQuade & Aikman, 1974). The hypothalamus coordinates the stress response by releasing corticotropin-releasing hormone (CRH). Recent evidence shows that CRH is released also as a neurotransmitter. CRH was discovered first as a hormone, hence its name. As a hormone, CRH controls the pituitary and the cortex of the adrenal gland. As a neurotransmitter, CRH controls behavior in higher brain centers and also appears to control the autonomic nervous system. The hypothalamus receives messages from peripheral nerves, the cortex, and the limbic system and sends messages out that induce the body's three characteristic types of response to stress: behavioral, autonomic nervous system, and endocrine system.

The behavioral responses to stress are numerous, complex, and only partially understood. One behavioral response is nervous eating. Another is alternately freezing and running in the face of danger. The message enters the ears and goes to the cortex and limbic system where it is recognized as a cause for concern. From here, the message is sent to the hypothalamus, which returns messages to the limbic system to stimulate complex behavioral patterns, such as fidgeting, tremors, and increased talkativeness. One of the hypothalamic messages is CRH, the same chemical that stimulates the endocrine and autonomic nervous systems. Consequently, one may also experience the autonomic symptoms of dilated pupils, sweaty palms, and increased heart and respiratory rates. The hypothalamus uses CRH as one of its messengers to coordinate the stress response.

A second type of response stimulated by the hypothalamus occurs in the autonomic nervous system. The autonomic responses are often the easiest to identify and may include increases in heartbeat, breathing, and the rate of the passage of food through the body; contraction of the bladder and the gut; and the influence of sweating and shivering on body temperature. The autonomic nerves send their messages to organs and glands by the sympathetic and the parasympathetic systems. These two pathways counterbalance each other, keeping the body in a steady state. The motor neurons in these systems are located outside the central nervous system (CNS) in small encapsulated clusters called *ganglia*. The sympathetic ganglia lie alongside the spinal cord.

Most of the autonomic nerve activity in the stress response is due to sympathetic nerves that release the Neoconservatives *norepinephrine*. Action of the parasympathetic system tends to restore the body to its state prior to the stressful stimulus (see Table 13.2).

The third type of response stimulated by the hypothalamus occurs in the endocrine system. In reaction to continued stress, the hypothalamus secretes CRH and thyrotropin-releasing hormone (TRH). These hormones are carried to the pituitary gland through the blood vessels of the pituitary stalk that connects the hypothalamus and the pituitary.

CRH and TRH stimulate the anterior pituitary to release two additional hormones into the blood of the systemic circulation. CRH stimulates the adrenocorticotropic hormone (ACTH) and TRH stimulates thyroid-stimulating hormone (TSH) release. ACTH stimulates the outer layer of the adrenal gland, called the *adrenal cortex*, to

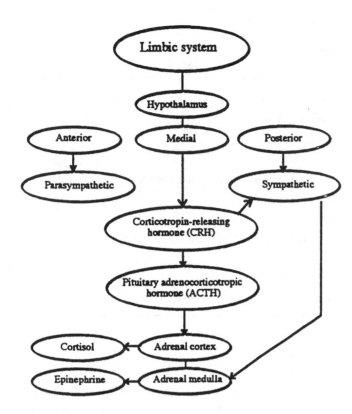

Figure 13.12. *Mediation of Stress*

release cortisol. Cortisol stimulates an increase in glucose available in blood for use by the body's cells. TSH stimulates the thyroid gland to release the hormone thyroxine. Thyroxine stimulates the cells of the body to use glucose at a faster rate. Together, cortisol and thyroxine help to supply energy to cells that are stimulated by stress stimuli and to cope with the increased metabolic demands on the cells brought on by increased activity (See Figure 13.12).

All three stress response systems—behavioral, autonomic, and endocrine—are coordinated in part by the hypothalamic release of CRH. These systems work together to help the body work at peak performance during athletically, intellectually, physiologically, or emotionally stressful activities. Acute stress is generally seen as beneficial in this way. However, during prolonged stress, the stress response may damage certain body tissues and functions. Cortisol acts as a negative feedback mechanism to prevent overreaction of the several CRH-stimulated stress response systems. This is fairly effective with acute stress, but long-term or chronic stress is still associated with harmful effects. It is generally best if one can manage a lifestyle with intermittent acute stress rather than continuous stress.

Nervous System Laboratory Investigation

Time Requirement:

A suggested time allotment follows:

Day 1

15 minutes: Perform Exploration 1 or Exploration 2.
15 minutes: Discuss results of Exploration in groups and as a class.
15 minutes: Write hypothesis and procedure to test it.

Day 2

30 minutes: Test hypothesis.

Materials:

For all phases of this lab, you will need the following for each group of four students:
1 watch or clock with second timer
1 stress sensor
1 thermometer
4 pairs of safety glasses (optional)
1 metric ruler
1 light meter (optional)
1 blood pressure sensor (optional)

Safety Notes:

Wear safety glasses when measuring eye pupil diameter.
Excuse students with heart or respiratory problems from exercise activities.
Parents should sign exercise exemption forms for all students.
Do not use any stressor that will cause a student any type of harm or that will provoke anger.

Method:

Focus Questions

Using your textbook or other materials supplied by your teacher, answer the following questions:

1. How do you think the stress sensor works?
2. What parts of your body are activated in times of danger?
3. How does the nervous system affect the parts of the body you named in Question 2?
4. What parts of the nervous system are involved in the stress response?
5. Explain how an EKG, measurement of heart activity; an EEG, measurement of electrical activity in the brain; and blood hormone analyses would help to measure stress levels.

6. State in words how stimulation of the sympathetic system affects all of the organs in the diagram at the same time, because fibers from different segments of the spinal cord innervate all the body systems simultaneously.

Lab Activity

You are going to have an opportunity to perform a simple activity in class and learn about the nervous system at the same time.

Exploration 1: Behavior Stress Activity— Colored Stress Sensor

You will work in groups of three. You have been given a stress feedback sensor with a color indicator:

1. Attach it to the tops of your hands if using the Biodot™ sensor, or
2. Hold it between your thumbs and index fingers if using the Stress Tester™.

Record the color of the stress sensor.

1. Place the sensors on top of your desks.
2. Place all books and notes under your desks or away and out of sight.
3. Take out a piece of paper and number it from 1 to 5 for a pop quiz.

When you have numbered your paper from 1 to 5, place the sensors again as you had them before, either on top of your hands, or between your thumbs and index fingers. After 15 seconds, write the color of the sensor next to number 1. Next, keep the sensor where it is—there is no pop quiz. After 15 seconds, record the color of the sensor beside number 2 on your "quiz" paper. What event was occurring when you answered numbers 1 and 2?

In groups of three, devise ways to elicit three additional color changes on the sensor and record the events and colors of the sensor on numbers 3 to 5. When you have completed this activity, answer the following questions:

What was the color of the sensor before you held it?
What color did it become after you held it?
Can you develop a relationship between the color of the sensor and the event that occurred?
What causes the sensor to change color? Does this have any relationship to the physiology of the body? If so, explain.
Are the color changes for each event consistent for all members of the class? Why or why not?

Exploration 2: Physical Stress Activity— Heartbeat (Pulse)

If stress sensors are not available, the wrist pulse can be taken by pressing two fingers, not the thumb, on the thumb side of the inside of the wrist.

A suggested procedure for this Exploration follows:

1. Form groups of three. Each of you will be assigned a role:
   Subject
   Time keeper
   Pulse recorder
2. The pulse recorder should locate the pulse of the subject.
3. To establish a baseline pulse, the pulse recorder should take the pulse of the subject for 1 minute. The time keeper should record this rate.
4. The subject should run in place for 3 minutes, then the pulse recorder should take the pulse again, as done in steps 2 and 3. The time keeper should record this rate.

Concept or Term Introduction:

Work in small groups to study the data you have collected, and make inferences about what the data tell you. Each group should share its ideas with the class, if time permits. After your sharing of ideas, the following questions could stimulate further discussion:

Why does your heart beat faster when you get excited?
Why do your hands sweat when you are afraid or nervous?
Why do you breathe faster when you are angry?
How do you feel when you are under pressure?
What systems of the body react to help protect you from danger? How would those systems change during this time and after the danger had passed?
Cite examples of the preceding item from the animal kingdom.

From the answers to the focus questions, you should be able to understand that stress is a reaction of the whole body.

Design Your Own Experiment

Experiments should assess other factors that influence stress reactions. These factors may include the following:

- Regular exercise
- Age
- Competition
- Gender
- Sleep deprivation
- Ingestion of soft drinks containing caffeine

- Ingestion of a safe dose of an over-the-counter drug, such as Ibuprofen, aspirin, or an antihistamine
- Meditation
- Mental imagery
- Counting backwards from 10 while thinking of relaxing specific body parts in sequence
- Taking several deep breaths
- Thinking positively about capabilities

Questions to help you start thinking about your own experiments:

- Will a person who exercises frequently show less of a stress reaction than a person who rarely exercises?
- Will consuming a soft drink containing caffeine 30 minutes before the "stressing event" increase the stress reaction?
- Will males show a stronger stress reaction than females of the same age?
- Will a person who is taking an over-the-counter antihistamine for a cold have a decreased stress reaction?

In addition to looking at the color of the stress sensor or measuring pulse rate, you may measure one of the following as an indicator of stress:

- Respiration rate
- Blood pressure
- The diameter of the pupils of the eyes in millimeters.

Application

Develop a hypothesis about a factor influencing stress. Design a procedure for an experiment to test your hypothesis. Make sure that the stress you apply is consistent from one student to the next as you do your test. Be sure you include enough details so that anyone could repeat your experiment. Make a data table to record data.

After the teacher has checked your design, measure and collect the data for the experiment you designed.

Teacher approval must be obtained before you begin this activity!

Analysis:

Use the following questions to analyze your data and record your results:

1. Was your hypothesis supported by your data? Explain.
2. Explain in detail how the stress you measured affected the nervous system.
3. Draw some tentative conclusions about the way the body responds to stress.
4. What classroom activities produced the most stress?
5. Did temperature affect stress levels?

For further consideration, your teacher may ask you to ponder the following questions:

6. Why is it important to develop ways of reducing stress?
7. Of what adaptive value is the stress response?
8. How can you tell if you are under too much stress?
9. Explain the positive and negative values of stress.
10. What other questions came up during your experiment? How could you answer these questions by experimentation?

Suggested Reading

Bieliausfas, L. A. (1982). *Stress and its relationship to health and illness.* Boulder, CO: Westview.

Chrousos, G. P., Loriaus, D. L., & Gold, P. W. (1988). *Mechanisms of physical and emotional stress.* New York: Plenum.

Newberry, B., Jaikins-Maden, J., & Gerstenberger, T. (1991). *A holistic conceptualization of stress and disease.* New York: AMS.

Sapolsky, R. M. (1994). *Why zebras don't get ulcers.* New York: Freeman.

Vander, A. J., Sherman, J. H., & Luciano, D. S. (1990). *Human physiology* (5th ed.). New York: McGraw-Hill.

Energy:
A Jug of Wine, A Loaf of Bread, and Yeast

Introduction:

Man's environment is full of the products of industrial technology, the majority of which came about through the original creative impetus of science. It was through such scientific breakthroughs as the discoveries of the properties of electricity and the structures of atoms that such technological developments as television and the hydrogen bomb were made possible.

However, discoveries of science have not always served as the impetus for technology. The word *technology,* which has come to mean "applied science," was derived from the Greek word *technologia,* which meant "systematic treatment of an art." Among the products of early technology were bread and wine, both of which use growing yeast cultures in their manufacture. Highly refined methods for making both bread and wine were practiced long before the functions of yeast were known. In fact, it was not realized until relatively modern times that yeasts are living organisms. Thus, the technologies of bread and wine making were developed as arts rather than as applications of science.

Leaven, which is mentioned in the Bible, was used in early bread making. It probably consisted of a mixture of yeasts and bacteria maintained in a dough medium. When a batch of dough was prepared for making bread, a small portion was retained for the inoculation of the next batch. In this way, the yeast culture was maintained indefinitely.

Bread yeast, *Saccharomyces cerevisiae* or baker's yeast, which is actually a type of sac fungi, reproduces by a process called *budding.* Bread yeast causes bread to rise by releasing carbon dioxide, which gets trapped in the dough. The Egyptians were the first to discover that allowing dough to ferment produced gases that made bread lighter (Microsoft, 1996).

Wine was known to man as early as Neolithic times; an inscription on an Egyptian tomb erected around 2,500 B.C. depicts wine making. Although the art of wine making had reached a highly perfected state by the beginning of the 19th century, science had not yet begun to explain the processes by which it occurred. In 1810, however, Joseph Lewis Guy-Lussac discovered the basic chemical reaction involved in the breakdown of sugars:

$$C_6H_{12}O_6 \rightarrow 2C_2H_5-OH + 2CO_2 + energy$$

$$sugar \rightarrow ethyl\ alcohol + carbon\ dioxide + energy$$

Following this discovery came a series of investigations on the fermentation process that revealed many of the basic functions of living organisms. The art of wine making thereby served as a stimulus for the science of biology.

Although the basic chemistry of fermentation was known much earlier, it was not until the 1850s that the correlation was made between fermentation and life processes. In a series of experiments at the beginning of his brilliant career, Louis Pasteur showed that yeasts were the agents of the fermentation process. He demonstrated that yeasts living naturally on the skin of grapes were responsible for fermentation and that yeast colonies could convert even simple sugar solutions into ethyl alcohol and carbon dioxide. In short, alcohol fermentation is yeast metabolism. But for what reasons do yeast cells cause this reaction to occur?

Investigations subsequent to Pasteur's showed that yeasts break down sugars to form the building blocks of protoplasm and convert the energy stored in the sugars to energy stored in adenosine triphosphate (ATP). Energy as stored in ATP is necessary to drive the biosynthetic reactions that form protoplasm. All of the ATP evolved from alcoholic fermentation is produced without oxygen-using steps. Alcoholic fermentation is therefore a form of anaerobic metabolism.

Aerobic metabolism gets its name from the fact that oxygen is required for the formation of ATP. The series of reactions involved in aerobic metabolism are identical to those involved in alcoholic fermentation to the point of the formation of pyruvic acid. In fermentation, pyruvic acid breaks down to form ethyl alcohol (C_2H_5-OH) and carbon dioxide (CO_2); whereas in aerobic metabolism, pyruvic acid is passed on the Krebs cycle to be broken down to carbon dioxide (CO_2) and water (H_2O).

Alcoholic fermentation is a process by which growing yeast colonies provide for two basic needs. Sugars are broken down into smaller molecules that are then incorporated, via other biochemical reactions, into yeast protoplasm; ethyl alcohol is the end product of this series of reactions. Also, energy stored in the chemical bonds of sugars is converted into energy stored in ATP. Because no oxygen-using steps are involved in alcoholic fermentation, it is a form of anaerobic metabolism.

Yeasts also are capable of aerobic metabolism and, in fact, aerobic metabolism occurs in dough production. To include oxygen from the atmosphere, "punching down" and other manipulations of the dough are used. These operations also serve to remove some of the waste products of metabolism from the dough. If allowed to accumulate, these compounds (including carbon dioxide and alcohol) can inhibit the normal growth and function of the yeast.

Yeasts serve three major function in bread making. First, dough volume is increased when the gaseous by-products of metabolism (mainly CO) are trapped during "rising." Second, the expansion due to the evolution of gases modifies the structure and texture of the dough by stretching it. Last, yeasts and yeast by-products modify the flavor of bread.

Purpose:

1. To learn about fermentative metabolism in making bread

Materials:

2½ cups (325 ml) warm water
2 pkgs. active dry yeast
1 tsp. (5 ml) clover honey
2 (10 ml) tsps. sea salt
¼ cup (33 ml) softened safflower margarine
¼ cup (33 ml) unrefined dark molasses or sorghum
¼ cup (33 ml) apple cider vinegar
1 sq. melted unsweetened chocolate
1½ tbs. (22.5 ml) crushed caraway seeds
2 tsps. (10 ml) instant Postum
½ tsp. (2.5 ml) crushed fennel seeds
2 cups (260 ml) unprocessed bran flakes
4 cups (520 ml) unsifted rye flour
31/4 cups (422.5 ml) stone ground all-purpose flour (unsifted)

1 cake yeast (dry)
¼ cup (33 ml) lukewarm water
1 cup (130 ml) milk
¼ cup (33 ml) honey
1 tsp. (5 ml) salt
1 egg, well beaten
½ cup (66 ml) melted shortening
4 cups (520 ml) flour

Method:

Basic Black Bread

Measure the warm water into a large mixing bowl. Add the yeast and stir until dissolved. Stir in all the remaining ingredients except the all-purpose flour. Beat until thoroughly blended. Add the all-purpose flour a little at a time until the dough becomes fairly stiff. Knead the dough on a floured board until it is smooth and elastic (about 10 minutes of steady kneading). Don't worry if the dough is slightly sticky.

Shape the dough into a smooth ball and place the mixing bowl, inverted, over it. After 15 minutes, cover the dough lightly with butter or margarine by turning it around in a greased mixing bowl. Leave the dough in the bowl, cover it with cloth, and let it rise in a warm, draft-free spot until it doubles in bulk (about 1 hour).

Punch down the dough with your knuckles and turn it out onto a board. Divide the dough in half and shape each piece into a tight round ball about 5 inches (13 cm) in diameter. Place each ball in the middle of a greased, 8-inch (20 cm) cake pan, and cover it with a cloth again. Let rise double until double in bulk (about 1 hour).

Bake the loaves at 350 degrees for about 45 minutes. Rap the bread with your knuckles—if you hear a hollow thump, the bread is ready. Remove the bread from the pans and cool it on wire racks, away from drafts. Brush the bread with butter or margarine if you want a soft crust. Makes two loaves.

Honey Bread

Soften the yeast in lukewarm water. Scald the milk, then add the honey and salt. Add 1 cup (130 ml) flour and beat well. Mix in the shortening and the remaining flour to make a soft dough.

Place the dough in a lightly greased bowl. Grease the top of the dough, cover it, and let it rise until doubled (about 1 hour). Punch down, knead, and mold the dough into two loaves. Put the dough into two well greased loaf pans. Bake at 400 degrees for 40 to 45 minutes. Makes two loaves.

Growth:
Embryology of the Chick

Introduction:

A fertile hen's egg provides a convenient "package" for the study of vertebrate embryology. Aristotle knew this and carried out a detailed study of the development of the chick about 2,300 years ago.

The early stages of the development of the chick are similar in many ways to your own early embryological development. By careful application of a few simple techniques, it is possible to observe living chick embryos in various stages of development.

Purpose:

■ To study the development of the chick embryo

Materials:

Incubator
Culture dishes
Forceps
0.9% saline solution
Scissors
Wide-mouthed pipette
Dissecting microscope
Thermometer
Embryology charts
Embryology models
24-hour egg
72-hour egg
Absorbent cotton
Dropping pipette
Petri dishes

Method:

There are many methods of preparing chick embryos for examination. The choice of method depends on personal preference and on what is to be done with the embryo. One method will be described here, and another method will be described in a subsequent step. Your teacher may suggest other methods.

1. Fill culture dish to two-thirds capacity with 0.9% saline solution at 38° Celsius. Put about ½ inch or 1 cm of the 0.9% saline solution at 38° Celsius in a petri dish.
2. Crack the broad end of 24-hour egg against the edge of the culture dish. Allow the contents of the egg to flow into the saline solution without breaking the yolk. If necessary, remove a section of the shell while holding

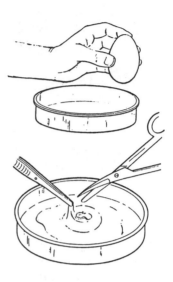

Figure 13.13. *Removing the Embryo*
SOURCE: From *Embriology of the Chick* by Edna R. Gree.© 1971 by Silver Burdett Ginn, Simon & Schuster Education Group. Used by permission.

the egg over the dish. The embryo will move to a dorsal position. You may observe the embryo while it is in the culture dish or carry out the procedure described in Step 3.

3. Carefully and gently, grasp the yolk on one side with forceps. With sharp-pointed scissors, cut the blastoderm disk loose (see Figure 13.13). Leave about 1 cm or ¼ in of yolk around the disk. With forceps, roll back the cut edge of the disk and adhering yolk so that you can separate the disk from the yolk mass and other adhering structures. With forceps or a wide-mouthed pipette, transfer the disk containing the embryo to the petri dish of saline solution. Observe with a dissecting microscope. This procedure, or one similar to it, is necessary if you intend to mount the embryo on a microslide.
4. Observe the embryo, and compare it with the one shown in Figure 13.14 and with embryos shown in other books that may be available. Try to find the structures illustrated in Figure 13.14.

What do you think the blood islands, notochord, and neural fold will develop into in later stages?

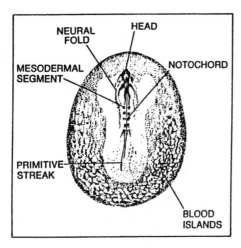

Figure 13.14. *24-Hour Embryo*
SOURCE: From *Embriology of the Chick* by Edna R. Gree.©
1971 by Silver Burdett Ginn, Simon & Schuster Education Group.
Used by permission.

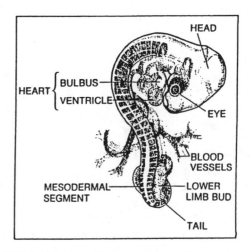

Figure 13.16. *72-Hour Embryo*
SOURCE: From *Embriology of the Chick* by Edna R. Gree.©
1971 by Silver Burdett Ginn, Simon & Schuster Education Group.
Used by permission.

5. Another method of preparing the embryo for observation is described here. Again, you may choose to use this method, the method described in Step 1, or any other method your teacher may suggest.

Place a 72-hour egg lengthwise on a pad of absorbent cotton or other soft material in a petri dish. Carefully insert the point of a pair of scissors through the shell at a point high on the shell (see Figure 13.15). Slowly and carefully, cut the shell completely around. Lift off the top portion of the shell with forceps (see Figure 13.15). The

embryo will be exposed but will be covered with albumen (egg white). With a dropping pipette, carefully remove albumen until the yolk on which the embryo rests is not covered. Carefully place the petri dish containing the egg on the stage of a dissecting microscope.

6. Compare the 72-hour embryo (see Figure 13.16 and charts and models) with the 24-hour embryo. Observe the beating of the heart.
   How can you distinguish between arteries and veins in the embryo?
   Locate the membranes and other structures shown in Figure 13.17.
   By means of lines from Figure 13.14 to Figure 13.16, point out the features on the 72-hour embryo that developed from corresponding features on the 24-hour embryo.

Figure 13.15.
A Method of Opening the Egg
SOURCE: From *Embriology of the Chick* by Edna R. Gree.© 1971 by Silver Burdett Ginn, Simon & Schuster Education Group. Used by permission.

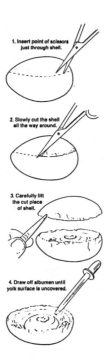

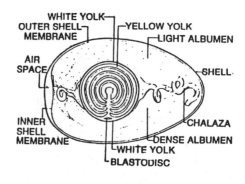

Figure 13.17. *Structure of the Egg*
SOURCE: From *Embriology of the Chick* by Edna R. Gree.©
1971 by Silver Burdett Ginn, Simon & Schuster Education Group.
Used by permission.

Linda S. Samuels, *Girls Can Succeed in Science!* Copyright © 1999 by Corwin Press, Inc.

Questions for Review:

1. What is the significance of the blood vessels opening into the yolk?

2. Is food digested in the embryonic stomach and intestine? Explain.

3. Do all parts of the embryo seem to increase in size at the same rate?

4. What organ seems to have shown the greatest degree of development in 24-hour to 72-hour period? Why do you think this is the case?

SOURCE: From *Embriology of the Chick* by Edna R. Gree. © 1971 by Silver Burdett Ginn, Simon & Schuster Education Group. Used by permission.

Nutrition:
Nutrition and Digestion: Testing Cereals

Purpose:

■ To question, test, observe, record data, and draw conclusions

Introduction:

What's in breakfast cereals? Which cereals are most flavorful? Which keep their crunch? Which are high in complex carbohydrates? Which are not? You'll find some answers by testing cereals, just as scientists at *Consumer Reports* might do.

The Four Basic Grains

Many cereals come chock full of ingredients from dried fruit to tiny marshmallows. But the most important ingredient is grain: oats, wheat, corn, or rice. How do the four main cereal grains differ in flavor?

WHAT ARE THE MAIN INGREDIENTS OF CEREALS? ARE SOME INGREDIENTS BETTER FOR YOU THAN OTHERS? WRITE YOUR HYPOTHESES HERE.

Materials:

Four single-grain, low-sugar cereals (oat, wheat, corn, rice), labeled W through Z
6 paper cups
Spoon
Milk
Water

Method:

1. Each tester should take ¼ (33 ml) cup of each cereal (dry), a cup (130 ml) of milk, and a cup (130 ml) of water.
2. Take a bite of cereal W, and chew it slowly. How does the cereal taste? Check off the words in Table 13.3 that apply. Note any other flavors you detect.
3. Add ¼ cup (33 ml) milk to the cereal, and taste again. Do you detect any additional flavors from the cereal? Record in Table 13.3.
4. Sip water to clean your mouth.
5. Repeat steps 2, 3, and 4 with cereals X, Y, and Z.
6. Can you identify the grain in each cereal? Write your hypotheses in Table 13.3. Then, decode the cereals to see if you were right.

TABLE 13.3 Grain Taste Flavors

	Cereal W	Cereal X	Cereal Y	Cereal Z
Sweet	_____	_____	_____	_____
Salty	_____	_____	_____	_____
Toasty	_____	_____	_____	_____
Nutty	_____	_____	_____	_____
Strong flavor	_____	_____	_____	_____
Aftertaste	_____	_____	_____	_____
Other flavors	_____	_____	_____	_____
Flavors brought out by milk	_____	_____	_____	_____
What grain? (your hypothesis)	_____	_____	_____	_____

The Taste Test

Most people like their cereals sweet, but sometimes, sweetness gets in the way of flavor. Which test cereals have the right amount of sweetness and plenty of grain flavor?

Materials:

4 test cereals, labeled A to D
5 paper cups per tester
Spoons
Water
Milk (optional)

Method:

1. Each tester should take 1/2 cup (66 ml) of each test cereal, a cup of water, and a spoon.
2. Take a bite of cereal A, and chew it slowly. Pay attention to its sweetness.
3. Give cereal A a Sweetness score from 1 (too much or too little sweetness) to 5 (just right). Record sweetness score in Table 13.4.
4. Take another bite of cereal A, and chew it slowly. This time, pay attention to its flavor. Does it have lots of real grain flavor or hardly any?
5. Give cereal A a Grain Flavor score from 1 (no grain flavor) to 5 (lots of grain flavor). Record the grain flavor score in Table 13.4.
6. Sip water to clean your mouth.
7. Repeat steps 2 through 6 with the other test cereals.
8. Does any cereal seem to have lots of grain flavor but not enough sweetness? Is that a problem? Why or why not?
9. Where does the sweetness in each cereal come from—is it on the outside or baked inside?
10. Can you figure out what grains are in each cereal?

WHICH GRAIN FLAVOR DID YOU LIKE BEST? WHY? WOULD OTHER PEOPLE AGREE WITH YOU? TEST YOUR HYPOTHESIS.

The Nutrition Test

More healthful cereals have lots of complex carbohydrates (which come from whole grains and other plant products) but go easy on fat, sugar, and sodium (nutrients that many people shouldn't eat too much of). There are two main types of carbohydrates—simple and complex. Sucrose and other sugars supply quick energy. Complex carbohydrates supply energy along with fiber, vitamins, and minerals. How much fat, sugar, sodium, and complex carbohydrates are in a serving of each cereal?

Materials:

Labels from test cereals
Calculator
Different colored pencils

Method:

1. Read each cereal's label, and record the grams of fat, sugar, and sodium per serving, in Table 13.5.
2. Rank each cereal for fat, from 1 (least fat) to 4 (most fat). Do a similar ranking for sugar and sodium.
3. Calculate each cereal's average "Easy Does It" ranking. Record Average rank.
4. Find the number of calories per serving for each of the cereals. Record in Table 13.5. Which has the most calories?

TABLE 13.4 Sweetness and Grain Flavor

	Sweetness[a]	Grain Flavor[b]
Cereal A	1 2 3 4 5	1 2 3 4 5
Cereal B	1 2 3 4 5	1 2 3 4 5
Cereal C	1 2 3 4 5	1 2 3 4 5
Cereal D	1 2 3 4 5	1 2 3 4 5

a. 1 = Too little sweetness or not enough sweetness; 5 = Just right
b. 1 = No grain flavor; 5 = lots of grain flavor

TABLE 13.5 Easy-Does-It Data

Nutrient		Cereal A	Cereal B	Cereal C	Cereal D
Fat	Grams/serving	g	g	g	g
	Rank				
Sucrose/Sugars	Grams/serving	g	g	g	g
	Rank				
Sodium	Mg/serving	mg	mg	mg	mg
	Rank				
Rank total (add three ranking)					
Average rank					
Calories/serving					

NOTE: 1 = least; 4 = most

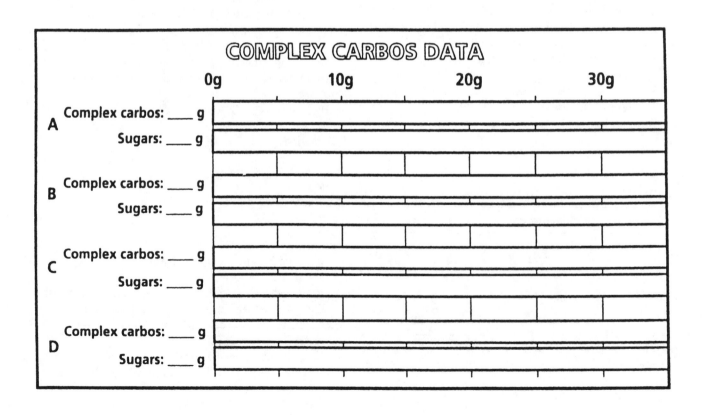

TABLE 13.6 Complex Carbohydrates Scores

Cereal	Score	Bonus
A	_____	_____
B	_____	_____
C	_____	_____
D	_____	_____

TABLE 13.7 Serving-Size Data

Cereal	Weight of actual serving	Weight of serving on label	Difference
A	_____ g –	_____ g =	_____ g
B	_____ g –	_____ g =	_____ g
C	_____ g –	_____ g =	_____ g
D	_____ g –	_____ g =	_____ g

Complex Carbohydrates Test

1. Read cereal A's label, and record grams of complex carbohydrates and sucrose and other sugars on the Complex Carbos Data graph (Figure 13.17). Then, draw bars on the graph to show these amounts. Use different colored pencils.
2. Repeat step 1 with cereals B through D.
3. Which cereal's complex carbohydrate bar is much longer than its sugar bar? Give that cereal a score of 5. Record in Table 13.6.
4. Which cereal's sugar bar is much longer than its complex carbohydrate bar? Give it a score of 1 in Table 13.6.
5. Give the other cereals scores in between, depending on how they compare.
6. Compare these scores to the cereals' Sweetness scores (Table 13.4). Does any cereal have plenty of sweetness without being loaded with sugar? Give that cereal a bonus point. Record in Table 13.6.

The Serving Size Test

Most people choose a cereal for its nutritiousness. But is what they actually pour into a bowl more than the serving size on the label? If so, they may be getting more calories and nutrients than they think. How do actual serving sizes compare with those given on cereal labels?

Materials:

Test cereals
Labels from those cereals
Cereal bowl
Balance (0.1 g)
Calculator

Method:

1. Weigh the empty cereal bowl. Record the weight.
2. Fill the cereal bowl with an actual serving of cereal A (the amount you would pour).
3. Weigh the filled bowl. Subtract the weight of the empty bowl from the weight of the filled bowl.
4. Record weight of the actual serving in Table 13.7.
5. Find the serving size given on cereal A's nutrition label. Convert the serving size to grams. (Multiply ounces by 28.4 or convert number of cups to weight, using the measuring-cup balance.) Record weight of serving on label in Table 13.7.
6. Subtract weight of serving on label from weight of an actual serving. Record the difference in Table 13.7.
7. Repeat steps 2 through 6 with cereals B, C, and D.

SUPPOSE THE SERVING SIZE YOU POUR OUT IS LARGER OR SMALLER THAN THE SERVING SIZE ON THE CEREAL BOX. HOW WOULD THIS AFFECT CALORIE AND NUTRIENT DATA?

IS THERE A RELATIONSHIP BETWEEN HOW SWEET A CEREAL IS AND HOW WELL IT KEEPS ITS CRUNCH? DOES IT MATTER WHETHER THE SWEETNESS COATS THE OUTSIDE OF A CEREAL OR IS BAKED INSIDE?

TABLE 13.9 Cost Analysis Chart

Cereal Name	Price per Box	Grams per Box	Grams per Actual Serving	Actual Servings per Box	Price per Actual Serving
A:_____	$_____	_____ g	+ _____ g	= _____	$_____
B:_____	$_____	_____ g	+ _____ g	= _____	$_____
C:_____	$_____	_____ g	+ _____ g	= _____	$_____
D:_____	$_____	_____ g	+ _____ g	= _____	$_____

The Crispy-Crunch Test

Many cereals claim to stay crispy in milk. This test will show how well the test cereals keep their crunch. Do some cereals stay crispier in milk than others?

Method:

1. Describe your test plan and the data you'll collect.
2. List materials needed.
3. List variables to control.
4. Conduct your test. Record data on a separate piece of paper. Then, use a scale of 1 (*soggy*) to 5 (*stays crisp*) to give each cereal a Crispy-Crunch score. Record scores in Table 13.8.

TABLE 13.8 Crispy-Crunch Scores

Cereal	Score
A	_____
B	_____
C	_____
D	_____

Cost Analysis

How much does a serving of each cereal cost? Use Table 13.9 to decide. Find the price and number of grams per box. Find the grams per actual serving (using the serving-size test).

Divide grams per box by grams per actual serving to find actual number of servings per box. Divide price per box by that amount. The answer is the price per serving.

Questions for Review:

1. Which cereal would you choose if you wanted lots of sweetness with the least amount of sugar?
2. Which would you choose if you wanted long-lasting crunch?
3. Which would you choose if you were on a fat, low-sugar, or low-sodium diet?
4. If you're looking for a cereal high in complex carbohydrates, which would you choose?
5. Which would you choose if saving money were the only object?
6. Rank the following in order of importance from 1 to 6.

Things to Consider	Ranking
Sweetness	_____
Grain flavor	_____
Crispy-crunchiness	_____
High proportion of complex carbohydrates	_____
Low proportions of fats, sugars, and sodium	_____
Cost	_____

What advice would you give others about choosing a cereal? Why?

_____

_____

_____

_____

SOURCE: From *Testing Cereals* by Consumer Reports. © 1993 by Prentice Hall, Simon & Schuster Education Group. Used by permission.

Nutrition:
Draw Your Body Image

Is Interdisciplinary
Relates to Real Life
Is an Age-Appropriate Activity
Incorporates Alternative Laboratory Assessment

Introduction:

Body image, or what you believe your body looks like, has become an important psychological concept in recent years. A distorted body image is often a precursor to anorexia nervosa—the intense fear of gaining weight leading to excessive weight loss from starvation diets and excessive exercise. Distorted body image can also lead to bulimia—whose sufferers ingest large quantities of food and then induce vomiting to remain thin. Both anorexia nervosa and bulimia can be fatal. Between 5% and 18% of known anorexia nervosa victims die of starvation. Bulimic sufferers' repeated vomiting depletes the body of fluids and potassium and can adversely affect heart function.

What's your body image? Do you often think about losing weight and restricting your diet? If you think you may suffer from one of these conditions, don't hesitate to ask your teacher what you can do about it: Among American teenage girls, both anorexia nervosa and bulimia are, unfortunately, as common as they are dangerous.

Purpose:

- To learn about body image and how it affects nutrition and eating habits
- To raise awareness about eating disorders

Materials:

Art supplies

Method:

1. Using your choice of colored pencils, crayons, and so forth, draw a picture of your body. You will hand in your picture to your teacher, but this picture won't be shared with the class.
2. Below your picture, write three things about yourself that you're proud of—they don't have to be about your body! In fact, they're probably more important if they're not.
3. On another piece of paper, draw what you think the ideal man and ideal woman should look like. Underneath each picture, write a "key" to the drawing, labeling each characteristic you think men and women should have. Your teacher will choose from among these drawings and present them to the class, interpreting them in terms of what they reveal about Americans' thoughts about body image.

For more information and advice on teaching about eating disorders, see the following resources:

Gilligan, C., & Rogers, A. (1993). *Strengthening healthy resistance and courage in girls: A prevention project and a development study.* Cambridge, MA: Harvard Graduate School of Education.
Fallon, P., Katzman, M., & Wooley, S. (1994). The politics of prevention. *Feminist Perspectives on Eating Disorders.* New York: Guilford Press.

Nutrition: Cafeteria Lab

Is a User-Friendly Lab
Relates to Real Life

Introduction:

Essential Nutrients

Nutrients are classified into five major groups: proteins, carbohydrates, fats, vitamins, and minerals. These groups comprise between 45 and 50 substances that scientists have established, mostly through experiments with animals, as essential for maintaining normal growth and health. Besides water and oxygen, they include about 8 amino acids from proteins, 4 fat-soluble and 10 water-soluble vitamins, about 10 minerals, and 3 electrolytes. Although carbohydrates are needed for the body's energy, they are not considered absolutely essential, because protein can be converted for this purpose.

Energy

The body uses energy to carry on vital activities and to maintain itself at a constant temperature. By using a calorimeter, scientists have been able to establish the energy amounts of the body's fuels—carbohydrates, fats, and protein. About 4 calories each are yielded by 1 g (0.035 oz) of pure carbohydrate and 1 gram of pure protein; 1 gram of pure fat yields about 9 calories. (A *kilogram calorie*, used in nutrition, is defined as the heat energy needed to raise the temperature of 1 k of water from 14.5° to 15.5°C (58.1° to 59.9°F).) Carbohydrates are the most abundant foods in the world, and fats are the most concentrated and easily stored fuel. If the body exhausts its available carbohydrates and fats, it can use proteins directly from the diet or break down its own protein tissue to make fuel.

Functions of Nutrients

The functions of the various categories of nutrients are described in the following sections:

Proteins

The primary function of protein is to build body tissue and to synthesize enzymes, some hormones such as insulin that regulate communication among organs and cells, and other complex substances that govern body pro-cesses. Animal and plant proteins are not used in the form in which they are ingested but are broken down by digestive enzymes called *proteases* into nitrogen-containing amino acids. Proteases disrupt the peptide bonds by which the ingested amino acids are linked so that they can be absorbed through the intestine into the blood and recombined into the particular tissue needed.

Proteins are usually readily available from both animal and plant sources. Of the 20 amino acids that make up protein, 8 are considered essential—that is, because the body cannot synthesize them, they must be supplied ready-made in foods. If these essential amino acids are not all present at the same time and in specific proportions, the other amino acids, in whole or in part, cannot be used for metabolizing human protein. Therefore, a diet containing these essential amino acids is very important for sustaining growth and health. When any of the essential amino acids are lacking, the remaining ones are converted into energy-yielding compounds, and their nitrogen is excreted. When an excess of protein is eaten, which is often the case with heavy meat diets in the United States, the extra protein is similarly broken down into energy-yielding compounds. Because protein is far scarcer than carbohydrates and yields the same 4 calories per gram, the eating of meat beyond the tissue-building demands of the body becomes an inefficient way to procure energy. Foods from animal sources contain complete proteins because they include all the essential amino acids. In most diets, a combination of plant and animal protein is recommended: 0.8 grams per kilogram of body weight is considered a safe daily allowance for normal adults.

Infants and young children require more protein per kilogram of body weight. A protein deficiency accompanied by energy deficits results in a form of protein-energy malnutrition called *kwashiorkor,* which is characterized by loss of body fat and wasting of muscle.

Minerals

Inorganic mineral nutrients are required in the structural composition of hard and soft body tissues; they also participate in such processes as the action of enzyme systems, the contraction of muscles, nerve reactions, and the clotting of blood. These mineral nutrients, all of which must be supplied in the diet, are of two classes: (a) the major elements, such as calcium, phosphorus, magnesium, iron, iodine, and potassium, and (b) trace elements, such as copper, cobalt, manganese, fluorine, and zinc.

Calcium is needed for developing the bones and maintaining their rigidity. It also contributes in forming intracellular cement and the cell membranes and in regulating nervous excitability and muscular contraction. About 90% of calcium is stored in bone, where it can be reabsorbed by blood and tissue. Milk and milk products are the chief sources of calcium.

Phosphorus, also present in many foods and especially in milk, combines with calcium in the bones and teeth. It plays an important role in energy metabolism of the cells, affecting carbohydrates, lipids, and proteins.

Magnesium, which is present in most foods, is essential for human metabolism and is important for maintaining the electrical potential in nerve and muscle cells. A deficiency in magnesium among malnourished people, especially alcoholics, leads to tremors and convulsions.

Sodium, which is present in small and usually sufficient quantities in most natural foods, is found in liberal amounts in salted prepared and cooked foods. It is present in extracellular fluid, which it plays a role in regulating. Too much sodium causes edema, an overaccumulation of extracellular fluid. Evidence now exists that excess dietary salt contributes to high blood pressure.

Iron is needed to form hemoglobin, which is the pigment in red blood cells responsible for transporting oxygen, but the mineral is not readily absorbed by the digestive system. It exists in sufficient amounts in men, but women of menstrual age, who need nearly twice as much iron because of blood loss, often have deficiencies and must take in absorbable iron.

Iodine is needed to synthesize hormones of the thyroid gland. A deficiency leads to goiter, a swelling of this gland in the lower neck. Goiter, which used to be common in the U.S. population, still remains prevalent in certain parts of Asia, Africa, and South America. Low iodine intakes during pregnancy may result in the birth of cretinous (see Cretinism) or mentally retarded infants (see Mental Retardation). It is estimated that worldwide, more than 150 million people suffer from iodine-deficiency diseases.

Trace elements are other inorganic substances that appear in the body in minute amounts and are essential for good health. Little is known about how they function, and most knowledge about them comes from how their absence, especially in animals, affects health. Trace elements appear in sufficient amounts in most foods.

Among the more important trace elements is copper, which is present in many enzymes and in copper-containing proteins found in the blood, brain, and liver. Copper deficiency is associated with the failure to use iron in the formation of hemoglobin. Zinc is also important in forming enzymes. A deficiency of zinc is believed to impair growth and, in severe cases, to cause dwarfism. Fluorine,

which is retained especially in the teeth and bones, has been found necessary for growth in animals. Fluorides, a category of fluorine compounds, are important for protecting against demineralization of bone. The fluoridation of water supplies has proved an effective measure against tooth decay, reducing it by as much as 40%. Other trace elements include chromium, molybdenum, and selenium.

Vitamins

Vitamins are organic compounds that mainly function in enzyme systems to enhance the metabolism of proteins, carbohydrates, and fats. Without these substances, the breakdown and assimilation of foods could not occur. Certain vitamins participate in the formation of blood cells, hormones, nervous system chemicals, and genetic materials. Vitamins are classified into two groups, the fat-soluble and the water-soluble vitamins. Fat-soluble vitamins include vitamins A, D, E, and K. The water-soluble vitamins include vitamin C and the B-vitamin complex.

Fat-soluble vitamins are usually absorbed with foods that contain fat. They are broken down by bile, and the emulsified molecules pass through the lymphatics and veins to be distributed through the arteries. Excess amounts are stored in the body's fat and in the liver and kidneys. Because fat-soluble vitamins can be stored, they do not have to be consumed every day.

Vitamin A is essential for the health of epithelial cells and for normal growth. A deficiency leads to skin changes and to night blindness, a failure of dark adaptation due to the effects of deficiency on the retina. Later, xerophthalmia, an eye condition characterized by dryness and thickening of the surface of the conjunctiva and cornea, may develop; untreated, xerophthalmia can lead to blindness, especially in children. Vitamin A can be obtained directly in the diet from foods of animal origin, such as milk, eggs, and liver. In developing countries, most vitamin A is obtained from carotene, which is present in green and yellow fruits and vegetables. Carotene is converted to vitamin A in the body.

Vitamin D acts much like a hormone and regulates calcium and phosphorus absorption and metabolism. Some vitamin D is obtained from such foods as eggs, fish, liver, butter, margarine, and milk, some of which might have been fortified with vitamin D. But humans get most of their vitamin D from exposure of the skin to sunlight. A deficiency leads to rickets in children or osteomalacia in adults.

Vitamin E is an essential nutrient for many vertebrate animals, but its role in the human body has not been established. It has been popularly advocated for a great variety of afflictions, but no clear evidence exists that it alleviates any specific disease. Vitamin E is found in seed oils and wheat germ.

Vitamin K is necessary for the coagulation of blood. It assists in forming the enzyme prothrombin, which, in turn, is needed to produce fibrin for blood clots. Vitamin K is produced in sufficient quantities in the intestine by bacteria but is also provided by leafy green vegetables, such as spinach and kale; egg yolk; and many other foods.

The water-soluble vitamins, C and B-complex, cannot be stored and therefore need to be consumed daily to replenish the body's needs. Vitamin C, or ascorbic acid, is important in the synthesis and maintenance of connective tissue. It prevents scurvy, which attacks the gums, skin, and mucous membranes, and its main source is citrus fruits.

The most important B-complex vitamins are thiamine (B1), riboflavin (B2), nicotinic acid or niacin (B3), pyridoxine (B6), pantothenic acid, lecithin, choline, inositol, para-aminobenzoic acid (PABA), folic acid, and cyanocobalamin (B12). These vitamins serve a wide range of important metabolic functions and prevent such afflictions as beriberi and pellagra. They are found mostly in yeast and liver.

Carbohydrates

Carbohydrates provide a great part of the energy in most human diets. Foods rich in carbohydrates are usually the most abundant and cheapest, when compared with foods high in protein and fat content. Carbohydrates are burned during metabolism to produce energy, liberating carbon dioxide and water. Humans also get energy less efficiently from fats and proteins in the diet and also from alcohol.

The two kinds of carbohydrates are starches, which are found mainly in grains, legumes, and tubers, and sugars, which are found in plants and fruits. Carbohydrates are used by the cells in the form of glucose, the body's main fuel. After absorption from the small intestine, glucose is processed in the liver, which stores some as glycogen, a starchlike substance, and passes the rest into the bloodstream. In combination with fatty acids, glucose forms triglycerides, which are fat compounds that can be easily broken down into combustible ketones. Glucose and triglycerides are carried by the bloodstream to the muscles and organs to be oxidized, and excess quantities are stored as fat in the adipose and other tissues, to be retrieved and burned at times of low carbohydrate intake.

The carbohydrates containing the most nutrients are the complex carbohydrates, such as unrefined grains, tubers, vegetables, and fruit, which also provide protein, vitamins, minerals, and fats. A less beneficial source is foods made from refined sugar, such as candy and soft drinks, which are high in calories but low in nutrients and fill the body with what nutritionists call empty calories.

Fats

Although scarcer than carbohydrates, fats produce more than twice as much energy. Being a compact fuel, fat is efficiently stored in the body for later use when carbohydrates are in short supply. Animals obviously need stored fat to tide them over dry or cold seasons, as do humans during times of scarce food supply. In industrial nations, such as the United States, however, with food always available and with machines replacing human labor, the accumulation of body fat has become a serious health concern.

Dietary fats are broken down into fatty acids that pass into the blood to form the body's own triglycerides. The fatty acids that contain as many hydrogen atoms as possible on the carbon chain are called saturated fatty acids and are derived mostly from animal sources. Unsaturated fatty acids are those having some of the hydrogen atoms missing; this group includes monounsaturated fatty acids, which have a single pair of hydrogens missing, and polyunsaturated fatty acids, which have more than one pair missing. Polyunsaturated fats are found mostly in seed oils. Saturated fats in the bloodstream have been found to raise the level of cholesterol, and polyunsaturated fat tends to lower it. Saturated fats generally are solid at room temperature; polyunsaturated fats are liquid.

In the following exercise, you will observe and catalog three different meals, either your own or your friends', and analyze whether they represent a healthy diet.

Purpose:

- To learn about nutrition
- To practice the scientific method
- To become aware of unhealthy eating habits and eating disorders

Materials:

A cafeteria
Students
A notebook
Chart of recommended daily nutritional allowances
Chart of calories and nutrients contained in common foods

Method:

1. Collect the data.

Bring a notebook to the cafeteria. Write down three example meals—You can use your own and two of your friends'. Be sure to write down everything contained in the meal, including condiments. Record the eater's age, sex, and how active he or she is. Save as many of the nutrition information labels as you can.

2. Analyze the data.

a. Using your data, your textbook, and other reference materials, fill out the following chart:

Age:_____ Sex:_____ Activity Level:_____

Nutrition Requirements:

Energy	_____
Calcium	_____
Folate	_____
Iron	_____
Magnesium	_____
Niacin	_____
Phosphorus	_____
Protein	_____
Riboflavin	_____
Thiamine	_____
Vitamin A	_____
Vitamin B12	_____
Vitamin B6	_____
Vitamin C	_____
Vitamin E	_____
Zinc	_____

Here is an example:

Age: 15-18   Sex: Female
Activity Level: Moderate

Nutrition requirements:

Energy	1754-2630 Calories
Calcium	1200.0 mg
Folate	400.0 µg
Iron	18.0 mg
Magnesium	300.0 mg
Niacin	14.0 mg
Phosphorus	1200.0 mg
Protein	46.0 gm
Riboflavin	1.3 mg
Thiamine	1.1 mg
Vitamin A	800.0 µg RE
Vitamin B12	3.0 µg
Vitamin B6	2.0 mg
Vitamin C	60.0 mg
Vitamin E	8.0 mg a-TE
Zinc	15.0 mg

b. Using your textbook, the nutrition information labels you collected, and other reference materials, calculate what amounts of each nutrient the foods in your three meals contain. Make charts like the following for each food item:

Food Item:

Nutrient	Amount
Energy	_____
Calcium	_____
Folate	_____
Iron	_____

Magnesium	_____
Niacin	_____
Phosphorus	_____
Protein	_____
Riboflavin	_____
Thiamine	_____
Vitamin A	_____
Vitamin B12	_____
Vitamin B6	_____
Vitamin C	_____
Vitamin E	_____
Zinc	_____

c. After you have completed charts for each food item, add up the totals for each nutrient so that you get a single table for each meal like the following example:

Nutrient	Amount	% RDA
Cholesterol	190.4 mg	63%
Carbohydrates	376.8 gm	126%
Dietary fiber	32.9 gm	132%
Energy	2265.9 Cal	113%
Fat	42.8 gm	66%
Potassium	6038.0 mg	173%
Calcium	1451.8 mg	121%
Folate	846.3 µg	212%
Iron	43.9 mg	244%
Magnesium	562.9 mg	188%
Niacin	48.6 mg	347%
Phosphorus	2334.4 mg	195%
Protein	118.0 gm	257%
Riboflavin	4.2 mg	327%
Thiamine	2.9 mg	266%
Vitamin A	2839.9 µg RE	355%
Vitamin B12	13.9 µg	463%
Vitamin B6	4.4 mg	221%
Vitamin C	575.3 mg	959%
Vitamin E	9.7 mg a-TE	121%
Zinc	12.7 mg	84%

d. Answer the following questions:

Which is the most nutritious meal?

Do any of the meals show evidence of an unhealthy diet? Why or why not?

Would any of the meals (if multiplied by 3) satisfy the RDA recommendations for all nutrients?

What are some suggestions for easy ways to make each meal more nutritious?

Do any of the meals show evidence of extreme eating behaviors: compulsive overeating, anorexia nervosa, or bulimia? If so, what signs can you recognize? If not, what are some clues that you would use to identify those eating disorders?

Nutrition: Food Fair

**Relates to Real Life
Is Interdisciplinary
Is a User-Friendly Lab**

Introduction:

Even though all kinds of people need the same basic nutrients to survive and thrive, people in different parts of the world (and even across the street) eat vastly different food. In this laboratory experiment, we'll evaluate some of the different ethnic and regional cuisines for nutritional value.

Purpose:

- To learn how to calculate nutritional values
- To learn how to choose balanced meals
- To learn about other cultures

Materials:

Plastic forks, knives, and spoons for all students
Disposable bamboo chopsticks
Cookbooks for each type of cuisine
Various ethnic or regional dishes (suggestions):

Indian: Basmati rice, Chicken or vegetable curry, Nan (Indian bread)
Chinese: Broccoli in oyster sauce, moo shu vegetables, sweet and sour fish
Thai: Pad Thai, tom yum seafood soup
Japanese: California rolls, soba noodles, tempura vegetables
Cuban: Fried plantains, red beans and rice
Mexican: Chile rellenos

Delegate students to bring in dishes. They can either prepare the dishes themselves or find them in local take-out restaurants.

Method:

Preparation

1. Divide the class into groups.
2. Based on availability, budget, and taste, decide which cuisines each group will provide for the food fair.
3. Each group should bring one dish per group member. They should bring a single portion (enough for a meal for one person) of each dish.

Research

4. Each group should prepare a short history (approximately one typewritten page) of the cuisine they've chosen to present. The history should include information about how the cuisine developed, why it was particularly suited to the region, and so forth.
5. The group should prepare 3 × 5 cards that list the name and nutritional content of each dish. Recipes should also be provided for display.

Food Fair

6. Students choose meals for themselves from the dishes provided, marking down the approximate amounts of each dish.
7. Each student calculates the nutritional value of the meal she or he designed.

Disease:
Disease Transmission Lab

Relates to Real Life
Fosters Collaboration

Introduction:

Since early civilizations, how diseases are transmitted from one individual to another has been a major health concern. In the Middle Ages, over a quarter of the world's population was eliminated by the bubonic plague. The medical minds of the era strove for decades to discover how the disease was transmitted. Finally, they found it was spread by the fleas on rats.

Today, the disease we are struggling to learn more about is AIDS. The AIDS virus, HIV, attacks cells of the immune system. As a result of this damage, the immune system's ability to fight disease is seriously weakened—so many AIDS sufferers eventually die of diseases that modern medicine could otherwise cure, such as pneumonia.

When a disease rapidly infects a growing proportion of the population, it is called an epidemic. Epidemiology is the study of epidemics and how they can be controlled. If there is no cure for a disease, the next best answer is to prevent people from catching it. Before epidemiologists can work to control an epidemic, however, they must understand how the disease they need to control spreads. After they understand that, they can work to ensure that the conditions for spreading occur as rarely as possible. In the case of the bubonic plague, for instance, cities could launch large-scale rat-extermination initiatives once scientists linked rats to outbreaks of the disease. Even though they couldn't cure the plague, they could prevent epidemics.

Through years of testing, scientists have learned that the AIDS virus is transmitted by the exchange of body fluids with an infected individual. In most cases, this exchange occurs through sexual contact or through sharing of hypodermic needles. Any exchange of body fluids can transmit the disease, however. Most people think that because AIDS is primarily a sexually transmitted disease, they have little chance of contracting it as long as they don't have sex with a lot of different partners. Unfortunately, as this lab will demonstrate, even a single sexual encounter can expose you to the body fluids of a large number of people—because you'll be exposed to every person to whom your partner was ever exposed.

Purpose:

- To learn how HIV is transmitted
- To practice basic laboratory skills
- To learn more about epidemiology

Materials:

1 test tube per student, each 3/4 full of distilled water and one of which also contains the sodium hydroxide listed
1 pipette or eye dropper per student
Phenolphthalein
25 ml of sodium hydroxide

Method:

1. Each student obtains a test tube containing "body fluids" and a pipette. (Be sure one and only one of the tubes contains the sodium hydroxide solution.)
2. Exchange one dropper full of "body fluids" with another student in the class. Do this by putting a dropper of your own solution into the other person's test tube and vice versa.
3. Record the name of the individual with whom you shared your fluids in Data Table 1 (Table 13.10). Label this the First Contact.
4. Repeat the exchange with another person, and record it as the Second Contact.
5. After two rounds of contact are completed, add a few drops of phenolphthalein to each test tube, one drop at a time. If the solution turns hot pink, the individual (represented by the test tube) is infected with the "virus." Record how many drops of phenolphthalein are required to turn your solution pink. Stop if you reach 15 drops.
6. Record all infected individuals on the board.
7. After all of the infected individuals have been identified, list in order the two individuals with whom they were in contact.

TABLE 13.10 Data Table 1

Name	Infected	Not Infected	Individuals Contacted
_____	___	___	_____
_____	___	___	_____
_____	___	___	_____
_____	___	___	_____
_____	___	___	_____
_____	___	___	_____
_____	___	___	_____
_____	___	___	_____
_____	___	___	_____
_____	___	___	_____
_____	___	___	_____
_____	___	___	_____
_____	___	___	_____

Did your solution turn pink?

Number of drops of phenolphthalein required?

Analysis and Conclusion:

1. You are now the health department investigator. You need to analyze the data you have collected and identify the source of the infection. (Before anyone exchanged body fluids, only a single individual was infected). How can you find the source?

2. Trace the transmission route of the disease. Try to deduce in what order the disease traveled to each person.

3. Explain three ways in which AIDS can be transmitted. Include in your answer an explanation of why AIDS is considered an epidemic.

4. If you were given the same set of test tubes as in the beginning of the lab and told that any 10 of the tubes must be mixed, how could you ensure that the disease would not be spread?

Evolutionary Adaptations: Floral Adaptations

Is a User-Friendly Lab
Relates to Real Life

Purpose:

- To observe floral anatomy and practice using scientific nomenclature
- To draw inferences about evolutionary adaptations through observation of modern flowers

Materials:

A large assortment of flowers, including primitive and advanced species

Method:

Basic Floral Anatomy

1. First, observe the anatomy of a relatively simple flower.

   You should find the following parts:

   a. Perianth—all the sepals and the all the petals (see b and c to follow).

   b. Calyx—all the sepals. The sepals are usually green, leaflike organs surrounding the petals. Sometimes, they are difficult to identify, because they resemble the petals. In this case, you can locate them by finding the outermost layer of petal-like organs. Count the number of sepals on your flowers, and record the number here:

   c. Corolla—all the petals. The petals are usually the colored, most obvious part of the flower. What structure of the vegetative plant do the petals seem to be related to?

   Count the number of petals and record here:

   d. Androecium—the male part of the flower, which makes up the next layer of structures inside the petals. All the stamens make up the androecium. The stamens are composed of the filament and the anther. The anther contains the pollen. What vegetative structure of the plant are the stamens related to? Count the number of stamens. Are the stamens adapted in any way to bring about or prevent self-fertilization of the flower?

   e. Gynoecium—the female part of the flower. Usually, the individual female parts or carpels are fused to form a pistil. The pistil is composed of a surface that receives the pollen, called the stigma, and leads to a tube called the style, which connects with the ovary at the base of the flower. The ovary contains ovules or future seeds. Can you see any evidence that the pistil of your flower is composed of fused carpels? Cut open the ovary to determine the number and arrangement of the ovules. Is the pistil adapted in any way to bring about or prevent self-fertilization of the flower?

   f. Pedicel—the stalk holding the flower.

   g. Receptacle—the tissue at the tip of the pedicel that serves to hold the flower. Sometimes, the ovary is embedded in the receptacle.

Variations in Floral Anatomy

You will be provided with as large a variety of flowers as possible. You should dissect a number of these flowers and attempt to find the parts and answer the questions listed asked earlier for each flower type. *Make a chart of the information.*

The following are possible variations in anatomy you might find:

1. Variation in number of parts—The number of sepals, petals, or stamens vary in flowers. In general, the floral parts of dicots occur in multiples of four or five. The floral parts of monocots occur in multiples of three. The primitive condition is large and the number of parts varies.

2. Color of perianth—Both sepals and petals vary widely in color. Does the color of the perianth give any clue about its function in sexual reproduction? The primitive color is green or white. Why?

3. Reduction or loss of some parts—Often, petals, stamens, or pistils are missing from a flower. If you find a missing part, try to explain why the flower has adapted this way.

4. Ovary superior to petals is a more primitive arrangement than ovary inferior to petals.

5. Bilateral and radial symmetry

Questions to Answer

After observing a number of flowers and noting the variations among them, try to answer the following questions:

1. Why is there so much floral variation? What is the primary purpose or adaptive reason for all this variation?

2. Try to arrange the flowers in evolutionary sequences based on their anatomy. What is the most primitive flower you have observed? Why? The most advanced flower? Why? Is it necessary that an advanced flower on the evolutionary scale be complicated? Can evolution move toward greater simplification or only toward more complication? List the flowers in order of evolutionary advancement.

3. Speculate what the fruit of each flower will look like. The fruit will be the seeds surrounded by some of the ovary and sometimes, by the receptacle. How is seed dispersal brought about in each type of plant?

14

The five activities in Chapter 14 take the study of science outside the classroom. They cover three topics, as shown in the list to follow, and address several levels of scientific proficiency. If necessary, use them as templates to work with to adapt for use with your local resources.

Evolution:
Natural History Museum Trip

Teaches Science Outside the Classroom
Relates to Real Life
Fosters Collaboration

Purpose:

- To learn to identify and explain evolutionary adaptations
- To see how the concepts learned in science class are used by professionals

Method:

1. Obtain a map of the museum. Go to the Invertebrate Collection.
   a. What is distinctive about the horny coral or sea fan *Eugorgia aurantsea?*
   b. Why are the Shaddish sponges in West Indian waters more coarse and have larger openings than those in the Mediterranean Sea?
   c. What are two structural differences and one structural similarity between the tropical fish *Malacanthus needit* and *Malacanthus plumerieri?*

2. Go to the Vertebrate Collection.
   a. Go to the fishes.
      1. On the skeleton of *Arapima gigas,* what is the relationship of the pelvic girdle to the rest of the skeleton? Why is this situation possible here and not in the majority of tetrapods (four-footed animals)?
      2. Why is the *Alopias vulpinus* called the "thresher shark"? What is its specialized tail for?
      3. Fish have adapted in many different ways. What are two structural adaptations that have made certain species of fish more efficient bottom dwellers?
   b. Go to the reptiles and amphibians.
      4. Judging from the skeleton of the cobra, how is the snake able to expand and flatten its neck? What might be a reason that the cobra's neck evolved to do this?
      5. What is peculiar about the reproductive habits of the Evans tree frog, *Hyla evans?* How is this peculiarity advantageous to the frog?

6. What differences can you see between the skull of the alligator and the skull of the crocodile?
7. On the various turtle skeletons, what has happened to the ribs? In what way is the leatherback turtle anatomically more primitive than other turtles?
8. Note the adaptations of geckonid lizards for arboreal and sand dune environments.
9. How are the skeletons of the Ridley, Hawksbill, and Green turtles modified for aquatic existence? Compare your results with the Galapagos turtles.
   c. Go to the collection of birds.
10. Do any of the birds have teeth? Find examples of two types of birds that eat fish or small mammals. What special structural adaptations do they possess?
11. Are there systematic differences in the beak morphology (structure) between insect-eating birds (e.g., warblers and flycatchers) and seedeaters (e.g., finches and sparrows)?
12. Feathers have adapted to suit many purposes. Can you suggest a probable function for the woodpecker's stiff tail feathers and the owl's soft tail feathers?
   d. Go to the collection of mammals.
13. On the bison skeleton, what is the functional advantage of the long neural spines on the cervical and anterior thoracic vertebrae?
14. Compare cervical vertebrae of giraffe, whale, and moose. Note differences in number of vertebrae and any obvious adaptations and their significance.
15. Examine the whales suspended from the roof. Note position and function of baleen. How do baleen whales differ from sperm whales in skull construction?
16. On the sperm whale skeleton, what is the relationship of the pelvic girdle and appendage to the rest of the skeleton? Compare this relation-

ship to the one you observed in the skeleton of the fish *Arapaima gigas*.

17. What are two structural differences and two structural similarities of humans and apes?

18. How do mastodons differ from mammoths and elephants?

19. How are walruses specifically adapted to their environment?

c. Go to the fossils.

20. Compare the posture of the legs in Epaphosaurus, Ophiacodon, and Dimetrodon with that of mammals.

21. Note the progressive modifications of feet and teeth in the exhibit of fossil horses. What changes of diet and habitat do they indicate?

Evolution: Zoo Exploration

Teaches Science Outside the Classroom
Incorporates Alternative Assessment
Fosters Collaboration

Purpose:

- To observe how animals of various species have adapted to their environments through natural selection
- To observe and analyze variation within species
- To make connections between knowledge of evolution and actual species

Method:

Evolution by natural selection states that particular individuals possessing certain characteristics, sometimes called adaptations, remain alive in a specific environment, whereas other organisms without those adaptations may die. If the environment changes, then different adaptations will become important for survival and reproduction, so the population will change as those unable to survive die out. Every environment favors different characteristics, so the organisms that thrive in each environment will be different.

Evolution does not *cause* changes to occur in the environment or the population. Rather, it is a *result* of pressure on the members of the population. Evolution does not follow a prescribed plan nor does it lead to some perfect end product (evolution never ends!). There is just a constant shifting balance between the nature of a population and its response to the environment in which it lives.

The activity you are about to perform primarily illustrates aspects of the Darwinian view of evolution by *natural selection*. Thoughts about evolution did not end with Darwin, however. There are many theories that compete with or modify Darwin's ideas—such as *punctuated equilibrium*. Although science is still trying to establish the best explanation for the process of change through time, no scientist seriously questions the evidence that change has indeed occurred.

Part 1: Variation Within a Species

In this part of the lab, you will study a particular type of organism and decide whether or not organisms of the same species will show some variation within that species. Remember that physical characteristics (size, color, etc.) are not the only factors that help some individuals to survive. There are also differences in physiology, behavior, and reproductive success. Although these and other factors may not be as apparent to the casual observer, they play just as big a role in the process.

1. Choose an animal (species) in the zoo that is represented by at least three (3) different individual specimens. Write the common and scientific names of the animal on the lines that follow. So we can learn as much as possible, each person should pick a different animal.

Animal A

_____

Common name

_____

Scientific name

2. What is the specific location of the animal within the zoo?

3. Examine your animals in detail, and list as many individual differences as possible for the species in question. If there is a great difference between the two sexes in the species you choose, you should compare only specimens of the *same sex*. Also, try not to compare a baby to an adult, because animals change as they grow up. Example: Hair characteristics (long, short, or medium); light brown versus dark brown fur color, and so forth.

4. In the space that follows, discuss the role of variation within a species in the process of evolution by natural selection.

6. Select and list those characteristics that you believe will help the animal fit into its environment. Example: Long fur, to help the animal to stay warm in the cold temperatures, and so forth.

Part 2: Adaptation to the Environment

In this section, you are to examine the environment in which the animal you have chosen naturally lives. Try to see what general characteristics make the animal fit well into that setting and suggest what other characteristics, if present, would make the animal less well-adapted to that particular environment.

5. Write a short paragraph that discusses the environment in which the animal you have chosen lives. Be very specific. Note: You may have to do some additional research here!

7. List a few general characteristics that would make the animal poorly suited to its normal environment.

8. In the following space, discuss the advantages and disadvantages of having particular characteristics in relation to the process of evolution by natural selection.

Part 3A: Convergent Evolution
Due to a Shared Environment

In its most general form, *convergent evolution* is a trend that produces similarities between unrelated organisms because they share a common environment. For example, whales and fish both have finlike structures that move them through their watery environment but that does not mean that they are closely related. Pressure from the environment has dictated that to survive, animals living there must share many "tools of the trade." Organisms coexisting in a given environment will often have a number of characteristics in common as a result of the processes of change working on both populations at the same time.

In this section, you are to find another animal that lives in the *same type* of environment as Animal A. Note: Sometimes, similar environments exist in different parts of the world: for example, a desert in Africa and a desert in North America. Your second animal does not have to live in the same environment, just the same type of environment.

9. Choose a new animal that lives in the same type of environment as Animal A. Write the common and scientific names of the animal on the following lines.

Animal B

_____
Common name

_____
Scientific name

10. What is the specific location of the animal in the zoo?

11. Examine Animal B, and list the characteristics that it has in common with the organism you chose at the beginning (Animal A). Both animals have these characteristics:

12. In the following space, define and discuss the term *convergent evolution.*

13. Why do you think the two animals that share a common environment have so many characteristics in common? How could this similarity have occurred?

14. What do you think might happen if the two animals you have identified lived in not only the same type of environment but in the same area?

Part 3B: Divergent Evolution
Due to Geographic Separation

15. To illustrate further the idea of convergent evolution, identify yet another animal that shares many of the same characteristics as Animal A. Write the common and scientific names of this new animal on the following lines.

Animal C

_____
Common name

_____
Scientific name

16. What is the specific location of the animal in the zoo?

20. Restate the common name of Animal A and the type of environment in which it now lives.

17. Examine Animal C, and list the characteristics that it shares with the organism you chose at the beginning (Animal A). Both animals have:

21. Suppose that for some reason, the animal's normal environment slowly changes. Choose a new environment into which the old one will change. Describe this new environment. *Specifically*, what will be different about it?

18. State and discuss the relationships, if any, between the two organisms that you have identified. Relationships include predator-prey, competitors, helpers (mutualism, symbiosis), no relationship (amensalism), and so forth.

22. Choose eight different characteristics seen in the animal at present. Show how these characteristics will have to change (if they must) as the environment changes, for the species to survive. Example: If a woodland slowly becomes a desert, the green coloration of a species of toad might shift to brown so it could hide more effectively.

19. In the following space, define and discuss the term *divergent devolution.*

23. Do you think that the animal in question will be able to evolve to live in the new environment proposed for it? To help you answer the question, think about the normal variation within the species (Part 1). Do any of the individuals that you have observed have any of the characteristics that would enable it to survive and reproduce as the environment changes?

Part 4: Future Evolution

Go back to the animal you chose first (Animal A), and try to imagine what evolution would do to this animal if its environment slowly changed toward one quite different from that seen at present. For example, you might examine an animal in a desert environment and predict how it would evolve if the environment slowly became more like a woodland.

SOURCE: Reprinted from *The American Biology Teacher*, Vol. 50, No. 6, with permission from The National Association of Biology Teachers.

Plants:
Greenhouse Trip for Advanced Biology Classes

Teaches Science Outside the Classroom
Incorporates Alternative Assessment
Fosters Collaboration

Purpose:

- To learn about the plants of other regions of the country and world
- To observe evolutionary adaptation in action

Method:

Tour the greenhouse and make your observations. You may start any place in your tour. Be sure to be sensitive to the overall atmosphere of the houses as well as appreciative of the fascinating details about the individual plants on display. (Please leave all doors between exhibits exactly as you found them.)

1. *Tillandsias* are members of the pineapple family, *Bromeliaceae,* with some 900 species found in the subtropics and tropics of America. You will see several more species in the Tropical House. *Tillandsias* are sometimes called "air pines" and are found in Georgia and Florida growing wild, festooning old live oak trees and even telephone wires. How do you suppose air pines got their name?

2. *Coleus* are raised for the interesting variations in leaf pigment patterns, which makes them decorative house plants. The green color comes from the chlorophylls, the reds and pinks, from anthocyanins, and the yellows, from carotenes. The purple color is a combination of red and green. What pigments are present in the white portion of the leaves?

3. A well-known refrain by Simon and Garfunkle, "Parsley, Sage, Rosemary and Thyme," comes to mind at this station with its collection of aromatic herbs. The fragrant oils are manufactured by the leaves and are sometimes volatile enough to be detected even without crushing the leaves. Gently press a leaf surface between your fingers and sniff.

4. Green plants are able to manufacture their organic food by means of photosynthesis. But there are some 500 different kinds of plants that, though green and perfectly capable of manufacturing their own food, have fashioned their leaves into unique traps for the capture of insects and other animals. More remarkable still, some of these carnivorous plants have glands that secrete digestive juices so that the animal remains are actually digested and absorbed in much the same manner as in the human digestive tract. Despite many entertaining stories of "man-eaters," all carnivorous plants are small, and the largest animals caught in their traps are dragonflies or small frogs. More frequently, the victims are ants, beetles, gnats, worms, various crustaceans, and larvae. List species of carnivorous plants you can find in this exhibit.

5. One conspicuous tendency among dicots has been the crowding of flowers into clusters, thus increasing and concentrating the mass of attractive color or scent that lures insects and other pollinators to the flowers. The climax of efficient flower clusters is found in the head of plants such as the Daisy, Dandelion, and Aster—all of which belong to the enormous family (13,000 species) known as the *Compositae.* Such a composite flower head (often mistaken for a single flower) is really several small flowers clustered on top of the stem. The head of the flower is composed of numerous tiny florets, each with a pair of fused carpels forming a single ovary, and fused anthers enclosed in a small corolla of fused petals. These fertile florets are in the center, or *disk,* of the composite flower. The *ray flowers* are around the outside, look like large petals, are often a different color from the disk florets, and are often sterile. Describe the flower of one Composite of your choice.

6. The *Crocus* is a member of the iris family. Its name means *saffron*—the expensive powder added to food for coloring and flavor and used as a dye. The stigmas of the flower are collected to be ground into this powder. The *Crocus* is a stemless plant with small grasslike leaves and showy clusters of funnel-shaped flowers that stand erect; the perianth is made from six equal segments. The flowers, which generally only open in the sunlight, bloom early in the spring or in fall. The 75 species of this genus are all native to the Mediterranean and southwestern Asia. The parallel leaf veination, six-part flower, fibrous roots, and single-cotyledon seed all serve to identify the *Crocus* as one example of a *monocot* plant.

7. The *Cyclamen* has beautiful flowers that look as though they have been turned inside out. Where are the reproductive organs located?

8. Find a climbing plant. Examine the *tendrils,* which are specialized tips of the leaves that look like feathers or corkscrews and enable the plant to climb. The tendrils are actually sensitive to shade and touch, which enables them to seek out and wind around any small structure (string, stick, etc.) that casts a shadow.

9. The desert house contains a collection of plants adapted to very dry environments. All these species, although belonging to more than five different families, evolved to use one of two strategies to survive. They either have thick, succulent leaves or thick, succulent, leafless stems (or reduced leaves called *thorns*). This parallel adaptation among different families is an example of *convergent evolution.* Use the posted information to list three other ways plants adapted to dry environments.

10. The Century Plant (agave) has many uses—it can be made into needles and thread for sewing, its fibers can be woven into rope, its meat is edible, and its juices can be fermented to make alcoholic drinks—pulque and mescal. Many species of agave flower just once after many years of growth and then die. They are commonly thought to flower "once in a century." The flowering stalk can be six m (20 ft) or more tall.

11. The Cacti are an exclusive American family of plants. The center of the cactus empire is the southwestern United States and Mexico, where cacti colonize rocky mesas and mountain canyons wherever there is good soil drainage. The only species native to New England is the Prickly Pear (*Opuntia*), which can be found growing wild on Cape Cod.

12. The most magnificent of the *Pterophyta* living today are the Tree Ferns (*Cyatheaceae*). They are a declining

plant type, restricted to humid tropical regions of Australia, New Zealand, Hawaii, Ceylon, East Africa, and South America. A fern forest is unique—feathery, quiet. Today, Tree Ferns are used chiefly as a starchy food for hogs and for building corduroy roads through tropical swamps.

How is the rhizome (stem) of the tree fern different from the rhizome of common ferns?

13. The Banana Plant (*Musa*) grows to be a small tree, even though its stem is below ground, and what looks like a trunk is actually the concentric leaf bases or the enormous, feather-veined leaves. This plant was cut back to the ground after it bore fruit. The leaves, a meter and a half long, are easily torn. The flowers will bloom on a huge, nodding, one-meter-long spike. Each flower becomes one banana, and each banana is grouped with several others into a "hand" (which is what you buy), and several hands are grouped together into a bunch. Each plant bears one bunch of fruit, then dies. A new plant then grows from the base. The banana is actually an elongated berry, with many infertile seeds (the black specks) in the pulp.

14. The Bird of Paradise Flower (*Strelitzia*) is a South African plant cultivated out-of-doors in Florida. It belongs to the same family as the banana and has similar large leaves. The unusual "flower" is actually half a dozen orange and blue flowers that bloom in a boat-shaped spathe resembling a bird in flight.

15. The Bromeliads all belong to the pineapple family. Most are *epiphytic* in habit, living suspended from the branches of the tropical forest canopy.

Many species have a unique leaf arrangement that traps rainfall. Describe how it works.

An unusual member of the family is Spanish or Florida Moss (*Dendropogon*). It is not a moss at all but a flowering plant. It is also an epiphyte, or Air Plant, with no roots and very tiny, silvery leaves. It photosynthesizes but depends on the rain and mist for moisture and minerals.

16. Locate and check off the following economically important plants. *Palms:* Palms of various species supply the primary needs of millions of people in tropical regions. Palms are a source of food (e.g., coconut), lumber, fiber, thatch, vegetable "ivory", oils, waxes, and starches. One of the magnificent palms here is the *Coconut Palm* ____. Notice its enormous leaves and

Linda S. Samuels, *Girls Can Succeed in Science!* Copyright © 1999 by Corwin Press, Inc.

burlaplike stem wrap. *Chicle* (*Sapota*) ____ is found in the jungles of Yucatan and Central America. Its sap is the plastic basis for chewing gums. The best supplier of natural rubber is the *Para Rubber Tree* (*Hevea*) ___, which is native to the Amazon jungles. Just beneath its bark is a network of vessels that produce a milky substance known as *latex*—it is a mixture of water and rubber. The latex is harvested by slicing the bark (look for the old scars) and collecting the ooze, which is then heated or dried to form rubber. You might also be able to find *Chocolate* or *Cacao* (*Theobroma*–"Tea for the Gods") ___, *Papaya* (*Carica*) ___, *Mango* (*Mangifera*) ___, *Breadfruit* (*Artocarpus*) ___, *Taro* ___ with its edible root, and *Ginger* (*Alpinea*)___.

17. The tropical plant house is a tiny sample of a biome that is threatened today—the tropical rain forest. Feel the high humidity, and listen for the quiet dripping of water. The beautiful broad leaves of these luxuriant plants create their own special environment—exhaling water vapor and oxygen to moisten and enrich the air, while tying up carbon dioxide in their plant tissues. Imagine the same house with its vegetation stripped and burned. Now imagine miles and miles of scorched rain forest—as far as you can see in all directions. That is what is happening to the rain forests of the world.

    Find the largest leaves you can. Describe them.

18. The Coffee shrub (*Coffea*) has clusters of fragrant white flowers that develop into dark red berries, containing two seeds buried in the fleshy pulp. After the fruits are picked, they are pulped, and the seeds are removed. To remove the skin covering the seeds, they are allowed to ferment for a few days. The seeds are later dried and roasted. The flavor of coffee is due in part to the development of the aromatic oil, *caffeine*, during the roasting process. It is also caffeine that causes you to feel stimulated after drinking coffee. Caffeine is closely related to the *theine* of tea or the *theobromine* of cocoa.

19. Blooming Citrus have a wonderful smell. At times, large areas of Florida and California smell of blooming citrus. All citrus species have an edible fruit that consists of an oily rind or skin surrounding a fleshy pulp that is divided into compartments. In this genus, we find the orange, lemon, grapefruit, citron, and lime, all of which have several varieties. How many can you count in this small area?

20. The Papaya Family (*Caricaceae*) includes a few tropical and subtropical shrubs and trees with edible fruit. The main trunk is unbranched and stout and can grow to a height of over six m or 20 ft. The top is crowned by a mass of large palmately compound leaves. The flowers and fruits grow just beneath the leaf cluster; each fruit is melon shaped, may weigh as much as seven kg or 15 lb, and has a muskmelon flavor.

21. The Powder Puff Tree is spectacular in bloom. Examine a cluster of flowers carefully. What flower part has enlarged to give the "puff" impression?

22. The Cinnamon Tree (*Cinnamonum*) is native to tropical Asia and Australia. The bark of young stems is harvested and dried for use as a spice. At first, the forest trees were wastefully stripped of their bark by the Portugese. Later, after intense fighting for control for the spice trade of the Indies, the British cultivated cinnamon trees in gardens. Today, most cinnamon comes from Ceylon. The Chinese have used cinnamon since 2700 B.C.

23. Floating on the surface of the pools are a couple of the tiniest true plants known. The tiny lacy leaves belong to the Water Fern (*Azolla*), sometimes called the *mosquito fern*, a truly aquatic fern relative. Some states have tried growing mats of these tiny plants on ponds to suffocate mosquito larvae. The Water Fern produces spores in the spring.

24. Orchids have often been called the elite of the plant kingdom; certainly, in their floral structure, they represent one of the culminations of plant evolution. Their often showy (even when in miniature), fragrant, uniquely constructed blossoms are fascinating to laymen and botanists alike. Their rarity, the peculiar relationship of their germinating seedlings with root fungi (mycorrhizae), and the exotic appeal of tropical epiphytic species combine to make Orchids especially interesting.

    The tropical ladyslipper orchids are the only terrestrial orchids in the collection. All the others are epiphytic, growing naturally on the branches of trees or hung on lattice (simulating their natural environment).

    The only orchid with any economic use is the Vanilla Plant (*Vanilla*). Notice that it is a vine with a ropelike stem. The flowers are not spectacular, but the elongated fruit capsule is the vanilla bean of commerce. The unripe capsules are picked and dried. The vanillin crystallizes on the outside of the capsule.

    Examine several different orchid flowers. Describe any patterns you observe that would help define the common characteristics of orchid flowers.

25. The Sugar Cane (*Saccharum*), a native grass of India, thrives only in hot regions. It has been cultivated in India and China since ancient times and was introduced to Europe after the Crusades and later, to America and the West Indies. In the United States, it is grown only in the Gulf States. The plants are propagated from stem cuttings and grow to more than 4 m or 15 ft tall. The sap is collected by crushing the stalks and then evaporating the juice. What doesn't make it as "refined" sugar is called *molasses*.

26. The Grass Family (*Poaceae*) is one of the most important families of food plants, many of which have been cultivated for over 5,000 years. With their narrow parallel-veined leaves, fibrous roots, and (in many species) underground stems that extend horizontally and sprout tufts of leaves, grasses form an ideal impediment to erosion by forming a carpetlike sod. Under the best conditions, grasses form extensive communities, such as our prairies, the Russian steppes, the South American pampas, and the African veldt or savannah. The fruit of the grass formed after pollination is a one-seeded *grain*, which is a husk (chaff) with a nourishing seed inside. The fruits of the cereal grains have furnished the "staff of life" for most cultures around the world.

    The cereal grasses have all been perfected through the years to have larger, more nourishing grains than their wild ancestors. The grains are a nearly perfect food, containing all the essential nutrients. Because they are produced as dry fruits, they can be stored and shipped successfully. What important grasses have you seen today?

27. Tobacco (*Nicotiana*) is a vigorous growing annual reaching a height of nearly 2 m or 5 ft. Its leaves contain the narcotic *nicotine*. Sadly, tobacco is perhaps one of the most important economic contributions of the New World. South American Indians were already cultivating tobacco for smoking when the first European explorers reached these shores. Today, of course, we discourage the use of this harmful plant.

28. Maize or Corn (*Zea*) differs from most other grasses because it has separate staminate and pistillate flowers. Staminate flowers are clustered to form the plumelike tassel at the top of the corn plant, whereas the pistillate flowers are grouped on an axis (the cob) lower down on the stalk. The entire pistillate axis is enclosed by leafy husks, and threadlike projections from each pistil (the silk) extend beyond the husk to catch the pollen. Special "prop roots" act as buttress supports for the tall plant. Maize is a subtropical and tropical American plant whose wild ancestors are

unknown. Modern corn is the result of thousands of years of selective breeding (by the Mayas and earlier tribes). We continue to develop new strains on an almost annual basis, such as the newest "supersweet" varieties.

29. Vegetative propagation is a way some plants multiply without sexual reproduction. Vegetative propagation works on two basic principles: the ability of plants to send out roots from an injured (i.e., a cut) surface and the ability of tissue from related plants to weld together and grow into a single plant when placed close together.

    A *cutting* or *slip* from a plant can be inserted in the right growing medium and will produce roots and eventually, a new plant. This method has been practiced since the ancient Greek civilization. A second method leaves the injured part of the parent plant covered with moss or soil until it produces roots, at which point, it is removed to grow into a new plant. Some stems will grow roots when they are simply covered with soil, a method known as *layering*.

    When a bud from one plant is welded to another so that it will grow using a foreign stem and root system, it is called *grafting*. It is commonly used with woody plants, such as apples and roses.

    Still another strategy of vegetative propagation is to split an existing clump of vegetation (grass), bulbs (onion), corms (crocus), tubers (potato), rhizome (Iris), or runners (strawberries). This method is called *division*.

30. The Spike Mosses (*Selaginella*) are closely related to Club Mosses and are a Fern relative (*Pterophyta*). Notice their mosslike bodies, which form matted growths over ground, trunks of trees, and rocks. These plants do not flower but reproduce by spores.

31. The most ancient of known land plants began their development in the middle of the Paleozoic Era. A small group of fern allies living today are considered a dwindling remnant of these early pioneers. The Whisk Fern (*Psilotum*) has stiff leaves. It is a tropical plant and is found in this country only in southern Florida, where it forms inconspicuous tufts at the bases of Cabbage Palms.

32. There is no other single plant that has influenced civilization as much as the Cotton Plant (*Gossypium*). Cotton was cultivated as long as 5,000 years ago in India, and Columbus found the American aborigines using cotton cloth. It ranks as the most important plant fiber and played an important part in bringing on the Industrial Revolution, which had far-reaching effects on civilization. In nature, cotton is tree sized, but cultivated cotton, with its heart-shaped leaves, is herbaceous (soft stemmed). The fruiting capsule, or *boll*, contains seeds that are covered with long, white unicellular hairs. The hairs have a natural twist that helps them to be woven into threads and yarns.

33. The Sensitive Plant (*Mimosa*) quickly reacts to touch. The movement seems to be related to changes in hydrostatic pressure in certain cells at the bases of the leaflets and leaves. However, there is still a mystery surrounding the transmission of the "touch" message. The plant has no nerves, yet it can be "put to sleep" with ether!

What selective advantage might be gained by this plant's peculiar behavior? (It is often found growing in grazing lands in subtropical areas).

34. When the early Spanish and Italian explorers discovered a flower with blood-red fringe around the inside of the corolla, spikelike stamens surrounding a central carpel, and numerous other flower parts, which to their imaginative minds looked like implements used for the crucifixion of Christ, they immediately named the plant "Passion Flower" (*Passiflora*). The ornamental passion flowers, derived from species native to Central America, Mexico, and Brazil, are highly prized for their extravagantly colored and constructed flowers.

SOURCE: Wayland High School (1991). Used with permission.

Plants:
Greenhouse Trip for Biology Classes

Teaches Science Outside the Classroom
Relates to Real Life
Fosters Collaboration

Purpose:

- To learn to identify various families and species of plant life
- To observe how plants have adapted to various environmental conditions

Method:

Tour the greenhouse and answer the following questions:

1. Identify four to five types of plants that are being grown as seedlings.

2. Why are some plants grown in soft peat pots?

3. Touch a Sensitive Plant. Come up with a hypothesis as to why they move.

4. Look at the sandy flats. They contain a number of different kinds of *cuttings* (pieces of parent plants). It is hoped that they will develop roots of their own and flourish. This is a means of *artificial propagation.* Can you identify some of the plants?

5. Some branch cuttings were brought into the greenhouse for the purpose of *forcing.* After a period of cold dormancy, plants will often bloom and leaf out if you bring them indoors. This is a great way to have fresh flowers in the winter.

6. Smell the Marigolds. They contain pyrethrum. Some people believe that this chemical keeps insects away from plants.

7. Find a Begonia. What kinds of flowers do these plants have? Look carefully. These flowers are *dioecious* (male and female flowers are separate and on different parts of the same plant). Corn is another example of a dioecious plant. Find the male and female flowers. What is unusual about a begonia's leaves?

8. Find a plant that is being *air layered.* Air layering allows a botanist to cut the stem a little around the cut area wrapped in a plastic bag. Roots will soon grow as the cells redifferentiate in the cut area. Sometimes, a hormone is placed in the cut area to speed up differentiation. Name a plant that is being air layered.

9. Foxglove (digitalis) is a medicinal plant with a long history of use in treating heart disease patients. What is the arrangement of the flowers in this plant?

10. Find Nicotiana, Nasturtium, and Sweet Pea flowers. Are these flowers monocots or dicots? Can you state two reasons why?

11. Are there any Mosses or Liverworts in this greenhouse? Keep your eyes focused low—to the floors and under the pots—for signs of any of these primitive land plants. They need to be close to water and in shaded areas because they have no vascular systems. Report any of these plants you see during the trip.

12. Look for African Violets. Some are being propagated in strange ways: by leaf cuttings. Find one, and briefly state what you notice at the base of the leaf cutting.

13. Examine the pigmentation (color) in the leaves around you. Name three plants with lots of green chlorophyll and three plants that are lighter in coloring.

14. What does the amount of green chlorophyll have to do with the capability of the plant to produce food?

15. Look for the Powder Puff Tree. What part of the flower provides coloration and the overall effect (petals? sepals? stamens?)

16. Observe the temperature and relative humidity (air moist or dry?) in the Cactus room.

    How is this house different from the others you have visited?

    How have the plants here adapted themselves to survive in a superdry environment?

    Do cacti have flowers?

    Spines are found on some cactus plants. What are spines? (roots, stems, or leaves?)

17. Compare the vegetation of the tropical plant house with that seen in the cactus house. How are the plants different?

18. Find a Banana Plant, and look to see if it has bananas on it. Why are the leaves of a banana plant so broad and long?

19. Find the Bird of Paradise plant.
20. Find a Cycad. What kind of reproductive parts can be seen on these plants?

21. Before seed plants evolved, Tree Ferns dominated the great forests of the earth. There are other plants in the center circle. Name two of them.

    Ferns and cycads (along with horsetails, such as *Equisetum*) are the plants that produced the petroleum and coal products we use today. They once ruled the earth—during the time of the dinosaurs, millions of years ago.

22. What are *Epiphytes*? I'll tell you! They are *air plants*. They grow by hanging on other plants. They are not attached directly to the ground. How do these plants get water?

23. There are a number of climbing plants in these greenhouses. What are the special adaptive characteristics of these plants? (How are they designed to climb?)

    How might this way of life (climbing) aid the plant to survive?

24. Many plants have aromatic oils in their tissues that give them characteristic fragrances. Sometimes, these smells are pleasant, other times, not so nice (Skunk Cabbage!). There are some fragrant leaves in this room. Find one, and lightly rub the leaf between your fingers (you may touch them), and then, sniff. Can you recognize the smell?

25. Check the following economically important plants if you can locate them.

    Rice   ____

    Bamboo   ____

    Sugar cane   ____

    Papyrus   ____

    Scouring rush ____

26. In the Orchid Room, you can observe many types of Orchid flowers. What characteristics can you identify that would group all of them together as orchids?

27. Plants can react to their environment but usually, very slowly. Find the Venus Fly Trap and the Sundew. What special adaptations do these plants have that would enable them to catch insects in the nutrient-poor soil that they live in?

    The Venus Fly Trap and the Sensitive Plant have basal cells that quickly lose turgor water pressure when disturbed. The water will soon build up again and reopen the leaves.

28. Look around you. Compare leaf characteristics of the different plants you see. Describe ways leaves may differ in terms of the following:

    a. Pigmentation:

    b. General shape:

    c. Edges:

    d. Surfaces:

    e. Attachments:

29. Look at the Coleus plants. How do the varieties differ?

30. If you wanted to make different varieties of foliage, would you perform your breeding experiments on the roots, stems, leaves, or flowers of the plants? Explain your answer.

31. What are some differences between spore-bearing and seed-bearing plants?

Review:

For homework, answer the following questions:

1. Choose one of the greenhouse plants that you found interesting. Please tell something special about it. Be specific and informative.

2. Name four plants we saw at the greenhouse that humans use for food.

3. Name at least two plants at the greenhouse that humans use in medicine. Then, tell how and in what medicines we use them.

4. List four monocots and four dicots that we saw at the greenhouse.

5. Choose two plants we saw in the greenhouse. State and explain their special evolutionary adaptations.

6. Did any of the greenhouses depict particular environments? If so, name one type of environment and some of the plants that grow in it.

CityLab Visit:
Mystery of the Crooked Cell

Note for the Teacher:

This activity was developed by CityLab, Boston University Medical School's biotechnology learning laboratory, which invites participation from area schools. Following is a partial list of centers in other parts of the country that teachers may contact about similar experiences for their students:

Biotechology Teaching Lab, Stony Brook, NY
DNA Learning Center, Cold Spring Harbor, NY
Eccles Institute, Salt Lake City, UT
Fernbank Science Center, Atlanta, GA
Mathematics and Science Education Center, St. Louis, MO
Tech Center of Innovation, San Jose, CA

Introduction:

Sickle cell anemia is a genetic disease that affects the hemoglobin molecule of red blood cells. The hemoglobin molecule is composed of four amino acid chains. The most common type of hemoglobin is called hemoglobin A. It consists of two alpha chains and two beta chains of amino acids. Sickle cell hemoglobin, hemoglobin S, is identical to hemoglobin A except the sixth amino acid in the chain is valine instead of glutamic acid. This single change in amino acids causes the molecule to stick together in long chains in the blood cell that distort the shape of the cell, giving it the characteristic sickle shape (see Figure 14.1). A low concentration of oxygen contributes to the formation of chains by hemoglobin S. The switch in amino acids also causes hemoglobin S to have a lower net negative charge.

The irregularly shaped blood cells lead to a cascade of symptoms. The sickled blood cells become hard and inflexible. Blood no longer flows freely through the capillaries and tends to clog, causing pain and swelling. This condition results in a lower concentration of oxygen being delivered by the blood that in turn, creates more sickling. The sickle-shaped red blood cells only last about 10 days as opposed to the 120-day cycle of healthy red blood cells. The bone marrow cannot produce enough red blood cells to keep up with the demand, resulting in anemia. With an abnormally high amount of red blood cells breaking down, there is an excess of bilirubin present (bilirubin is a yellow pigment that results from the breakdown of hemoglobin). The liver usually removes bilirubin from the blood. If the liver cannot break bilirubin down fast enough, it builds up, and jaundice results. Bilirubin can harden and cause gall stones.

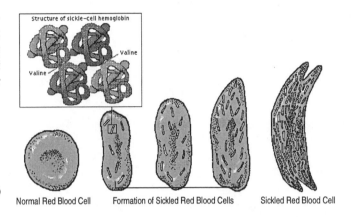

Figure 14.1. *Sickle-Cell Anemia*
Sickle cell anemia arises from a mutation in hemoglobin, the protein that carries oxygen in the bloodstream. A substitution in its amino acid sequence (valine, where glutamic acid should be) causes the four-chained hemoglobin molecule to form incorrectly when oxygen is low. Defective hemoglobins bind together, forming long rods that stretch the red blood cell into a crescent. These "sickled" red blood cells cannot fit through small blood vessels.

SOURCE: Microsoft Illustration: "Sickle-Cell Anemia," Microsoft® *Encarta® 96 Encyclopedia.* (c) 1993-1995 Microsoft Corporation. All rights reserved.

A sickling episode, or crisis, can be brought on by infection, dehydration, overexertion, high altitude, chills, or cold weather. Sometimes, there is no apparent precipitating factor. Often, people with sickle cell anemia are more susceptible to fevers and infection.

There is no cure for sickle cell anemia. Hydration, bed rest, pain killers, and antibiotics are often prescribed. Recently, Dr. Susan Perrine of Children's Hospital Oakland Research Institute in Oakland, California, has tested butyrate on patients with sickle cell anemia. Initial results indicate that butyrate, a fatty acid produced by the body and found in certain foods, may turn on the gene that produces fetal hemoglobin in the blood. The production of fetal hemoglobin usually decreases after birth and is replaced by adult hemoglobin. Fetal hemoglobin in patients with sickle cell anemia may replace the diseased hemoglobin and offer some relief for people with the disease.

There are three tests for sickle cell anemia. They are called sickle cell prep, the sickle dex, and hemoglobin electrophoresis. The first two can produce a high percentage of false positives. Hemoglobin electrophoresis is the most accurate and can identify sickle cell trait as well as sickle cell anemia.

In this activity, students will visit stations to obtain clues about a mystery disease described to them. Each station challenges the students to explore a different aspect of sickle cell anemia. Working in groups, they will manipulate models and gather data to try to figure out what is causing the symptoms that have been described to them by the patient. The instructor will lead a discussion about the disease and how it causes the symptoms described. At CityLab, they will use hemoglobin electrophoresis as a tool to diagnose a fictional patient with either sickle cell anemia or sickle cell trait.

Previsit

Purpose:

■ To explore the connection of hemoglobin to the symptoms exhibited in sickle cell anemia

Objectives:

1. Observe prepared normal and sickle cell slides.
2. Manipulate models of blood cells to gather data and make inferences about sickle cell anemia.
3. Analyze an inheritance pattern using a pedigree.
4. Work cooperatively to develop an explanation for the symptoms exhibited in sickle cell anemia.

Materials:

Four microscopes
Prepared slides of sickle cell blood and normal blood (2 each)
Two models, one of normal hemoglobin and one of affected hemoglobin in red blood cells
One model of capillary made from tygon tubing
Several clay models of round and sickled red blood cells

Teacher Preparation:

Make a copy of the station guide sheets for each group (see samples at the end of this two-part activity).

Set up each station as follows:

Station A: Four microscopes and the prepared slides of sickle cell blood and normal blood

Station B: One model of capillaries represented by clear tubing; clay models of round and sickled red blood cells

Station C: Two models, one of normal hemoglobin and one of affected hemoglobin in red blood cells

Station D: Key of symbols used in the pedigree

Method:

1. Engagement:

Working in teams of four, students will be given the following description of a patient in which various symptoms are described. The students will be asked to learn more about the disease to find out what is causing the symptoms.

In 1904, a student from the West Indies came to a Chicago physician, Dr. James Herrick, with a puzzling condition. Following is a summary of some of the observations Dr. Herrick made. Your job is to learn more about this condition and to find out how the disease is affecting this person's body. Read the description to follow, and underline the information that you may think may provide important clues that will help you understand the disease.

The patient reports feeling well most of the time. But he also reports odd recurring events. For instance, one day, after a short swim, he became so tired that he could hardly move. He became short of breath and complained of pain in his joints and muscles, especially the arms and legs. He felt unusually weak and required bed rest lasting a few weeks. These symptoms occurred repeatedly during this youth. He also had frequent fevers and infections.

The patient complained of fatigue and soreness in the joints. On inspection, the whites of his eyes had a yellowish tint. He complained of pain in the left abdominal area, which was tender to the touch.

A family history revealed that he has two brothers and three sisters. None of them have this problem. His uncle and his grandmother used to have similar attacks. His grandmother died a young woman. His parents do not have this condition.

2. Exploration:

After the students have read the story, tell them they will investigate this disease in the lab today.

Their challenge is to learn as much as they can about the disease and try to establish what is happening in the patient to cause the symptoms. They will begin learning about the disease by investigating questions at a series of stations in the room. Each team of four will be responsible for recording their observations and conclusions at each station. Before proceeding, give each team a station sheet that will describe each station and the questions posed. The students are to alternate recording the group's findings at each station. They will write their responses on the station sheet. Allow 15 minutes for each group at a station.

a. Station A

Six microscopes are set up, each with a slide marked "P" for patient's blood or "N" for normal blood. Every team member observes each sample. They draw and describe what they see. When everyone is finished, the drawings and descriptions are shared such that the students determine how the patient's blood differed from the normal blood.

b. Station B

Students are given models that represent blood vessels and red blood cells from a person with sickle cell anemia. They are asked to find the effect the patient's cells will have on the flow of blood through the blood vessel system. The team will be required to record the conclusions they have made from their observations.

c. Station C

Models representing red blood cells are present. One set represents the patient's blood, the other set represents normal blood. Each set contains pieces that represent hemoglobin. The response of normal and sickle cell hemoglobin in conditions of low oxygen concentration are described. Based on this information, students use the models to determine how the cell shape is altered by the different hemoglobin structures.

d. Station D

A pedigree of sickle cell anemia in the patient's family will be available (Figure 14.2). Students will use it to investigate the pattern of inheritance of the disease. (Figure 14.2 can be found at the end of the activity with the other sample materials.)

3. Explanation:

After each group completes all four stations, they will put outlines of their findings about sickle cell anemia on the board.

Each team will present an oral summary of their results to the class. Some main points are these:

a. The blood cells are irregularly shaped.
b. The irregular shape of the red blood cells interferes with their ability to
   • Flow through the blood pathways
   • Carry oxygen
c. The blood cells are irregular because the Hgb protein is altered.
d. The condition is inherited.

The instructor will lead a discussion about the class findings. Some sample questions and suggested answers follow.

What observations did you make when you observed the blood samples using the microscope?

Patient sample usually has a lower concentration of red blood cells. This indicates anemia. The patient sample may have irregularly shaped cells although this is not always readily apparent.

What clues may account for the anemia observed?

The cells with abnormal hemoglobin are more likely to break prematurely due to repeated sickling.

Why do the symptoms seem to be brought on during times of exertion, such as running, swimming, or climbing a mountain?

Low oxygen concentrations cause hemoglobin to sickle.

How do you think one gets the disease?

It's inherited.

What do you think the disease is called?

Sickle cell anemia

If you were looking for a cure for sickle cell anemia, what would you try to fix?

The hemoglobin

The main point to be made is that the altered hemoglobin is the source of the cascade of symptoms. Laboratory investigation will focus on the analysis of hemoglobin as a method for identifying sickle cell anemia.

4. Closure:

Ask the students to make a concept map depicting what they learned today about sickle cell anemia.

Medical Laboratory Visit

Purpose:

■ To understand the molecular basis for sickle cell anemia
■ To use gel electrophoresis as a research tool

Objectives:

1. Perform gel electrophoresis to separate normal hemoglobin from sickle cell hemoglobin.
2. Interpret results of gel electrophoresis.
3. Make inferences about genotype from observed phenotypic expression of hemoglobin.
4. Demonstrate the process and concept of protein electrophoresis.

Method:

1. Engagement:

Remind students that yesterday, they investigated sickle cell anemia. As a brief review, ask the class what they discovered.

After the discussion, ask the students what they would do to confirm that someone had sickle cell anemia. A common response is to examine the blood and look for anemia or sickled cells. However, anemia is not an exclusive symptom nor are the blood cells necessarily sickled unless the patient is in crisis. It makes more sense to look at the hemoglobin because that is the component that is affected.

Hold up a microfuge tube with a sample of hemoglobin. It has been taken from a patient who has symptoms of sickle cell anemia. Tell the students that each person will test the hemoglobin in the lab today and use the evidence to diagnose the patient. Each student will be given a sample of normal hemoglobin to use as a control. They will use a technique called *protein electrophoresis* to identify the patient's hemoglobin.

To demonstrate the concept of protein electrophoresis, have two groups of five students come to the front of the room. Each group represents a hemoglobin molecule (one of millions in the tube) from Sample A and Sample B, respectively. Each person represents an amino acid. Note that both molecules have the same number of amino acids and are therefore the same size. Ask the students if there are any distinguishing characteristics displayed so far. Then, give each student a card with a number representing a charge of –1 or 0 written on it. To Sample A, give three people –1 charges and two people 0 charges. To Sample B, give three people 0 charges and two people –1 charges. Ask the students how the two molecules differ now. They can see that Sample A has a net charge of –3 and Sample B has a net charge of –2. Ask the students how the difference in overall charge can be expressed in an electric field. To illustrate the concept, ask the class to imagine the classroom as an electric field. There is a negative pole at the same end as the hemoglobin molecules and a positive pole at the opposite end of the room. Ask in which direction the molecules will go when the electric current is turned on. The negatively charged hemoglobin molecules will migrate toward the positive pole. Ask which molecule will move fastest toward the positive pole. Sample A, with the net charge of –3, will get there first. Have the students move as the molecules would, with Sample A moving ahead of Sample B. Stop the students before Sample A has reached the end to demonstrate that the samples have been distinguished by the rate at which they move through the electric field. Figure 14.3 can be used as an overhead projector image and summarizes the process. (Figure 14.3 can be found at the end of the activity with the other sample materials.)

2. Exploration:

In the lab, the students will use techniques that enable the concept described earlier to be applied to hemoglobin. Using the demonstration equipment provided, briefly describe the procedures used in the lab:

a. Make the gel. The purpose of the gel is as a media to slow the rate of movement of the hemoglobin and to provide a lane for the hemoglobin to travel in a straight line, much like a track. Pass a gel around the class for students to observe.
b. Put the gel in the electrophoresis box where the electric current will be applied.
c. Add the hemoglobin to the gel.
d. Close the lid of the electrophoresis box and turn on the electricity.

The process just described will be applied by each student to test the sample of hemoglobin given to them. They will need to diagnose the patient based on their results and their knowledge of the process. Before entering the lab, review the safety procedures. Give each student a lab procedure guide (a sample guide prepared by Boston University School of Medicine's CityLab will be

found at the end of this activity). Remind them to keep accurate notebooks.

The instructor will work with the laboratory staff while in the lab to guide and coach the students. The laboratory procedure identifies when techniques can be demonstrated for the students. The degree of coaching and demonstration will vary with the capabilities of the class.

3. Explanation:

When the gels are completed, the students can return to a room where they will analyze the gels. Results will vary. Some samples will produce two bands representative of sickle cell trait, others will be positive for sickle cell anemia, and some will be negative for sickle cell anemia. Students will write their analyses in their notebooks with evidence to support their results.

To facilitate discussion, choose a representative gel of each outcome and put the gels on the overhead projector. Highlight the bands projected on the board with a marker. Some sample questions for discussion follow:

What can be concluded about the differences of each protein based on what you understand about how the process of protein electrophoresis works?

The diseased hemoglobin has a lower net negative charge.

How do you explain the presence of two bands in some patient samples?

Two proteins were expressed. The patient has both types of hemoglobin. He or she is a carrier.

What does this tell you about the inheritance of sickle cell anemia? Is it dominant, recessive, codominant, incompletely dominant?

Codominant

4. Closure:

Have the students write a letter to the fictional patient explaining the results of the test and the precautions the patient may want to consider taking.

Follow Up:

1. Sickle cell anemia is an example of one genetic condition for which there is a test but no cure. Have groups of students research other inherited conditions for which there is a test but no cure: for example, cystic fibrosis, Huntington's disease, muscular dystrophy, and fragile x syndrome. Each group can make an informative display about the disease. The display could be in the form of a poster, mobile, booklet, radio broadcast, interview, role play, and so forth. After each group has

made a presentation about the disease, create a role play in which a genetic counselor presents a scenario. For example,

Both parents are carriers for sickle cell anemia, cystic fibrosis, or any recessive disorder. The couple decides whether or not to try to have children.

One spouse's parent has been diagnosed with Huntington's disease. The couple has two younger children. The counselor asks whether they want to be tested.

The role plays can lead to interesting discussions among the students. The teacher can facilitate by writing down ideas and issues on the board as they come up.

2. Invite a genetic counselor to speak to the class.
3. Use the follow-up worksheet, "A Closer Look at the Cause of Sickle Cell Anemia," to help students discover the connection between a point mutation and its effect on protein synthesis.

Note for the Teacher:

Sample sheets follow for Stations A through D, used in the Previsit segment, and Figure 14.3, useful for the Lab Visit segment.

SOURCE: Activity reprinted with permission of CityLab, Boston University School of Medicine, Boston. CityLab is a fully equipped biotechnology learning laboratory at the Boston University School of Medicine for use by high school teachers and their students. It is funded by the National Institutes of Health and the Howard Hughes Medical Institute. The participation of more than 500 teachers and 7,000 students at CityLab since 1992 has provided valuable input for the development of this activity.

Station A

At this station, you will use a microscope to observe blood samples magnified 1000X. The slide marked "P" represents the patient's blood sample. The slide marked "N" represents the normal blood sample.

Describe the differences you see between the two blood samples.

Station B

The tubing at this station represents the pathways of blood in the body. Pieces representing the patient's red blood cells are given. For blood to do its job of delivering oxygen and picking up wastes, red blood cells must flow freely through the body. Use these models to show the effect the patient's red blood cells will have on the flow of blood.

What symptoms do you think are caused by the abnormal red blood cells?

Station C

At this station, you will be given two sets of models. Each model represents a blood cell. One model is labeled "patient's blood." The other model is labeled "normal blood." The pieces inside the blood cells represent blood proteins called *hemoglobin units.* This model uses only a few pieces to represent the millions of hemoglobin units found in real blood cells.

Hemoglobin has two functions: (a) It carries oxygen, and (2) it gives the red blood cell its shape. In the patient's blood cells, the units of hemoglobin connect together when oxygen levels are low.

Show what would happen to the shape of both these cells if oxygen levels were low in the blood. Record your results on this page.

Linda S. Samuels, *Girls Can Succeed in Science!* Copyright © 1999 by Corwin Press, Inc.

Station D

Given the family history shown in Figure 14.2, can you
explain how the patient got the condition?

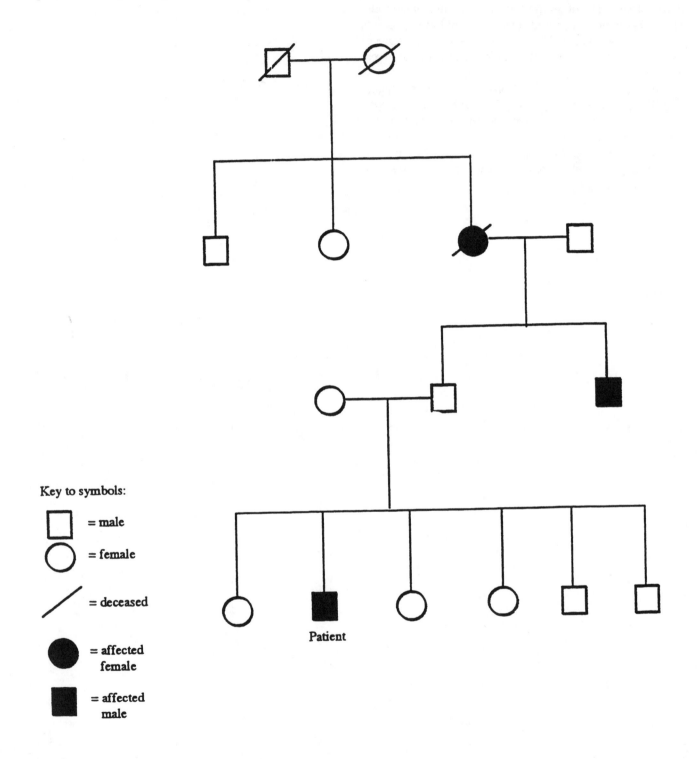

Figure 14.2. *Station D*

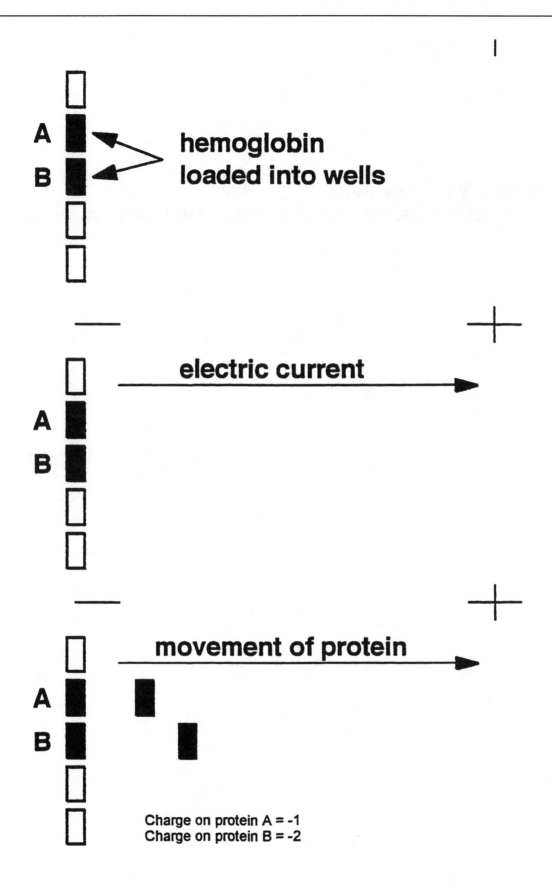

Figure 14.3. *Protein Electrophoresis*

SOURCE: Reprinted with permission of CityLab, Boston University School of Medicine, Boston.

NOTE: Charge on Protein A = –1; charge on Protein B = –2.

Laboratory Procedure

I. Preparing the gel

Equipment needed:

10-ml pipette with a pipette pump
Test tube
Electronic balance
Vortex
Water bath
Casting deck
Casting tray
Combs

Chemicals needed:

Agarose
Electophoresis buffer

At your station, you will find two numbered test tubes, one for each person. These will be used to mix the agarose powder and the buffer solution. The agarose powder is located next to the balances. The electrophoresis buffer solution is in a bottle at your station. Wait for the instructor to demonstrate the use of the equipment. Then, follow the instructions in the order given.

A. *Mix the agarose and electrophoresis buffer.*

1. Bring the numbered test tube at your station to the electronic balance. Use the electronic balance to measure 0.2 g of agarose. Add the agarose to your test tube.
2. Return to your station. Use the 10-ml pipette to add 15 ml of electrophoresis buffer to the agarose powder in your test tube (see Figure 14.4).

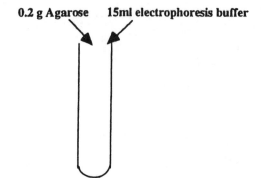

0.2 g Agarose   15ml electrophoresis buffer

Figure 14.4. *Test Tube With 2 Arrows*

3. Use the vortex to *gently* mix the agarose-buffer solution. Mix carefully so that the agar does not spill.
4. Give the test tube containing the agarose-buffer solution to an instructor who will put it into a hot water bath. Keep it in the water bath until the agarose

powder is completely dissolved. When the solution is clear, you can take it out. While you are waiting for the agarose to dissolve, proceed to Part B.

B. *Set up the casting deck and casting trays.*

The casting deck and tray are used to mold the gel into a rectangular shape as it hardens. The casting tray is nothing more that the glass slide that will support the gel. The casting deck acts as the actual mold into which you will pour the gel.

1. Place the casting tray into the casting deck (see Figure 14.5).
2. Put the casting tray on a level surface.

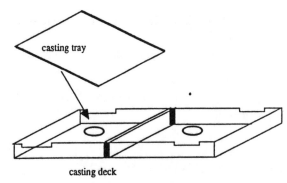

casting tray

casting deck

Figure 14.5. *Casting Deck and Casting Tray*

C. *Pour the agarose solution into the casting deck.*

1. When the agarose is dissolved, remove the test tube from the water bath.

   Caution: The test tube is hot. Hold the test tube by the top. Do not grab it around the tape.

2. Pour the agarose solution into one side of the casting deck (see Figure 14.6).

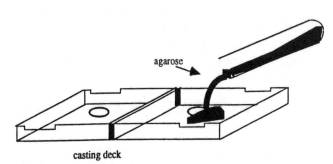

agarose

casting deck

Figure 14.6. *Casting Deck and Liquid Pouring From Test Tube*

3. Insert a comb into the slots in the end of the casting deck. Make sure the long side of the comb faces the center of the casting deck (see Figure 14.7).

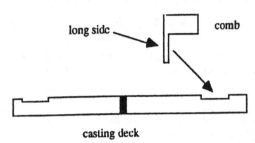

Figure 14.7. *Casting Deck and Comb*

Wait for the gel to cool until it is opaque in color and firm to the touch.

5. Wash the test tube. Follow the washing instructions at the sink.

Watch for the demonstration on how to use the equipment for Part II.

II. Preparing the gel electrophoresis box

Equipment needed:

Electrophoresis box
Casting deck and casting tray

Chemicals needed:

Electrophoresis buffer

A. *Remove the hardened gel from the casting deck.*

1. Remove the comb from the tray. The depressions left in the gel are referred to as *wells.*
2. Put your thumb through the hole in the bottom of the casting deck and gently push on the casting tray (the glass slide) until the gel comes out. (If you have difficulty, you may need to "score" the sides of the gel with a spatula. Ask an instructor for assistance.)

B. *Place the gel and casting tray in the electrophoresis box.*

1. Keep the gel on the casting tray and place it on the central platform of the electrophoresis box so that the wells are at the *negative* (black electrode) end (see Figure 14.8). Note: Two gels will fit in each electrophoresis box.

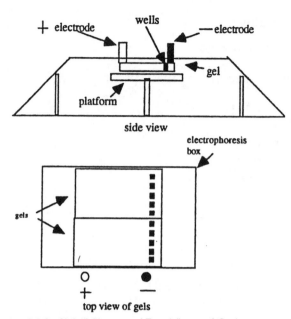

Figure 14.8. *Side View and Top View of Gels*

2. Slowly pour the contents of the bottle labeled "Hgb Buffer" into the electrophoresis box until the gels are covered with a 2-mm to 3-mm layer of buffer. You can pour the buffer directly from the bottle (see Figure 14.9).

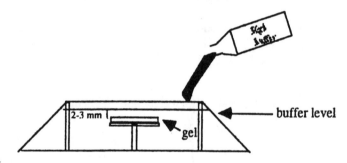

Figure 14.9. *Buffer Level*

III. Loading the samples of hemoglobin into the wells

Equipment needed:

Micropipette P20
Micropipette tips

Samples needed:

Hemoglobin samples A and B

Use the micropipettes as demonstrated previously by the instructors.

1. Use a micropipette (P20) to put 15 μ of hemoglobin from Sample A into a well. Keep a record of the well you put Sample A into in your notebook.
2. Use a micropipette (P20) to put 15 μ of hemoglobin from Sample B into a well. Keep a record of the well you put Sample B into in your notebook.

Caution: After loading your gel, gently *close the lid* of the electrophoresis box to avoid exposure to high voltage.

IV. Connecting the cables and turning on the electricity

Equipment needed:

Electrophoresis box
Power source
Positive and negative cables (red and black, respectively)

A. Connecting the cables

Caution: *High voltage* will be used. Be sure the lid on the electrophoresis box is in the closed position before proceeding.

1. Connect the red cable to the red electrode on the electrophoresis box.
2. Connect the black cable to the black electrode on the electrophoresis box.
3. Connect the other end of the red cable to the red plug on the power source.
4. Connect the other end of the black cable to the black plug on the power source.

B. Turning on the power

Before turning on the power, have an instructor check your connections. He or she will instruct you as to how to turn on your power supply.
Return to the classroom and eat lunch!

VI. Removal of the gel from the electrophoresis box

1. Turn the *power off.* Disconnect the cables.
2. Open the lid of the electrophoresis box.
3. Gently lift the casting tray and the gel out of the box.
4. Slide the gel off the casting tray into a plastic bag. Write your name across the top of the bag.
5. Use a "sharpie" marker and mark on the bag where your "A" and "B" hemoglobin samples are on the gel.

6. Rinse the electrophoresis box with *only* deionized water! Also, rinse the glass plates with soap and water.

VII. Analysis of the gel

Return to the classroom with your gel in the plastic bag.

1. Observe the banding patterns on your gel and record the results on your data sheet. Record your observations on your data sheet.
2. What is your conclusion? Compare your results with some other student "clinicians."

Follow-Up: A Closer Look at the Cause of Sickle Cell Anemia

Your research has determined that sickle cell hemoglobin differs from normal hemoglobin in the net negative charge on the proteins. This discovery is an important one; it identifies a characteristic that can be used to diagnose sickle cell anemia. However, it does not tell us what causes sickle cell anemia or why the proteins are different. Advanced in molecular biology and our understanding of DNA in the past two decades have provided us with more insights into the cause of sickle cell anemia. See if you can use the data obtained from research in molecular biology, provided in the following three pages, to uncover more information about sickle cell anemia.

The DNA base sequence of the first amino acids for both hemoglobins
A chart of mRNA codons and their corresponding amino acids (see Figure 14.10)
The structural formulas for the amino acids and their corresponding charges (see Figure 14.11)

DNA Base Sequences for Normal and Sickle Cell Hemoglobin

The DNA sequence of bases for the first seven amino acids in normal hemoglobin is

C A C G T G G A C T G A G G A C T C C T C

The DNA sequence of bases for the first seven amino acids in sickle cell hemoglobin is

C A C G T G G A C T G A G G A C A C C T C

SOURCE: CityLab is a fully equipped biotechnology learning laboratory at the Boston University School of Medicine for use by high school teachers and their students. It is funded by the National Institutes of Health and the Howard Hughes Medical Institute. The participation of more than 500 teachers and 7,000 students at CityLab since 1992 has provided valuable input for the development of this activity.

AMINO ACIDS

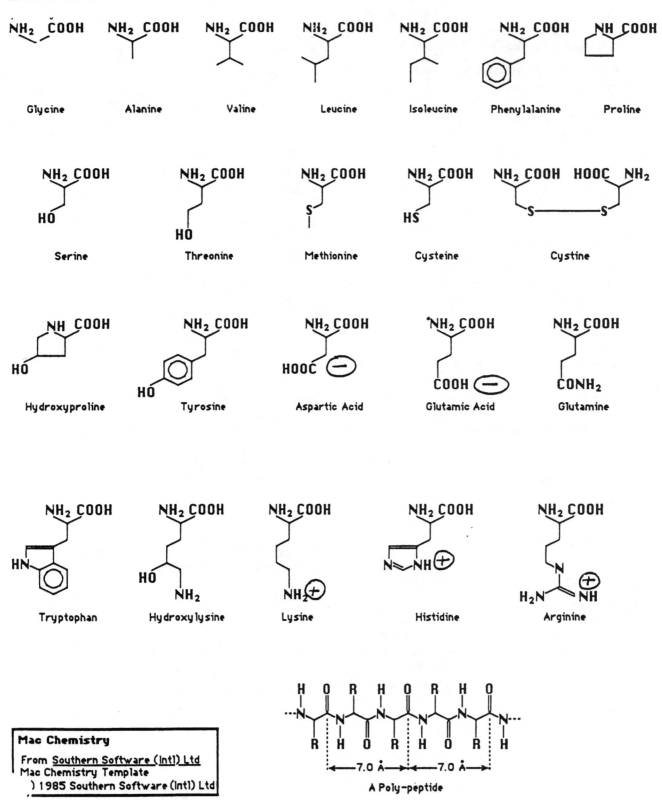

Figure 14.10. *Amino Acids*

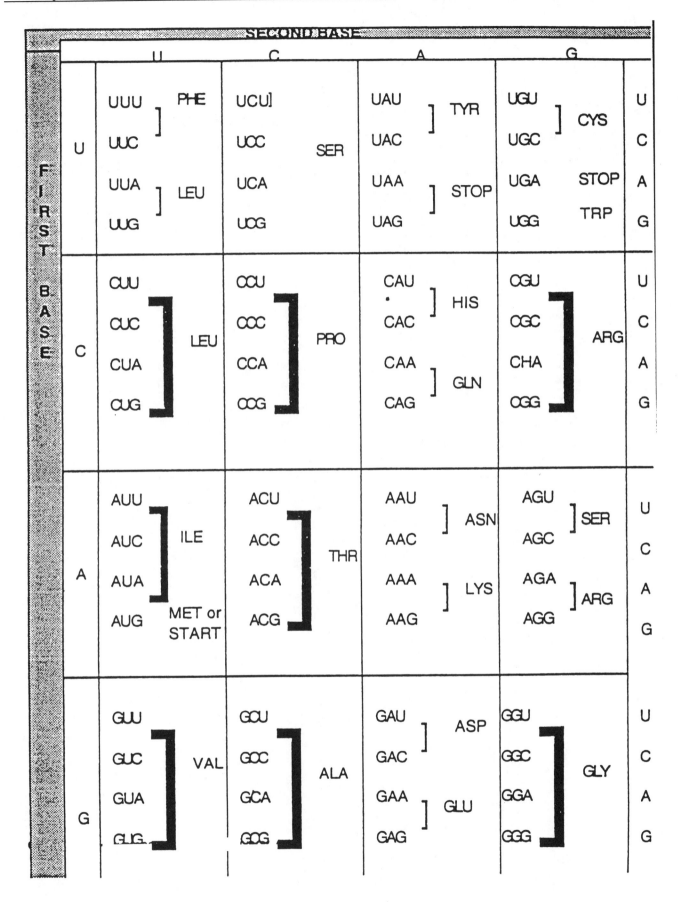

Figure 14.11. *Messenger RNA Codons and the Amino Acids They Code For*

Linda S. Samuels, *Girls Can Succeed in Science!* Copyright © 1999 by Corwin Press, Inc.

Principal Investigator

Dr. Carl Franzblau

Project Co-Director

Ms. Constance Phillips

Dr. Douglas Zook

Written for CityLab by

Mr. Don DeRosa, CityLab Education Coordinator

Dr. Leslie Wolfe, CityLab Laboratory Supervisor

Teacher Contributors

Mr. Fred Sculco
   Science Department Chairperson, Noble and
   Greenough Academy, Dedham, MA

Ms. Nancy Topalian
   Science Department Chairperson, Hope High School,
   Providence, RI.

Ms. Anita Bijan
   Former chemistry teacher, Boston Latin Academy,
   Boston, MA

15

Home Activities

This final chapter of the book takes the study of science outside the classroom and integrates it into the home environment. The eight activities fall into four areas, as seen in the list to follow. These offer excellent opportunities for the adults in your students' home lives to participate actively in their learning of science.

**Immunology:
Immunization Analysis**

**Teaches Science Outside the Classroom
Relates to Real Life**

Purpose:

- To determine whether you've been immunized properly
- To understand why immunization is necessary

Materials:

Each student's immunization record

Method:

1. First, obtain a copy of your immunization record from your doctor, parents, or like source.
2. Complete the Personal Immunization Record (Form 15.1).
3. On a separate page, list all the infectious diseases you have had in your lifetime.
4. Did you contract any diseases because you did not have the proper immunization?

5. Explain what a vaccine in and how it works to protect you.

6. Which of your immunizations are permanent? Which require periodic renewal?

7. If you were going to the Ecuadorian Amazon, what additional immunizations would you need?

8. List any new vaccines that have been developed in the past 5 years. Speculate on any vaccines that should be produced within the next 5 years.

TABLE 15.1 Personal Immunization Record

Name: _____ Sex: _____ Birth Date: _____

Address: _____

Vaccine	Date Given (Month/Day/Year)	Doctor or Clinic (with phone number)	Date Next Dose Is Due
Tetanus and Diphtheria toxoids (Td) for adult use	_____	_____	_____ _____
	_____	_____	_____
	_____	_____	_____
	_____	_____	_____
	_____	_____	_____
	_____	_____	_____
Pneumococcal	_____	_____	_____
	_____	_____	_____
Measles[a]	_____	_____	_____
	_____	_____	_____
Mumps[a]	_____	_____	_____
	_____	_____	_____
Rubella[a]	_____	_____	_____
	_____	_____	_____
	_____	_____	_____
Polio (specify OPV or eIPV)	_____	_____	_____
	_____	_____	_____
Hepatitis B	_____	_____	_____
	_____	_____	_____
	_____	_____	_____
Influenza	_____	_____	_____
	_____	_____	_____
	_____	_____	_____
	_____	_____	_____
	_____	_____	_____
Other	_____	_____	_____
	_____	_____	_____
	_____	_____	_____

NOTE: a. These vaccines are frequently combined as measles-mumps-rubella (MMR) or measles-rubella (MR).

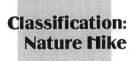

Classification: Nature Hike

Teaches Science Outside the Classroom
Relates to Real Life

Purpose:

- To learn about the plants and animals of a specific region
- To learn some of the basic techniques of scientific observation
- To learn that science can be FUN!

Materials:

A guidebook to plants, flowers, and trees of your region
A bird identification book
A sketchpad and sample bag for each participant

Method:

1. Find the following organisms. Draw and describe them. Name them if possible.
   a. Two kinds of birds
   b. Leaves from four kinds of deciduous trees
   c. Three kinds of flowers
   d. Two kinds of insects
   e. Two kinds of pine cones
   f. One shrub
   g. Any two other organisms you choose
2. Write a poem, song, or story describing the ecosystem you investigated.

Classification: Zoo Explorer

Relates to Real World
Teaches Science Outside the Classroom
Is Interdisciplinary

Purpose:

- To learn about zoology, taxonomy, morphology, and comparative anatomy and evolution
- To practice observation skills
- To practice forming hypotheses

Introduction:

As you probably know, a zoo is a place where wild animals are kept and displayed. Most large zoos exhibit mammals, birds, reptiles, and amphibians from all parts of the world. Some also feature fish and insects.

Part of the purpose of zoos is, of course, to entertain. Zoos also help teach ordinary people about animals and help scientists learn more about animal habits and diseases. In a way, a zoo is like a laboratory, where scientists can "test" how animals react to certain conditions. In addition, wildlife conservation has become one of the most important functions of zoos. The breeding of animals in captivity may offer the only means of survival for many species that face extinction in nature. Zoos breed endangered species in the hope that someday, these creatures may be reintroduced to the wild.

The word *zoo* stems from zoology, the science or study of animal life. Together with botany, the study of plant life, it forms the science of biology, the study of living things. Zoology is a vast subject, including many specialized fields. *Taxonomy*, for example, is the science of naming and classifying animals. *Morphology* studies animal form and structure. *Comparative anatomy* compares the body structures of different animals and is useful for formulating theories about evolution. There are many more branches of zoology, but these are the ones we will be practicing today.

Method:

Taxonomy

1. Obtain a zoo map from the visitors' center. Examine how the zoo is organized. You'll notice that each section has both a Latin and a common name: For example, the snake house is also called a *herpetarium*.

Latin names such as herpetarium come from the study of taxonomy, the science of naming and classifying animals. Every animal has a two-part scientific name. They may be known by different common names in different regions, but each has only one correct scientific name. Examine some of the two-part scientific names of the animals grouped together. What do you notice about them? Some of the "first names" of different animals are the same, aren't they? The first name of an animal's scientific name is called its *genus*. Members of the same genus are very similar, but different animals within one genus usually cannot breed with one another. The second term of the scientific name is the *species*. Members of a species can breed with one another, and the young grow up to look like the parents.

Choose your favorite animal, and proceed to that section of the zoo.

2. Read the plaque describing the animal you chose. What does it say about other animals that are closely related to it? What similarities are there between those closely related animals?

You will notice that not all of the related animals belong to the same genus. Taxonomy requires more classifications than just genus and species because its job is not only to name every animal but also to show relationships between different kinds of animals. Animals of the same family and order have easily observed similarities, too.

Scientific classification begins by grouping animals together by their most basic similarities. Then, it gradually divides the groups further through identifying more and more shared characteristics. Examine the diagram shown in Figure 15.1.

Scientific Classification

Kingdom

Kingdom is the largest group in the classification system. There are five kingdoms: Animalia, Plantae, Protista, Monera, and Fungi (animals, plants, protists, mon-

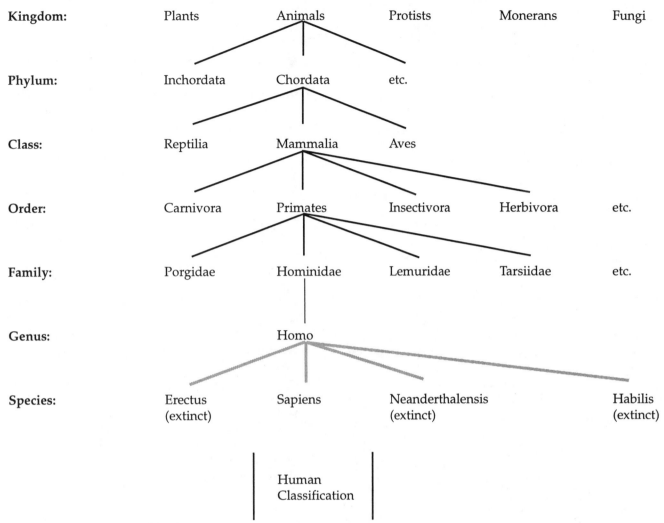

Figure 15.1. Taxonomy Chart

erans, and fungi). The Animalia kingdom includes all animals.

Phylum

Phylum is the second largest group. The animal kingdom may be divided into 20 or more phyla. One phylum, Chordata, includes all animals with a notochord, a rodlike structure in the back that develops into a backbone among vertebrates.

Class

Class members have more characteristics in common than do members of a phylum. For example, mammals, reptiles, and birds all belong to the phylum Chordata, but each belongs to a different class. Dogs, monkeys, bears, and mice all belong to the class Mammalia, and are commonly called "mammals." Mammals have hair on their bodies and feed milk to their young. Reptiles, members of the class Reptilia, have scales covering their body and don't feed milk to their young. Reptilia includes lizards,

snakes, and turtles, among others. Birds belong to the class Aves. Members of the class Aves have feathers on their bodies and do not feed milk to their young.

3. Is the animal you picked a member of the phylum Chordata? If not, can you determine what phylum it belongs to?
4. What class does your animal belong to?

Order

Animals within the same order are more alike than animals within the same class. In the class Mammalia, for example, all the animals produce milk for their young. Lions, bats, moles, and raccoons are all mammals. Dogs and raccoons both eat flesh and therefore are grouped together in the order Carnivora with other flesh-eating animals (commonly called carnivores). Bats and moles both eat insects and so belong to the order Insectivora. Plant eaters belong to the order Herbivora.

5. What order does your animal belong to? Does it eat flesh, insects, or plants? Can you observe any food inside its habitat? If not, the plaque should tell you about its eating habits.

Family

Members of the same family are even more alike than members of the same order. For example, wolves and lions are both in the order Carnivora, but wolves are in the family Canidae. All members of this family have long snouts and bushy tails. Lions belong to the family Felidae. Members of this family have short snouts and short-haired tails.

6. What family does your animal belong to? Can you think of some other animals in the same family?

Genus

A genus consists of very similar groups, but members of the same genus cannot usually breed with one another unless they are of the same species. Both the coyote and the timber wolf are in the genus Canis, but coyotes and timber wolves generally do not breed with one another (actually, in artificial conditions, coyotes and wolves could produce young).

7. What genus does your animal belong to? (Hint: Check its "first name") Can you think of other animals that belong to the same genus? Some of them should be nearby.
8. What are some of the characteristics that animals within your animal's genus share? Can you tell which of those characteristics separates that genus from the rest of the family?

Species

Species is the basic unit of scientific classification. Members of a species have many common characteristics, and they differ from all other species in one or more ways. Members of a species can breed with one another, and the young grow up to look like the parents. No two species in a genus have the same scientific name. For example, the coyote is *Canis latrans* and the timber wolf is *Canis lupus*. Sometimes, groups within a species differ enough from other groups in the species that they are called subspecies or varieties.

9. Are there any subspecies of the animal you chose?

Morphology and Comparative Anatomy

1. On the first page of your Explorer's Journal, draw a picture of your animal. Be as accurate as you can, but don't worry if you're not an artist. You can probably find a picture of the animal in your identification book or on a postcard at the zoo gift shop.
2. Watch what the animal does. Note down anything you observe about how the animal uses its body on your drawing. For example, if you've chosen a monkey that hangs by its tail, note that on your sketch, with an arrow pointing to the tail. If you've chosen the polar bear, take note of its thick fur coat. Try to determine how the animal uses each part of its body, especially if that part is unusual in some way (e.g., the rhino's horn, the elephant's trunk, the monkey's hand, etc.).
3. After you've observed the animal for 10 or 15 minutes, marking down how it uses the various parts of its body on your sketch, write a short description of what the animal does for the next 5 minutes. If the animal is inactive, your description may be very short! Zoologists sometimes have to observe animals for weeks or months to gather interesting observations about their behavior.
4. Look around the animal's habitat. Most modern zoos attempt to make the artificial environment of the enclosure as similar as possible to the area where the animal lives naturally. What kind of habitat does your animal live in? Can you notice any characteristics of the environment that seem to "require" some of the body characteristics you observed in #3?
5. Now, look at some of the animals of the same genus as your animal. What makes them different from your animal? Do they live in the same environment or a different one? Are they larger or smaller? Do they eat the same food or different food? What about their anatomy? Do they have longer or shorter legs, larger or smaller ears, or other differing characteristics?
6. Now that you've made some initial observations about your animal, turn over the page in your Explorer's Journal and write down your hypothesis, or informed guess, about why your animal looks and behaves the way it does. Imagine that at one time, your animal and another animal of the same genus (pick one that's very similar) were part of the same species. Can you think of some reasons why they might have become more and more different over time?

Evolution

Evolution means gradual development. In zoology and biology, the theory of evolution describes how life on earth began from nonliving matter and gradually multiplied and developed, becoming more and more diverse. The differences you observed in the last section are all caused by evolution.

Evolution is based on two main principles: *natural selection* and *heredity*. Natural selection simply means that, in nature, some animals live and reproduce, whereas others die. This is often called the survival of the fittest. Often, the animals that survive and reproduce have special characteristics that help them to live. Over thousands or even millions of years, those characteristics help to change the nature of the species. The second principle, heredity, is also necessary if the species is to evolve. Heredity means that characteristics, such as size, strength, color, and so on, can be passed on from the parent animals to the young. Characteristics that cannot be passed on through heredity cannot help the species to evolve.

1. Look back over your notes about your animal. What characteristics did you observe that would help it to survive better than other animals without that characteristic?

Evolution through natural selection causes a species to change so that it can adapt to changes in its environment. However, natural selection does not entirely explain how several species develop from one common ancestor species. This type of species development is called *speciation*.

Speciation begins when members of a single species get separated into two or more isolated populations. Each of these isolated populations develops through natural se-lection, but because the survival characteristics for each population are different, eventually each population evolves enough so that they can no longer interbreed. Then speciation has occurred.

2. Think about the differences you noticed between your species and similar members of the same genus. You developed a theory about why they became different. Does your theory make sense, according to what you have learned about speciation?

The isolation that marks the beginning of speciation may be geographic, ecological, or genetic. In geographic isolation, populations are separated by physical barriers, such as mountains, deserts, or bodies of water. In ecological isolation, the separating populations live in the same area but occupy different survival niches. For example, a population of birds may be divided if part of the population survives on nuts and seeds and another part feeds on nectar from flowers. Two different kinds of characteristics (a strong beak for seed eaters and a long beak for nectar eaters) will evolve. Eventually, these two populations will become separate species. Genetic isolation results from mutations that affect sexual traits. Organisms with such mutations may be able to breed with one another but not with other members of the same species.

3. What kind of isolation do you think separated your species from the similar animal of the same genus?

Environment: Camping Trip

Relates to Real Life
Is Interdisciplinary
Incorporates Hands-On Activity

Introduction:

Camping is an excellent form of recreation and education. While living in the woods, you are intimately connected to the various life cycles of nature and can observe an ecosystem in action. There are millions of fun things to do while you're camping—a lot of them scientific. These are only a few suggestions.

Purpose:

- To learn about the classification and identification of plants, animals, and insects
- To learn about conservation and the environment
- To practice observation skills

Materials:

Homemade compass
    Cork (1 per participant)
    Small bowl or cup for the cork to float in
    Needle
    Magnet
    Water source
Flora and fauna identification
    Wildlife identification books for your area: bird book, insect book, plant book
    Notebook
    Pencil
Water purification
    Water from spring or stream
    Water-purifying pump (or iodine tablets)
    Jug or canteen

Method:

Magnetic Compass

In its simplest form, the magnetic compass consists of a magnetized needle mounted on a pivot at the center of a fixed graduated card so as to permit the needle to swing freely in the horizontal plane. Because the northern pole of the earth is magnetic, the magnetized needle is attracted northward.

1. Rub the point of the needle briskly back and forth across the magnet for several minutes. This procedure will magnetize the needle.
2. Force the needle through the cork lengthwise.
3. Fill the cup or dish with water deep enough so that the cork floats.
4. Place the cork, with needle inserted, into the dish, and observe. The point should rotate toward magnetic North. Test to make sure, by turning the cork in another direction with your hand. Did the cork spin back to its original direction?

Water Purification

Because of its capacity to dissolve numerous substances in large amounts, pure water rarely occurs in nature.

During condensation and precipitation, rain or snow absorbs from the atmosphere varying amounts of carbon dioxide and other gases as well as traces of organic and inorganic material. In addition, precipitation carries radioactive fallout to the earth's surface.

In its movement on and through the earth's crust, water reacts with minerals in the soil and rocks. The principal dissolved constituents of surface and groundwater are sulfates, chlorides, the bicarbonates of sodium and potassium, and the oxides of calcium and magnesium. Surface waters may also contain domestic sewage and industrial wastes. Groundwaters from shallow wells may contain large quantities of nitrogen compounds and chlorides derived from human and animal wastes. Waters from deep wells generally contain only minerals in solution. Almost all supplies of natural drinking water contain fluorides in varying amounts. The proper proportion of fluorides in drinking water has been found to reduce tooth decay.

In addition to concentrated amounts of sodium chloride, or salt, seawater contains many other soluble compounds, because the impure waters of rivers and streams are constantly feeding the oceans. At the same time, pure water is continually lost by the process of evaporation, and as a result, the proportion of the impurities that give the oceans their saline character is increased.

Purifying Water

Suspended and dissolved impurities present in naturally occurring water make it unsuitable for many purposes. Objectionable organic and inorganic materials are removed by such methods as screening and sedimentation to eliminate suspended materials, treatment with such compounds as activated carbon to remove tastes and odors, filtration, and chlorination or irradiation to kill infective microorganisms.

In aeration, or the saturation of water with air, water is brought into contact with air in such a manner as to produce maximum diffusion, usually by spraying water into the air in fountains. Aeration removes odors and tastes caused by decomposing organic matter and also industrial wastes, such as phenols and volatile gases, such as chlorine. It also converts dissolved iron and manganese compounds into insoluble hydrated oxides of the metals, which may then be readily settled out.

Hardness of natural waters is caused largely by calcium and magnesium salts and to a small extent by iron, aluminum, and other metals. Hardness resulting from the bicarbonates and carbonates of calcium and magnesium is called temporary hardness and can be removed by boiling, which also sterilizes the water. The residual hardness is known as noncarbonate, or permanent, hardness. The methods of softening noncarbonate hardness include the addition of sodium carbonate and lime and filtration through natural or artificial zeolites that absorb the hardness-producing metallic ions and release sodium ions to the water. Sequestering agents in detergents serve to inactivate the substances that make water hard.

Iron, which causes an unpleasant taste in drinking water, may be removed by aeration and sedimentation or by passing the water through iron-removing zeolite filters, or the iron may be stabilized by addition of such salts as polyphosphates. For use in laboratory applications, water is either distilled or demineralized by passing it through ion-absorbing compounds.

Exercise:

Obtain your water-purifying kit and follow its instructions. What method of purification are you using? Does it have any drawbacks?

Identifying Flora and Fauna

See instructions for the flora and fauna identification in the "Nature Hike" activity and adapt them to your camping locale.

Environment: Fishing Trip

Relates to Real Life
Fights Gender Stereotypes

Introduction:

Modern sportfishing may be broken down into two basic categories: freshwater fishing and saltwater fishing. Freshwater fishing takes place in lakes, ponds, rivers, and streams, whereas saltwater fishing is done in the ocean, estuaries, and rivers influenced by tides. Game fish in fresh water are, with many exceptions, generally smaller than those species found in salt water; consequently, they are caught with lighter rods, reels, and lines and with smaller baits or lures.

Popular game fish caught in fresh water include the bass, trout, salmon, walleye, bluegill, pike, and catfish; popular saltwater species include the striped bass, bluefish, tuna, marlin, weakfish, drum, flounder, yellowtail, tarpon, and bonefish.

Saltwater and freshwater anglers both often use the same basic angling techniques, although locale and size of equipment differ. The three most favored fishing tactics are bait fishing (often called *still fishing* in North America and *bottom fishing* in England), spin fishing, and fly-fishing.

Materials:

Fishing rod, reel, and tackle
Notebook and pencil
Fish identification book

Method:

1. Catch fish!

To fish successfully, you have to be a good biologist, or at least an icthyologist—someone who studies fish! You have to know what kind of fish you can expect to find in the waters you're fishing; their eating habits; their spawning (reproductive) cycles; and what areas of the lake, river, or ocean they like to frequent.

You can find out these things several ways: (a) from books, (b) from experienced fishermen, or (c) by experimentation. If you're reading this in the car to the water or if you're already in the boat, you'll only have recourse to (b) and (c)—maybe even only to (c)! That's OK—experimentation is the key to any science, and that's what fishing is: half science, half sport.

Because today you're practicing your scientific as well as your fishing skills, take a moment to copy the following chart (Table 15.1) into your notebook, and fill in the blanks about the locale where you'll be fishing. If you don't know the answer to a question, ask your mom, dad, or whomever you think does know.

Based on the information you placed in the chart, what kind of bait or lure do you hypothesize will catch the most fish? What areas of the water should you find fish in? Write your hypothesis in your notebook. Example: Because it is early spring and the water temperature is still low, the fish are probably still in the deepest water of the lake. We will most likely catch fish by trolling or bait fishing in deep water.

By the way, there's another way that fishing is like science: In both arenas, hypotheses are often proven wrong! The difficulty with fishing, however, is that, *unlike* laboratory science, we can't control all the variables. That means that sometimes, even if we fail to catch fish in the way or area we expected to, we can't be completely sure why. Can you think of a way that a scientist could set up a controlled experiment to test different fishing techniques under different conditions?

What Technique Will You Use?

Bait Fishing

Bait fishing, as the name implies, involves the use of live or dead bait with a hook attached. Using a short rod, reel, and heavy line, the bait angler casts the bait from shore or boat and lets it sink. Lead weights are frequently attached to the line to help the bait reach bottom. Depending on the species one hopes to catch, the angler then either lets the bait sit on bottom, hoping that a game fish will be attracted by the bait's odor or size; jigs the bait up and down off bottom so that the action may attract fish; or else reels the bait a good distance off bottom, with the intention of enticing fish schooled at middepth. Stream anglers also let their baits drift in the current to likely fish-holding spots, such as pools, undercut banks, or riffles. Anglers who fish with live bait, such as minnows, often let their offerings swim freely on the end of the line and try to guide their bait where fish might be.

TABLE 15.2 Fishing Chart

Today's Conditions:

Sky:	Overcast	Partly cloudy	Partly sunny	Clear
Air temperature: _____				
Water temperature: _____				
Season:	Spring	Summer	Fall	Winter
Water:	Deep ocean	Ocean surf	Fresh river	Fresh lake pond

Fish species known to be in habitat: _____

_____

_____

Spawning cycle:

Spin Fishing

When spin fishing with artificial lures, anglers cast their offering from boat or shore into areas where game fish might be. Once the lure has landed in the water, the angler retrieves it by turning the reel handle. If a fish should strike the moving lure, it will usually hook itself. The angler then reels in the fish and lands it with a net or gaff (a sharp, hooklike instrument). Some sporting anglers also prefer to land their fish by hand if possible.

Today, artificial lures simulate almost everything that game fish eat. Worm, frog, snake, and bait fish imitations are just a few. Made of balsa wood, plastic, metal, or rubber, such lures may contain anything from a single hook to three treble (triple) hooks. Depending on their weight and design, artificial lures may be used on the bottom, in middepths, or on the surface.

Fly-Fishing

Perhaps the most sporting and difficult angling method is fly-fishing, widely used for catching trout. The fly angler uses a rod much longer—up to 3 m (10 ft)—and lighter than rods used for bait and spin fishing. Fly reels are also different; in contrast to baitcasting and spinning reels, they are single action. Such reels have a frame and revolving spool, but the handle is attached directly to the spool. One turn of the handle turns the spool one time.

Fly lines also differ from the nylon and Dacron lines used in other methods of fishing. Coated with various plastics, different fly lines can float, sink rapidly, or sink slowly. Once the fly line has been wound onto the reel spool, the fly angler then adds a nylon leader to the end of the line. Fly leaders are much lighter, with a smaller diameter, than the actual fly line. Their purpose is to let the angler cast easily and to give hooked game fish a fair, fighting chance.

To the end of the leader is attached a fly, which may imitate an insect or bait fish that game fish feed on. Made of feathers, hairs, or synthetic materials tied onto a single hook, the fly has virtually no weight. Bait-fish-imitating flies, or streamers, are generally 5 to 13 cm (2 to 5 in) long. Insect imitations, which may simulate aquatic insects in their nymphal, pupal, or adult stage, may be as large as a golf ball or as small as a pencil eraser. Anglers choose flies according to what fish are feeding on at the moment.

To cast such a small offering, the angler whips the fly rod back and forth until a considerable amount of line is in the air. Whereas a spin angler depends on the weight of the lure to take out the cast, the fly angler's cast is dependent on the weight of the line. Casts are made to likely looking spots, such as pools and pockets in streams, where the fly is allowed to touch the water and then float (dry-fly fishing) or sink (wet-fly fishing). If a fish strikes, the angler pulls in line while raising the rod tip to set the hook in the fish's mouth. The angler fights the fish by pulling in the line by hand or by reeling line onto the reel.

Clearly, the more scientific knowledge fly-fishers have, the more successful they are. They must know (a) what type of insects or larvae are present in the water, (b) what habitats the fish like, and (c) what type of lure action will simulate the fly or larvae.

In your notebook, copy down the names of the different types of baits and lures you will be trying, according to the following chart:

Number and species of fish caught

Location caught

Bait 1:

Bait 2:

Bait 3:

Lure 1:

Lure 2:

Lure 3:

Lure 4:

Lure 5:

Results and Conclusions:

Go ahead and catch some fish. Good luck. Fill in your chart as you go, and when you're finished, compare your results (how many fish you caught, where, and with what lures or baits) to your hypothesis. What conclusions can you draw? Write them down for the next time you go fishing. The more times you fish scientifically, the better fisherman you'll become!

Fish Facts

Trout

Trout is the common name for many species of fish belonging to the salmon family. Some, called sea trout, are anadromous—that is, they ascend the rivers from the sea to breed. Most of the species, however, live exclusively in fresh water and are found in most of the lakes and streams of northern regions. Their food consists of almost any sort of fresh animal matter, such as smaller fishes, crustacea, and insect larvae. Trout, like salmon, spawn during the spring or occasionally in the autumn, depending on the latitude and the species. The most widely distributed species in North America is the common brook trout, or speckled trout, which is similar to the brown trout of Europe. It is recognized by its large mouth, violet mantle, dark mottlings, and red lateral spots, the general coloring being dark gray or green. The male has a reddish band running along the side of the body. Brook trout are found from the Alleghenies in Georgia to the Arctic Ocean, varying in size according to the extent of water and the amount of food they procure, the average weight being about 1 kg (about 2 lb). The spawning season begins in September and lasts until December, when the female uses her tail to scrape out a hole in the gravel where she deposits her eggs, the male afterward dropping the milt on them. Only about 5% of the eggs become fertilized in the natural state; the rest are generally washed out and devoured by other fish. However, as many as 90% can be hatched by artificial means.

The most important of the trouts is the rainbow trout, native to the lakes and streams of the western United States and introduced widely throughout the world. Rainbow trout are highly prized as game fish because they fight hard to free themselves, leaping high out of the water. Steelhead, the anadromous form of the rainbow trout, is also a prized game fish. Another species, found in the Rocky Mountains region, is the cutthroat trout, known also as mountain trout. In the southern United States, the weakfish and the largemouth black bass are sometimes called trout.

Scientific Classification

Trouts belong to the family Salmonidae. Chars make up the genus *Salvelinus* and true trouts, the genus *Salmo*. The common brook trout is classified as *Salvelinus fontinalis*, the brown trout of Europe as *Salmo trutta*, the Dolly Varden trout as *Salvelinus malma*, and the Mackinaw trout as *Salvelinus namaycush*. The rainbow trout is classified as *Oncorhynchus mykiss* and the cutthroat trout as *Oncorhynchus clarki*. The weakfish is classified as *Cynoscion regalis* and the largemouth black bass as *Micropterus salmoides*.

Bass

Bass (fish) is the common name for many food fishes but not corresponding to any particular scientific classification. Various bass are known by such local names as black, white, or rock bass.

In the United States, there are 9 genera and 30 species of fish in the family containing bass and sunfish. The calico bass, also called black crappie, is found from the Great Lakes and upper Mississippi Valley to New Jersey and southward to Florida, Louisiana, and Texas; it reaches a length up to 36 cm (14 in) but rarely weighs more than 0.2 kg (0.5 lb). The rock bass rarely exceeds that weight and is a poor food fish. It is abundant west of the Allegheny Mountains, south to Louisiana, and north into Manitoba, Canada. The most important basses in this family are the black basses. The largemouth black bass is also called bayou, lake, or straw bass, and sometimes, in the southern United States, trout. The smallmouth black bass resembles the largemouth bass, and the spotted bass is found in the Mississippi basin. Largemouth bass are found throughout the central United States and may reach a weight of 9 kg (20 lb). Smallmouth bass are found from Lake Champlain southwest to the Appalachian region; they reach a maximum weight of about 2.3 kg (about 5 lb).

Members of a second family, the sea bass family, are *hermaphroditic*—that is, individuals have both male and female reproductive organs. Although part of the sea bass family, some of these family members are freshwater fishes.

Scientific Classification

Bass belong to the order Perciformes. Most bass are included within the sunfish family, Centrarchidae; the sea bass family, Serranidae; and the temperate bass family, Percichthyidae. Of those belonging to the family Centrarchidae, the calico bass is classified as *Pomoxis nigromaculatus*, the rock bass as *Ambloplites rupestris*, the largemouth black bass as *Micropterus salmoides*, the smallmouth black bass as *Micropterus dolomieu*, and the spotted bass as *Micropterus punctulatus*. Bass in the family Serranidae include the black sea bass, classified as *Centropristes striata*, and the kelp bass, classified as *Paralabrax clathratus*. In the family Percichthyidae, the striped bass is classified as *Morone saxatilis*, the white bass as *Morone chrysops*, and the yellow bass as *Morone mississippiensis*. The red drum, or channel bass, is classified in the drum family, Sciaenidae, as *Sciaenops ocellatus*.

Bluefish

Bluefish is common name for a fish living in warm seas throughout the world. Bluefish are voracious, and large schools enter the coastal waters every spring to prey on other fish when they come inshore to spawn, sometimes leaving a trail of blood for miles. Young bluefish are called snappers. Bluefish are among the most important food fish of the Atlantic seaboard, and catching bluefish is a highly regarded sport. The largest specimen on record weighed more than 11 kg (more than 25 lb), but the usual weight is 2 to 7 kg (5 to 15 lb).

Scientific Classification

The bluefish is classified as *Pomatomus saltatrix*.

Technology: Oil Change

**Relates to the Real World
Is Gender Neutral**

Purpose:

- To learn about friction
- To learn how basic laws of physics apply to automobile engines
- To prove that girls can understand machines

Introduction:

Have you ever noticed that when you rub your hands together, heat is produced? This heat results from *friction*, the property that makes objects resist being moved across one another.

Quick Experiment 1

Try a quick experiment. Place your palms together and rub them briskly across one another. You will feel your hands getting warm. Now, try repeating the same motion while pressing your hands together firmly. What happens? Now try rubbing your hands while holding them only loosely against one another. Did they get warm faster or slower than when you pressed them together tightly? What does this tell you about friction?

Quick Experiment 2

Now, try another experiment. Place a coin, a marble, and an ice cube on your kitchen counter. Lay a pencil on the counter so that its long edge rests against all three objects. Now, gently push the objects forward with an abrupt movement of the pencil. Which object went farthest? Why do you think it did so? Which object went the next farthest? Why?

There are three main kinds of friction. *Sliding* or *kinetic friction* is produced when two surfaces slide across one another (as with the coin, the ice cube, or your palms). *Rolling friction* is the resistance produced when a rolling body moves across a surface (the marble or an automobile tire rolling along a road). *Fluid friction*, or *viscosity*, is the friction between moving fluids or between moving fluids and a solid. Viscosity is the property that makes some fluids feel thicker than others—for example, oil is more viscous than water. Rub a drop of oil between your index finger and thumb. With your other hand, rub a drop of water. Oil has greater viscosity than water.

Friction has many important uses. Without friction, the tires of the car could not grip the road, and the car could neither speed up, slow down, or turn. Without friction, you couldn't walk—it's hard enough to walk on ice, where the friction is low.

Friction also has disadvantages. It limits the efficiency of all kinds of machines: Just as when you pushed the marble, coin, and ice cube, friction stopped them from moving forever, so friction slows and eventually stops machines. If friction didn't exist, a single gallon of gasoline could start the engine of a car turning, and it would turn forever! In addition, the heat produced by friction can cause objects to wear out. For both of these reasons, designers of machines try to reduce the amount of friction in their designs to increase efficiency.

The most basic way that designers reduce friction is through the use of *lubricants*. A lubricant is a liquid that reduces friction and makes the parts move more easily and produce less heat. One of the most common lubricants is motor oil. Remember when you rubbed a drop of oil between your fingers? It felt slippery—that is, it reduced the friction between your fingers. The same thing happens inside an engine. As the various moving parts slide or roll across one another, motor oil reduces the friction and the amount of heat produced so that the parts last longer and the engine runs more efficiently.

How Motor Oil Works

When the surfaces in contact are coated with oil or another liquid, the amount of friction depends much more on the viscosity of the liquid than on the two surfaces. Because oil is sealed inside the engine, the moving parts never rub directly against one another. Instead, each part rubs against the oil.

Over time, even the lesser friction between the oil and the moving parts is enough to cause minor wear in the metal parts. You can notice this wear if you examine the oil.

Method:

Checking the Oil

It is important to check the amount of oil in the car every two fill-ups or so, because friction actually causes oil to burn up over time. It is also possible for cars to develop leaks in their lubrication systems. Used oil will be black and opaque, whereas fresh oil is golden and translucent. The blackness is caused by tiny pieces of debris from wear. That debris increases the amount of friction in the engine and, if let go too long, can damage the car.

1. Take out the owner's manual, and turn to the section about oil. You may find it under a heading such as "Inspection and Maintenance." Read the instructions for checking the oil, and examine any diagrams.
2. Open the hood, and locate the oil dipstick. This is a long, metal stick that dips into the oil reservoir. You can tell how much oil is in the crankcase by looking how far up the stick it travels, just as if you dipped a ruler into a puddle of water.
3. Pull out the oil dipstick, and look at it. Because the oil sloshes around while the engine is running, this won't give you an accurate idea about how much oil is in the crankcase, but you can see whether the oil is in good condition or not. Is the oil dirty and black or golden brown and see-through? If it is black, you may need to change the oil (the owner's manual will tell you how many miles the car can go between oil changes). If the oil is very dirty or the mileage indicates it is time for an oil change, skip Steps 4 and 5 and proceed to the instructions for changing the oil.
4. With your rag, wipe all the oil off the dipstick. Now, push it all the way back into the hole and remove it again. The oil on the stick should be between the upper and lower limits shown on the stick (usually marked by two holes in the stick). If the oil is nearer the lower limit, add enough oil to bring it up to the higher limit. Bear in mind that it takes about one qt (or one l) of oil to bring the level from the lower limit to the upper limit, although the engine may hold five quarts (or liters) or more in total. Be careful not to overfill. Too much oil is almost as bad as too little.
5. Have your mother or father start the engine and let the car idle for about a minute. After he or she has turned off the engine, wait 2 or 3 minutes, and check the oil again (repeat Step 4).

Changing the Oil

If the oil is very dirty or if the mileage indicates it is time for an oil change, you should perform the following steps:

1. You should drain the engine oil while the engine is still warm. Be very careful, however, because the oil may be hot enough to burn your fingers.
2. Remove the oil filler cap (refer to owner's manual for location).
3. Place a drain pan under the drain plug (see owner's manual for location).
4. Using a wrench, remove the drain plug, and drain out the engine oil.
5. Reinstall the drain plug and gasket. Tighten the plug with a wrench according to the specifications in your owner's manual.
6. Using an oil filter wrench, turn the oil filter counter-clockwise, and remove it.
7. Using a clean rag, wipe off the mounting surface on the engine where the new filter will be seated.
8. Smear a little engine oil around the rubber gasket of the new oil filter. What do you think this gasket is for?
9. Screw on the new filter (specified in the owner's manual) by hand until the filter gasket contacts the mounting surface.
10. Tighten the filter a three-quarter turn from the point of contact with the mounting surface using an oil filter wrench.
11. Refill the engine with oil. Fill the engine with the amount of oil specified in the owner's manual through the filler hole, and screw on the filler cap.
12. Ask your father or mother to start the engine, and then (with an adult to help you), look carefully at the oil filter and the drain plug for leaks. The engine should run at various speeds for 5 minutes.
13. Ask your father or mother to stop the engine and wait a few minutes. Check the oil level again (see Step 4 of "Checking the Oil") and add oil if necessary. Check for leaks again.

Technology: Internet Scavenger Hunt

Relates to Current Science
Fosters Independent Activity
Presents Material in New Ways

Introduction:

What is the Internet, anyway?

Everyone's talking about the Internet, but do you know what it is or how it works? Few people do. The Internet is like a giant community of computers. No single computer holds all the information on the system—none would be powerful enough. Instead, the information is spread throughout all the computers that make up the Internet. Therefore, when you connect your computer to the Internet, you connect via the closest "hub," not to some distant all-powerful mainframe. And as soon as your computer is connected, it becomes part of the Internet.

Most computers connected to the Internet are called *hosts*. Computers that route data, or data packets, to other computers are called *routers*. Networks and computers that are part of the global Internet possess unique registered addresses and obtain access from Internet service providers.

The Internet technology was developed principally by U.S. computer scientist Vinton Cerf in 1973 as part of a United States Department of Defense Advanced Research Projects Agency project managed by U.S. engineer Robert Kahn. In 1984, the development of the technology and the running of the network were turned over to the private sector and to government research and scientific agencies for further development.

Since its inception, the Internet has continued to grow rapidly. In early 1995, access was available in 180 countries, and there were more than 30 million users. It is expected that 100 million computers will be connected via the public Internet by 2000 and even more via enterprise Internets. The technology and the Internet have supported global collaboration among people and organizations, information sharing, network innovations, and rapid business transactions. The development of the World Wide Web is fueling the introduction of new business tools and uses that may lead to billions of dollars worth of business transactions on the Internet in the future.

Right now, the World Wide Web allows users to create and use point-and-click hypermedia presentations. These documents are linked across the Internet to form a vast repository of information that can be browsed easily

(Rutkowski, 1996). In this exercise, you'll explore the World Wide Web and access some of that information!

Purpose:

- To learn to use the Internet as a research tool
- To learn to pose scientific questions and use research methods to answer them

Materials:

A computer with Internet access
Netscape Navigator® or other web browser

Method:

Designing Your Search

1. Choose a topic that interests you. Your teacher may provide certain limitations (for example, he or she may stipulate that your topic must relate to a specific chapter in your textbook). Write your topic in the space provided:

Be sure to choose a topic that is very specific. Because the Internet's resources are so vast, a general topic, such as "Medicine," will generate far too much information for you to read.

EXAMPLE TOPICS	
Too General	*Specific*
Drugs	Teenage drug abuse
Anatomy	Prosthetic limbs
The heart	Heart transplants
Genetics	Cloning
Sex	Advancements in birth control
AIDS	Treatments for AIDS
AIDS	Civil rights of AIDS sufferers

2. Let's say, for example, that your topic is "Hemophilia." How will you construct your search? You know that hemophilia is a disease that prevents blood clotting and that hemophiliacs have relatively recently had another concern added to their disease. Because they often need blood transfusions, they have to worry about contracting AIDS from infected blood. Now, the Red Cross tests its blood supply for HIV and AIDS, so in advanced countries, hemophiliacs have little to worry about. That makes you think of a question that you'd like to answer: "How do hemophiliacs in Third World countries cope with the dangers of contracting AIDS from infected blood?"

Think about the topic you've chosen. What question do you want to answer?

Question:

3. Connect to the Internet using Netscape Navigator® or a different web browser. If you are familiar with web-browsing programs, proceed to Step 4.

Orientation

All web browsers work essentially the same way: The user types a specific web address in the status line and the browser "goes" to that location, or the user constructs a web search and the browser finds all the sites that match the search criteria.

a. Locate the status line. It should be a long bar near the top of your screen. To the left of it will be written "URL." Inside the status line will be written the URL of the web page where the web browser is currently located. If you're using Netscape Navigator®, this will read something like "http://www.netscape.com/home". Whatever program you're using, the status line will have something written in it that begins with "http://."

Type a sample URL in the status line. Try typing "http://www.learner.org/content/k12/jnorth."

Now, press return.

Your web browser should take you to a web site called Journey North. If you get a message saying this site no longer exists, don't worry. If you get a message saying you can't access the server or another error message, you may have a problem.

You probably noticed that typing the entire name of the URL manually was inconvenient. It was a lot of seemingly meaningless letters, and the chances that you would mistype it were good. If you know exactly what web site you want to visit, however, typing the URL is usually the fastest way to get there.

b. Now, locate the "Web Search" button. Netscape Navigator's® Web Search button is just beneath the status line and labeled "Search the Web." On other programs, look for a square that looks like a button (a little) labeled with "Search." Click it with the mouse.

You should now see a dialogue box that allows you to input your search criteria. It will probably have a bar labeled "Search." Put the cursor in the search box and type "hemophilia." Press return.

You will now get a list of web sites that relate to hemophilia. If you glance through them, you'll see that only some appear to be relevant to the question we posed earlier. You'll also notice that there are a lot of sites to visit—a lot of articles to read. You could read all the articles to find out which ones will be useful, but it'd be smarter to let the computer do that work for you, right?

Limiting Your Search:

The most basic way to limit your search is by using *Boolean operators.* Boolean operators are key words and symbols that the computer recognizes. They include the following:

a. AND. Example: hemophilia AND AIDS—computer will search for all sites where both hemophilia and AIDS occur in the subject heading.

b. OR. Example: hemophilia OR AIDS—computer will search for all sites where either hemophilia or AIDS occurs in the subject heading.

c. NOT. Example: hemophilia NOT AIDS—computer will search for all sites where hemophilia occurs in the subject heading but AIDS does not.

You can also combine Boolean operators: hemophilia AND AIDS NOT United States

There are many other ways to limit your search. For more instructions, use your program's help function.

4. Search for information about your topic. Find 10 web sites that provide good information, and answer the question you posed for yourself. Record that information in the following spaces.

Web sites:

Answer:

TABLE 15.3 Web Site Review

Name of site:

URL:

Main topic or theme of site:

Graphics, videos, and multimedia presentations:

Information presented:

Most interesting fact:

Rating:

---

5. Choose the web site you found most interesting, and write a web site review using the format shown in Table 15.2.

Check it out!

List of Interesting Web Sites

The Heart: An Online Exploration
    http://sln.fi.edu/biosci/biosci.html

Visible Human Project
    http://www.yahoo.com/science/biology/anatomy/visible_human_project

Medical Students Dissect Cadavers
    http://meded.com.uci.edu/anatomy/willed_body/labs.html

Evolution and Behavior
    http://ccp.uchicago.edu/jyin/evolution. html

Journey North
    http://www.learner.org/content/k12/jnorth

Animal Behavior and Welfare Sites (links to other sites)
    http://www.wam.umd.edu/jaguar/

Bioethics Discussion Pages
    http://www-hsc.usc.edu/mbernste/

Genetics and Ethics Home Page (links to other sites)
    http: //mistral.ere.umontreal.ca/williamg/genetics.html

Yahoo-Cloning (links)
    http://www.yahoo.com/science/biology/biotechnology/cloning

Yahoo-Ecology (links)
    http://www.yahoo.com/science/ecology

HMS Beagle (On-Line Magazine)
    http://biomednet.com/hmsbeagle/

Nature Meetings Guide (On-Line Magazine)
    http://meetings.nature.com

The Scientist (On-Line Magazine)
    http://www.the_scientist.com/

Vita Marina and Spitula (On-Line Seashell Gallery)
    http://home.pi.net/spirula/

Biology of Reproduction
    http://www.ssr.org/ssr/bor/bor.html

Continuity of Life (DNA)
    http://home.ust.hk/bo_mkc

Virtual Library–Developmental Biology (links)
    http://www.ucalgary.ca/fvdhorn/fvdh.html

Abortion Issues (links)
    http://www.yahoo.com/health/reproductive_health/abortion_issues/

Birth (links)
    http://www.yahoo.com/society_and_culture/birth

Birth Control (links)
    http://www.yahoo.com/health/reproductive_health/birth_control

Pregnancy
    http://www.yahoo.com/health/reproductive_health/pregnancy

Zoology (links)
    http://www.yahoo.com/science/zoology/

Substance Abuse (links)
    http://www.yahoo.com/health/mental_health/diseases_and_conditions/substance_abuse/

Women's Health (links)
    http://www.yahoo.com/health/women_s_health/

**Technology:
Why Mountain Bike?**

**Relates to Real World
Demonstrates Abstract Concept
Fosters Hands-On Activity**

Introduction:

It's no wonder that bicycling has become more and more popular in recent years. Bicycling is great exercise and a great way to get around. But you knew that.

What you might not know is that the bicycle (in crude form) was popular as early as the second half of the 17th century! In 1690, a Frenchman invented the *célérifère*, consisting of a wooden beam to which the wheels were affixed. The vehicle had no handlebar; the rider sat on a cushion on the beam and propelled and steered the machine by pushing his or her feet against the ground.

About 1880, the so-called safety, or low, machine was developed. The wheels were of nearly equal size, the pedals, attached to a sprocket through gears and a chain, drove the rear wheel.

In the 1960s and 1970s, as air pollution from automobile exhaust caused great concern and the energy crisis worsened, the popularity of the bicycle increased tremendously. Some areas set up bike lanes and special bike paths. An emphasis on physical fitness in the 1970s and 1980s added to this popularity, and an estimated 82 million bicycles were in use in the United States in the mid-1980s. Most popular was the lightweight 10-speed touring bike, modeled after European racing models, with cable-and-caliper hand brakes and narrow, high-pressure tires.

The mountain bicycle has eclipsed the touring bike in the 1990s, as bicycling becomes more and more popular and cyclists redefine the ways they use the machine.

What Is a Mountain Bike?

If you bought your bike within the past few years, chances are, it's a mountain bike. What are the differences between it and other bikes? What is it designed to do? The true mountain bike has a sturdier (though still lightweight) frame than the touring or racing bicycle, it has flat handlebars for a midupright riding stance, and knobby tires for traction. Most important, mountain bikes have twice as many gears as touring bikes (or more!). The addition of gears makes it easier for the rider to climb hills—hence the name mountain bike. In this exercise, we'll figure out how these gears work.

Materials:

2 mountain bicycles (1 mountain bike and 1 ordinary bike will also work)
Stopwatch or watch with second hand
A hill where it's safe to ride your bike

Method:

Gear Basics

1. Take your bicycles outside where you can look at them. Flip them upside down so that they're standing on the seat and handlebars. Notice the two groups of metal wheels that hold the chain. Each toothed wheel is a *gear*, and each group of gears is called a *sprocket*. When you "shift gears" by moving the lever near the handlebars, the chain moves from one gear to another, and it becomes easier or harder for you to pedal.

2. With the gear lever, shift the bike to its highest gear. Notice the movement of the two derailers (devices that force the chain from one gear to another), one on each of the two sprockets. With your hand, turn the pedals. As the chain moves, it should slide from the largest gear on the front sprocket (attached to the pedals) to the smallest gear on the rear sprocket (attached to the rear wheel).

3. Count the number of teeth on each of the two gears where the chain is. Record the numbers in the following spaces:

_____   _____

Front Sprocket   *Rear Sprocket*

4. Write this number in the form of a ratio. For example, if there are 25 teeth on the front sprocket and 5 teeth on the second sprocket, you write the ratio 25:5. But because 25 is divisible by 5, you can reduce the ratio to 5:1.

5. Now, count the number of teeth on each of the gears of each sprocket and record the numbers on the following table.

Front Sprocket	Rear Sprocket
1	1
2	2
3	3
4	4
5	5
6	6
7	7
8	8

On a traditional 12-speed bike, this chart might look like the following one:

Front Sprocket	Rear Sprocket
1. 100 teeth	1. 70 teeth
2. 80	2. 60
	3. 50
	4. 40
	5. 30
	6. 20

There are 12 speeds because the gears can be arranged in 12 different configurations:

Front Sprocket	Rear Sprocket
1. 100	1. 70
2. 80	2. 60
	3. 50
	4. 40
	5. 30
	6. 20

6. Using a crayon, marker, or colored pencil, draw lines through your own gear chart. Count them to be sure you found all the combinations. (You should find the same number of combinations as the number of speeds your bike is advertised to have.)

7. Now, figure out the gear ratios for each of your bike's speeds, with the method you used in Step 5 and record them in the following chart:

Speed	Gear Ratio
1	
2	
3	
4	
5	
6	
7	
8	
9	
10	
11	
12	
13	
14	
15	
16	
17	
18	
19	
20	
21	
22	
23	
24	

Questions:

1. What relationship is there between speed and gear ratio?
2. Are the pedals harder or easier to turn when the gear ratio is high?

Power and Speed

In this exercise, you will test the relationship between speed and gear ratio with a series of races.

Short Race

1. Flip your bikes upright.
2. Measure a short racing course (roughly 20 yd or 18 m) on level ground.
3. One person should put her bike in the highest speed (e.g., on a 10-speed bike, put it in 10th gear). The other participant should put her bike in the lowest speed. Neither participant is allowed to shift gears during the race.
4. Race!

Who won?
Why? (hypothesis)

Distance Race

1. Measure a long racing course (at least 200 yd or 180 m) on level ground.
2. Keep one bike in its highest gear and the other bike in its lowest gear.
3. Race!

   Who won?
   Why? (hypothesis)

Uphill Race

1. Mark out an uphill racing course.
2. Keep one bike in its highest gear and the other bike in its lowest gear.
3. Race!

   Who won?
   Why? (hypothesis)

Conclusions:

Appendix

Real Life 1 Test
Middle School Life Sciences

1. Negative and positive stress

   a. Please list three similarities between positive and negative stress.
   b. What is the main difference between positive and negative stress?

2. Which method of relaxation do you prefer? Please describe this method and the benefits of its use.

3. Aerobic exercise should be approached properly to maximize benefits and safety.

   a. What are the three main components of an effective aerobics program?
   b. Please list three safety precautions that you should take while exercising.

4. Asthma

   a. What are some common misconceptions about asthma?
   b. Why does it become more difficult for an asthma sufferer to breathe while having an attack? Please give two reasons.

5. Why is acne commonly a problem among teenagers and women before their menstrual period?

Extra Credit:

1. Based on what you have eaten and recorded over the past few days, do you think that you eat "normally"? What could you do to improve your eating habits?

Reproduction Test: Biology

1. Define the word *puberty* and name the gland that is responsible for most of the changes adolescents experience during puberty.

2. The Female System

   a. When do females begin to experience puberty, and what are three physical indications?
   b. Please draw the female reproductive system and label the diagram with the these terms: fallopian tubes, vagina, ovaries, uterus, and cervix.

3. The Male System

   a. When do males begin to experience puberty, and what are three physical indications?
   b. Please draw the male reproductive system and label the diagram with these terms: vas deferens, penis, testes, scrotum, prostrate gland, urethra, and epididymis.
   c. Define the terms *erection* and *ejaculation*. In your definition, describe the pathway of sperm using your diagram.

4. Reproduction

   a. How many chromosomes are present in an egg? In a sperm? In a fertilized egg?

   b. Explain the process of fertilization in your own words. Include when and where it is most likely to occur.

5. Name and define the two types of abortion.

6. Family Planning

   a. Why is family planning important?

7. STDs

   a. Give the definition of *STD*. Include where they generally occur and how they are transmitted.
   b. Name two STDs and give two characteristics about each.

8. Please name the two forms of sexual harassment and give an example of each. How would you respond to sexual harassment?

Extra Credit:

1. Define *TSS*, and explain how it can be contracted.

2. Define *amniocentesis*. Explain the pros and cons of this procedure.

Biology Test 1: Biochemical Genetics Test

1.a. Express the following number in scientific notation:

0.000000348

b. Convert the following scientific notation into a number:

2.976×106

c. Express the following number in scientific notation:

$1, 985, 000, 000, 000$

2. What happens to the surface to volume ratio as the size of a cell increases? Why is this significant (please cite two reasons)?

3. Please define each of the following words with a very complete and detailed description:

a. Chromosome
b. Chromatin
c. Chromatid
d. Centromere
e. Centriole
f. Histone
g. Nucleosome

4. Label the diagrams on this page with the words from Question 3. Please use arrows to point to a particular part of the diagram.

i.

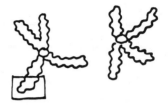

ii.

iii.

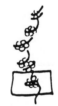

iv.

5. Please illustrate and explain all of the parts of the *cell cycle* using the following table.

Phase	Drawing	Events That Occur
Interphase		
Mitosis		

6. Please match the following scientists with their accomplishments:

Hershey and Chase	a. Took the X-ray diffraction photograph of DNA
Watson and Crick	b. Determined that the molecules responsible for transformation were made of DNA; Used a series of enzyme treatments
Avery	c. Discovered the "transforming factor"
Griffith	d. Determined the purine and pyrimidine content of DNA
Chargaff	e. Constructed the model of DNA
Rosalind Franklin	f. Determined that DNA was the hereditary material of a virus

7. Essays on famous scientists

a. Please write a brief essay on Griffith *or* Hershey and Chase. Include in the essay the scientist(s) responsible, a detailed description of the experimental procedure, the results, and the main conclusion.

b. Please choose one of the other four scientists listed in Question 6 on which to write a brief essay. Include in the essay the scientist(s) responsible, a detailed description of the experimental procedure, the results, and the main conclusion.

Fifteen Multiple Choice Questions: Choose the letter of the answer that best completes each statement.

1. In most cases, a living thing grows because it produces

    a. useless cells.
    b. more cells.
    c. larger cells
    d. smaller cells.

2. Which cells in the normal human body rarely divide?

    a. Skin
    b. Bones
    c. Digestive tract
    d. Nerves

3. Which term includes the others?

    a. Synthesis
    b. Interphase
    c. Gap 1 phase
    d. Gap 2 phase

4. The spindle fiber and the centriole are composed of

    a. RNA.
    b. chromatin.
    c. histones.
    d. microtubules.

5. The rate at which materials enter and leave through the cell membrane is dependent on the cell's

    a. volume.
    b. weight.
    c. mass.
    d. surface area.

6. Cancer cells placed in a petri dish containing nutrient broth

    a. will not start to grow.
    b. stop growing when they contact each other.
    c. continue to grow until the nutrients are used up.
    d. continue to grow until they are destroyed.

7. Which of the terms includes the others?

    a. Chromosomes
    b. Histones
    c. Proteins
    d. DNA

8. During mitosis, chromosomes become visible as the result of the

    a. condensing of chromatin.
    b. formation of the spindle.
    c. destruction of the nuclear membrane.
    d. duplication of the centrioles.

9. Bacteriophages are

    a. tiny bacteria.
    b. bacteria of the same type.
    c. coils of ribonucleic acid.
    d. viruses.

10. A nucleotide does not consist of

    a. polymerase.
    b. 5-carbon sugar.
    c. phosphate group.
    d. nitrogenous base.

11. The backbone of a chain of nucleotides consists of

    a. sugar and phosphate groups.
    b. nitrogenous bases.
    c. nitrogenous bases and phosphate groups.
    d. deoxyribonucleic acid.

12. Adenine and thymine

    a. are joined by weak hydrogen bonds.
    b. are joined by ionic bonds.
    c. alternately bond with a sugar.
    d. alternately bond with a phosphate group.

13. The genetic code in DNA depends on the order, or sequence, of

    a. nucleotides.
    b. phosphate groups.
    c. sugars.
    d. purines.

14. The force that holds two strands of the DNA double helix together is known as

    a. enzyme attraction.
    b. base pairing.
    c. codons.
    d. anticodons.

15. The part of the bacteriophage that is injected into a bacterium is the

    a. DNA core.
    b. protein coat.
    c. tail fibers.
    d. phosphate group.

Extra Credit:

1. Please explain cancer in terms of cell growth and division.

2. Define and draw a nucleotide. Explain how a DNA molecule is constructed.

Biology Test 2: Classical Genetics

Multiple Choice: Choose the letter of the answer that best completes each statement.

1. If an organism has 24 chromosomes in each body cell, its diploid (2N) number is
   a. 3.
   b. 6.
   c. 12.
   d. 24.

2. Any hybrid organism is
   a. recessive.
   b. purebred.
   c. heterozygous.
   d. homozygous.

3. A tetrad consists of four
   a. alleles.
   b. chromatids.
   c. homologs.
   d. homologous chromosomes.

4. Meiosis of a single cell results in the formation of
   a. two identical cells.
   b. three identical haploid polar bodies.
   c. four identical gamete cells.
   d. four unlike gamete cells.

5. Which is more likely to occur when genes are far apart on a chromosome?
   a. Crossing over
   b. Translocation
   c. Deletion
   d. Insertion

6. A change that affects a single nucleotide causes a (an)
   a. germ mutation.
   b. somatic mutation.
   c. inversion mutation.
   d. point mutation.

7. Linked genes do not
   a. undergo independent assortment.
   b. occur in linkage groups.
   c. occur on the same chromosome.
   d. show dominant and recessive traits.

8. When two pink carnations are crossed, the offspring are 25% red, 50% pink, and 25% white. This is known as
   a. complete dominance.
   b. incomplete dominance.
   c. codominance.
   d. polygenic inheritance.

9. Recombinants result from
   a. independent assortment of chromosomes.
   b. segregation of chromosomes.
   c. crossing over of chromosomes
   d. nonhomologous chromosomes.

10. Mutation in which a segment of a chromosome is repeated is a (an)
    a. deletion.
    b. inversion.
    c. translocation.
    d. duplication.

11. Most inherited human traits are determined by
    a. complicated gene interactions.
    b. dominant genes.
    c. recessive genes.
    d. codominant genes.

12. In humans, egg and sperm cells contain
    a. 2 sex chromosomes.
    b. 23 autosomes.
    c. 23 chromosomes.
    d. the diploid chromosome number.

13. In humans, sex is determined by the
    a. presence of two X chromosomes.
    b. number of chromosomes.
    c. presence or absence of an X chromosome.
    d. presence or absence of a Y chromosome.

14. Which term is least closely related to the others?
    a. Gamete
    b. Zygote
    c. Egg
    d. Sperm

15. The red blood cells of a person with type AB blood have
    a. A antigens only.
    b. B antigens only.
    c. A and B antigens.
    d. neither A nor B antigens.

Matching:

16. Please match each of the following human conditions with its mode of inheritance by writing the appropriate letter in the blank beside the condition name. You may use a particular mode of inheritance more than once. Please choose *only* eight conditions to match!!

Conditions	Inheritance:
Albinism	a. Codominance
Hairy ears	b. Polygenic
Hemophilia	c. Multiple alleles
Muscular dystrophy	d. Incomplete dominance
ABO blood types	e. Completely dominant or recessive
Height	f. Sex linked
Huntington's chorea	g. Sex influenced
Sickle cell anemia	
Color blindness	
Cystic fibrosis	
Dwarfism	
Male pattern baldness	

Short Answer:

17. Mendel found that the allele for tallness in peas (T) is dominant to its allele for shortness (t). What would be the expected genotypic and phenotypic ratios for a heterozygote X a homozygous short?

    Genotypic ratio:
    Phenotypic ratio:

18. A kennel owner has a magnificent Irish setter that he wants to hire out for stud. He knows that one of its ancestors carried a recessive allele for atrophy of the retina. In its homozygous state, this gene produces blindness. Before he can charge a stud fee, he must check to make sure his dog does not carry this allele. How can he do this? Please explain in words.

19. Sniffles, a male mouse with a colored coat, was mated with Esmerelda, an alluring albino. The resulting litter of six young all had colored fur. The next time around, Esmerelda was mated with Whiskers, who was the same color as Sniffles. Some of Esmerelda's next litter were white. What are the probable genotypes of Sniffles, Whiskers, and Esmerelda?

20. In tomato plants, the gene for purple stems (A) is dominant to its allele for green stems (a) and the gene for red fruit (R) is dominant to its allele for yellow fruit (r). If two tomato plants heterozygous for both traits are crossed, what fraction of the offspring are expected to have

    a. purple stems and yellow fruits?
    b. green stems and red fruits?
    c. purple stems and red fruits?

21. a. A couple are both phenotypically normal, but their son suffers from hemophilia. What fraction of future children are likely to suffer from hemophilia? What fraction are likely to be carriers?

    b. Under what circumstances is it possible for both a father and his son to be hemophiliacs?

22. Wilma, Fred, Bam-Bam, and Pebbles Flintstone lead a happy life in the town of Bedrock. Bam-Bam has Type O blood and Pebbles has Type AB blood.

    a. What are the genotypes and phenotypes of their parents?

    b. What is the probability that Wilma and Fred's next child will have Type B blood?

Essay:

23. Please discuss in a well-organized essay how nondisjunction, crossing-over, and deletion mutations contribute to genetic variability. Be sure to address the following points:

    a. When do each of the three events occur?
    b. How does it occur?
    c. What are the effects of this event on the organism?

    Be specific, and give examples of certain human disorders or conditions when possible. Please write the essay on a separate piece of lined paper and attach it to the test when finished.

Extra Credit:

1. You just graduated from medical school and decide to set up a family practice in Bedrock. You are the Flintstone family doctor and are asked to determine whose blood types are compatible in case of emergency. The payment for your consultation will be in the mail.

    Please use all relevant information from Question 22, and write your answers in the following space. You will need to arbitrarily assign the parental blood types to Wilma and Fred.

Recipient	Possible Donor(s)
Fred	
Wilma	
Bam-Bam	
Pebbles	

Biology Test 3: Digestion, Nutrition, and Eating Disorders

1. Please complete the following table on the "Nutrient content of average servings of fast foods."

   a. Which foods are high in fat content?

   b. Why are these foods high in fat content?

   c. Which food has the lowest protein content?

   d. Considering that you should not eat more than 1,800 mg of salt per day, which foods are high in salt content?

   e. If you ate a hamburger, a medium-sized portion of french fries, and a milk-shake, what percentage of your recommended daily calorie intake would you be receiving?

   f. Could a milk shake, french fries, and a piece of cheese pizza be considered a balanced meal? What is a balanced diet, and why is it important?

2. It is 7:00 p.m., and your stomach is growling. You go to McDonald's and order a quarter pounder with cheese. The ingredients include a sesame seed bun, ¼ lb (or approximately .25 kg) of ground beef, lettuce, tomatoes, and one slice of cheese. Please write an essay to describe the digestive process from the time the hamburger enters your mouth until it is excreted. Include the following in your essay:

   a. All parts of the digestive system that you labeled in Question 3

   b. Mechanical and chemical digestion

   c. Enzymes and digestive fluids:

   Mouth: Name one enzyme and its function.
   Stomach: Name one enzyme and one digestive fluid and their functions.
   Small intestine: Name one enzyme and its function.
   Pancreas: Name three enzymes and their functions.
   Liver: Name one digestive fluid and its function.

   Please write the essay on a separate piece of lined paper and attach it to the test when finished.

3. Why are anorexia and bulimia considered to be "abnormal" forms of eating? Briefly describe each eating disorder and list 4 warning signs or characteristics of each disorder.

Extra Credit:

1. List four characteristics of "normal" eating.

2. Based on what you have eaten and recorded over the past week, do you think that you eat "normally"? What could you do to improve your eating habits?

Biology Test 4: The Human Respiratory System

1. Please define the following vocabulary terms, and explain their functions in relation to the respiratory system.

   a. Nose
   b. Pharynx
   c. Larynx
   d. Vocal cord
   e. Trache
   f. Bronchus (left and right)
   g. Lung (left and right)
   h. Bronchiole
   i. Alveolus
   j. Diaphragm

2. Please draw and label a diagram of the respiratory system. Please include the 10 parts of the respiratory system listed in Question 1.

3. Gas exchange: It is almost the end of the period, and Ms. Kunz has just given a stimulating lecture on the respiratory system. You, however, are very tired and begin to yawn. This gasp of air eventually makes it to your lungs. Please answer the following questions related to gas exchange in the alveolus.

   a. Draw arrows on Figure R.2 to indicate the direction of carbon dioxide and oxygen movement immediately following inhalation.
   b. Why is hemoglobin important to gas exchange?

4. Control of Respiration:

   a. What section of the brain controls respiration?
   b. What is the importance of the following equations for respiratory control?

   $$CO_2 + H_2O \rightarrow H_2CO_3$$
   $$H_2CO_3 \rightarrow H^+ + HCO_3-$$

   c. Explain how carbon dioxide and acidity regulate breathing.

Extra Credit:

1. You have tried to persuade your friend to play a school sport; however, she says that she does not have the time. Please explain why regular exercise is an advantage from a respiratory point of view.

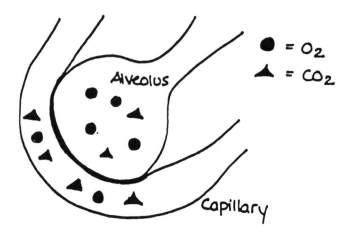

Figure R.2. *Gas Exchange*
SOURCE: Used with permission by Emily Chin.

Biology Test 5: Molecular Biology

Multiple Choice: Please write the letter of the correct response in the blank.

1. The term that is least closely related to the others is
   a. selective breeding.
   b. transformation.
   c. inbreeding.
   d. hybridization.

2. Chromosomal DNA fragments are separated by
   a. sequencing.
   b. radioactive labeling.
   c. electrophoresis.
   d. ultraviolet radiation.

3. Radiation and chemicals can be used to
   a. sequence DNA.
   b. cause mutations.
   c. hybridize animals.
   d. inbreed plants.

4. Your complete DNA sequence makes up your
   a. genome.
   b. DNA fingerprint.
   c. recombinant DNA.
   d. transgenic DNA.

5. A series of bands revealing lengths of various repeats in DNA is the basis of
   a. DNA sequencing.
   b. recombinant DNA.
   c. DNA fingerprinting.
   d. DNA chimeras.

6. A large number of identical bacterial cells grown from a single bacterium is a
   a. clone.
   b. plasmid.
   c. mutant.
   d. sequence.

7. Bacteria often contain small circular structures known as
   a. mutagens.
   b. restriction enzymes.
   c. luciferase.
   d. plasmids.

8. DNA fingerprinting is based on the fact that individuals have different numbers of
   a. genes on their X chromosome.
   b. repeated sequences between working genes.
   c. genes on their Y chromosome.
   d. genes on given chromosomes.

9. When individuals from different species are crossed to produce a species hardier than either parent, it is known as
   a. mutagenesis.
   b. sequencing.
   c. hybrid vigor.
   d. genome production.

10. The term least closely related to the others is
    a. DNA fragments.
    b. clones.
    c. "sticky ends."
    d. restriction enzymes.

11. Genes can be cut at specific DNA sequences by
    a. restriction enzymes.
    b. mutagens.
    c. plasmids.
    d. transgenic CDNA.

12. Purebred dogs are maintained by a process known as
    a. selective breeding.
    b. mutagenesis.
    c. hybridization.
    d. inbreeding.

13. The first step is moving a gene from one organism to another is
    a. combining the desired gene with DNA from the recipient cell.
    b. cutting the desired gene from the genes around it.
    c. inserting the combined DNA into a living cell.
    d. growing many organisms that contain recombinant DNA.

14. Which is a benefit of producing insulin with biotechnology?
    a. It is mass produced.
    b. It is nonallergenic.
    c. It is less expensive.
    d. All of the above

Short Answers:

15. Use the diagram in Figure R.3 to answer the following questions.

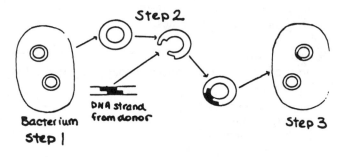

Figure R.3. *DNA-Cutting Diagram*
SOURCE: Used with permission by Emily Chin.

   a. What is used to cut the DNA in Step 2?
   b. What is the name of this circular DNA?
   c. What is the name of the "new" circular DNA in Step 3?
   d. How is this process different from hybridization and selective breeding?

16. A given strand of DNA is as follows:

   5' ATGTTATAACTTGCTGGCTAACTTGGTAC 3'
   3' TACAATATTGAACGACCGATTGAACCATG 5'

   This strand is treated with a restriction enzyme that cuts the sequence:

   5'AACTT 3'
   3'TTGAA 5'

   In the space that follows, draw the pieces that will result when this enzyme acts on the DNA segment. Label any "sticky ends."

17. A woman has a child and claims that Fred is the father. Fred claims that the father is Frank, his younger brother. The court orders that Fred and Frank both give blood samples and DNA testing be used to determine who the father really is. The results are shown in Figure R.4.

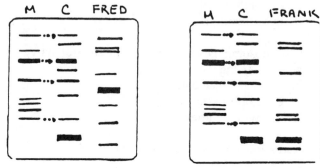

Figure R.4. *Blood Samples*
SOURCE: Used with permission by Emily Chin.

   a. Who is the father? State the reasons for your answer.
   b. What is it about sexual reproduction that makes DNA testing possible?

18. On December 20, 1990, at 3:00 a.m., Samantha left the library after finishing some research. As she walked alone to her apartment, she was abducted and raped by a tall, heavyset male in his late twenties. Fortunately, Samantha survived the rape and immediately went to the hospital. The doctors evaluated Samantha's condition and collected a semen sample. Samantha felt that the rapist might be her ex-boyfriend, Joe. The police obtained blood samples from Joe and two other suspects who had patterns of abuse in their pasts.

   The blood and semen samples were sent to Forengen, Inc., in San Francisco, CA, for testing. The results were as follows:

Well 1: Blood from Samantha
Well 2: Semen collected on Samantha
Well 3: Blood from Joe
Well 4: Blood from suspect X
Well 5: Blood from suspect Y

Draw the DNA fingerprint that would convict Joe.

a. Can you determine the identity of the rapist? Please explain how you reached your answer.

b. Based on the following article, "Strengths and Weaknesses Apparent in 2 DNA Tests," what do you think the future holds for the use of DNA fingerprinting to identify suspects? Please explain your answer.

19. a. Would a mutation in an intron affect gene expression in eukaryotes? Please include a brief description and drawing of eukaryotic gene expression in your response.

b. During prokaryotic gene expression, what happens during the presence and absence of a repressor? Please include a brief description and drawing of the process of prokaryotic gene expression in your response.

Strengths and Weaknesses Apparent in 2 DNA Tests

By Gina Kolata

Each of the two DNA tests at the center of today's sparring between prosecutors and O. J. Simpson's defense team has strengths and limitations.

The more conclusive of the two tests, used to determine whether two tissue samples came from the same person, is known as R.F.L.P., for restriction fragment length polymorphisms. It examines regions of the genetic material—from blood, saliva, tissue or a hair follicle—where particular small segments of DNA are repeated over and over, a sort of molecular stutter. Different people have different numbers of repeated segments. If one person has a segment repeated, say, 300 times, that would distinguish him or her from someone whose segment is repeated 100 times.

But the R.F.L.P. test requires a relatively large sample, about 5,000 cells, or a one-twentieth of a drop of blood. And the sample must be in good condition, said Dr. Robert E. Gaensslen, director of the forensic science program at the University of New Haven in West Haven, Conn.

The second test, a newer method known as the P.C.R. test, for polymerase chain reaction, can use as few as 50 cells, which could be found in a minute speck

of blood, and the cells can be somewhat degraded. It can determine with certainty if a defendant's blood is not in the sample, but it is less definite than the R.F.L.P. test in identifying whose blood is in the sample. In criminal cases, that often means it is more definitive in proving someone not guilty than in establishing guilt.

The P.C.R. test looks at several distinct genes with sequences that can vary slightly from person to person. Using an enzyme that copies each gene over and over again, investigators can build up enough copies of the genes to accurately ascertain their sequences. If the gene sequences in the tissue samples at the crime scene do not match a defendant's sequences, the cells could not have come from the defendant. If they do match the defendant's gene sequences, there is a good chance that they are his cells.

The R.F.L.P. test can make a positive match of two samples with the odds of an error ranging from one in tens of thousands to one in hundreds of thousands. When the P.C.R. test indicates a match, however, the chance that the sample came from a different person is more like one in thousands, Dr. Gaensslen said.

Mr. Simpson's lawyers argue vehemently that they need to do their own independent tests of the forensic samples. The prosecution argued yesterday that with certain items of evidence, it must first ascertain whether enough material is available to perform the R.F.L.P. test before giving samples to the defense. The defense team argues that although the DNA tests are powerful, laboratories can make mistakes.

Dr. Gaensslen agreed that independent testing was important. If two independent labs get the same results in a DNA testing, that is "a very good check on the results," Dr. Gaensslen said.

Extra Credit:

1. Give two examples of how biotechnology affects our lives, and describe them.

2. Read the following case study, "Cloning," and write a thoughtful and eloquent essay on a separate sheet of paper. Use the questions as a guideline to formulate your response.

Cloning

It was all over the news, newspapers screamed the headlines, everyone was talking about it—*a sheep had been cloned.* An exact duplicate of a sheep was made from its body cell. The photo wasn't too clear, and all sheep look alike anyway. It wasn't like they worked on humans.

However, it seems as though many people had mixed feelings about cloning. In the sheep cloning, a body cell (from the udder) was removed, and its nucleus was placed into another sheep's zygote. Then, an electrical current was sent through the cell, and it started dividing.

In Ms. Schwartz's biology class, everyone was talking about it. She explained carefully how it was done and what the benefits might be and why many people were against cloning of animals. But her class wanted to know what all the papers, magazines, and television shows were asking: Can we do this with humans? Should we?

So Mrs. Schwartz broke her class into two groups. One group had to argue that cloning of humans was acceptable; the other group had to argue that cloning was not acceptable.

Questions for Case Study on Cloning

1. Which group would you choose to be on?

2. Give four arguments for the acceptance of cloning of humans.

3. Give four arguments for the outlawing of cloning of humans.

4. The Congress of the United States has written a bill to outlaw cloning of humans. Should the government get involved in scientific experimentation? Why or why not?

5. If we do not consider cloning of humans, do you think it is acceptable to clone animals? Why or why not?

6. If cloning of humans were allowed, what possible uses could you see for this technology?

7. Do you think that people would actually have themselves or their children cloned? Why or why not?

SOURCE: Taken from *Case Studies in Bioethics II* by Ronnee Yashon with permission.

Real Life 1 Test
Middle School Life Sciences

1a. Answers will vary: feelings of anxiety; sense of physical & emotional change; when faced with new and/or challenging situations.

1b. Positive: once challenges are met, individuals can relax and enjoy their achievements to build up reserves for the next challenge; can improve performance; helps individuals to better focus, etc. Negative: when individuals cannot relax to enjoy achievements; stress is a way of life and is detrimental to health.

2. Answers will vary.

3a. Warming up; aerobics; cooling down.

3b. Use your target heart rate (your safe effective exercise pulse).
Set realistic fitness goals.
Space out workouts throughout the week.
Stretch to warm up and to cool down.
Use comfortable clothing and good equipment.

4a. Asthma is an emotional or psychological disease. The way parents raise children may cause asthma. Exercise is bad for those with asthma.

4b. During an attack, the bronchial tubes become constricted, making it difficult to take in enough air. In addition, the linings of the air passages may swell and become filled with mucus. Sometimes small tubes collapse, making it more difficult to exhale than it is to inhale.

5. This may be a result of the changes in hormone levels in the body that accompanies menstruation cycles.

Extra Credit: Answers will vary.

Reproduction Test:
Biology

1. Puberty is the time of life during which the secondary sex characteristics begin to appear and the capacity for sexual reproduction is possible; usually occurs between the ages of 10 and 15. The pituitary gland is responsible for most adolescent changes.

2a. Some characteristics are the development of breasts, menstruation, widening of the hips, etc. Age 12.

2b. See Diagram 1.

3a. Some characteristics are the deepening of the voice, facial hair growth, increase in height, etc. Age 14.

3b. See Diagram 2.

3c. *erection:* when the spongy tissue of the penis is filled with blood, making it more rigid.
ejaculation: stimulation of the mechanoreceptors of the penis and scrotum sends nerve impulses through reflex arcs in the lower spinal cord to motor neurons innervating different muscles of the reproductive system; the muscle encircling the epididymus and vas deferens contracts to move the spermatozoa into the urethra and the seminal vesicles secrete a nutrient fluid; the prostate gland adds milky alkaline fluid; these contractions then initiate in muscles around the bulb and propel the sperm and fluid through the urethra.

4a. Egg and sperm contain 23 chromosomes; a fertilized egg contains 46 chromosomes.

4b. Fertilization takes place when sperm travel up the female reproductive tract to fuse with the egg at the fallopian tubes; the fertilized egg then travels down to implant in the uterine wall.

5. Spontaneous abortion: when mother's body recognizes fetus as abnormal.
Induced abortion: suction, dilation & curettage, saline procedure, or rarely hysterotomy.

6. Even with carefully chosen contraceptives, pregnancy is still possible. It is important for individuals to be informed about unintended pregnancy before engaging in sexual activity.

7a. STD: sexually transmitted diseases; they are generally transmitted by the exchange of bodily fluids, such as during sexual intercourse; unmonitored blood transfusions; sharing of needles with infected persons, etc.

7b. *Chlamydia*—a bacterial infection causing vaginal bleeding and discharge and burning sensations during urination

Hepatitis B—a viral infection that causes fever, vomiting, diarrhea, decreased appetite, and yellowing of the skin

Syphilis—a bacterial infection causing painful sores on genitals, cervix, lips, mouth, or anus, or body rashes

HIV—a viral infection leading to AIDS

Genital herpes—a highly contagious viral infection causing burning, itching sensations, vaginal discharge, and blistery sores

Gonorrhea—a bacterial infection causing a burning sensation, pelvic pain, vaginal discharge

8. Answers will vary:

Verbal harassment: suggestive gestures, looks, jokes, comments, sexual notes, or pictures.

Physical harassment: physical contact like grabbing, pinching, groping.

Recommended responses include talking to an advisor, counselor, or friend about the incident.

Extra Credit 1: Toxic Shock Syndrome (TSS) is a rare but dangerous bacterial infection associated with the use of highly absorbent tampons. Signs and symptoms include high fever, nausea, diarrhea, dizziness, rashes, etc.

Extra Credit 2: Amniocentesis is a procedure where amniotic fluid, which surrounds a fetus, is removed through a needle that is inserted into a mother's womb. Analysis of the fluid can be done to test for various genetic disorders. Cons include: danger to the fetus; takes time; and cost.

Biology Test 1:
Biochemical Genetics Test

1a. 3.48×10^{-7}

1b. 2,976,000

1c. 1.985×10^{12}

2. The surface to volume ratio decreases as the size of the cell increases. This is significant because this can affect the cell's ability to transport nutrients and wastes.

3a. Chromosome—the genetic material of a cell; thread-like structures that can be seen under a microscope only after being stained with dyes.

3b. Chromatin—the piece of DNA that is studied and analyzed.

3c. Chromatid—one of two longitudinal subunits of all replicated chromosomes; visible during prophase and metaphase.

3d. Centromere—specialized region of a chromosome that is important in the activities of chromosomes during division.

3e. Histone—protein complexed with DNA in chromosomes; plays a large role in determining the structure of eukaryotic nuclear chromosomes.

3f. Nucleosome—the basic structural unit of eukaryotic nuclear chromosomes consisting of 140 base pairs of DNA wound around an octamer of histones.

4. See Diagram 3.

5. See Table 1.

6. Hershey and Chase—f
Watson and Crick—e
Avery—b
Griffith—c
Chargaff—d
Rosalind Franklin—a

7a. Frederick Griffith was an English microbiologist who discovered genetic transformation of the bacterium (1928) and called the agent responsible the "transforming principle." It was the first step toward identifying DNA as the genetic material. Griffith injected mice with R bacteria (rough pneumococcus) and observed that the mice did not die from pneumonia. When injected with S bacteria (smooth), the mice developed pneumonia and died. Heat-killed S bacteria did not kill them, however. Then, Griffith proceeded to inject both R bacteria and heat-killed S bacteria, which still contained intact DNA. These mice died from pneumonia and living deadly R bacteria were recovered. The conclusion of the experiment was that the DNA passed from type S bacteria to type R, enabling it to manufacture the smooth polysaccharide coat necessary for virulence.

7b. Alfred Hershey and Martha Chase were American microbiologists who, in 1950, confirmed DNA to be the genetic material. The two researchers "labeled" the batches of virus, or bacteriophage, one with radioactive sulfur (which marked protein) and the other with radioactive phosphorus (which marked DNA). They infected two batches of bacteria, each containing one type of labeled virus. After infection, they shook off empty protein virus coats (previously containing DNA) and then the samples were centrifuged to separate the bacteria from the virus coats. In the tube containing virus labeled with sulfur, the virus-infected bacteria were not radioactive. However, in the other tube, where the virus had incorporated radioactive phosphorus, the infected bacteria were radioactive. The conclusion made was that the component of the virus that could enter bacteria and direct production of more virus was the part that had incorporated the phosphorus label—the DNA. The genetic material, therefore, was DNA, and not protein.

1. b
2. d
3. b
4. d
5. d
6. c
7. a
8. a
9. d
10. a
11. a
12. a
13. a
14. b
15. a

Extra Credit 1: Cancer can occur when differentiated cells revert to an undifferentiated state and instead of remaining in the nondividing state, divide mitotically to form tumors or abnormal tissue masses that can invade surrounding tissues.

Extra Credit 2: Nucleotide—monomer molecule of RNA and DNA that is composed of three parts: a pentose, a nitrogenous base, and a phosphate group. DNA and RNA are formed from the combining of these nucleotide units (in DNA the pentose is deoxyribose and in RNA the pentose is ribose). The pentose sugars and the phosphate groups of the nucleotides serve as the backbone of the molecule. In DNA the nitrogenous bases form hydrogen bonds with corresponding bases of another chain of nucleotides to form the double helix.

Biology Test 2:
Classical Genetics

1. c
2. c
3. b
4. d
5. a
6. d
7. a
8. b
9. c
10. d
11. a
12. c
13. d
14. b
15. c
16. albinism—e
    hairy ears—b
    hemophilia—f
    Duchenne's muscular dystrophy—f
    ABO blood types—a, c, e
    height—b
    Huntington's—e

Sickle cell anemia—e
colorblindness—f
cystic fibrosis—e
dwarfism—e
male pattern baldness—g

17. Genotypic ratio = 1:1 (Tt:tt)
    Phenotypic ratio = 1:1 (Tall:Short)
18. He can breed his Irish setter with a blind setter (one that is homozygous for the gene he thinks that the Irish setter may carry) and see if any of the offspring become blind.
19. Let B=dominant colored fur allele and b=recessive albino allele.
    Probable genotypes of
        Sniffles: BB
        Whiskers: Bb
        Esmeralda: bb
20a. 3/16
20b. 3/16
20c. 9/16
20d. 1/16
21a. Hemophilia is a sex-linked trait. 50% of their male children will have hemophilia and 50% of their female children will be carriers of the disease.
21b. This is possible only if the mother is either a carrier or is a victim of hemophilia. The father cannot pass on a sex-linked trait to his son.
22a. One parent has AO blood and the other has BO blood.
22b. 25%
23a. Meiosis.
23b+c. Nondisjunction is an error in the segregation of replicated chromosomes to daughter cells during cell division. It occurs when the centromere fails to function properly. If absent, the chromosome cannot attach itself to the spindle and will migrate through the cell randomly during cell division. Aneuploidy, monoploidy, and polyploidy can result from nondisjunction, i.e., Down's Syndrome.

Crossing-over is an exchange between two non-sister chromatids during meiotic prophase, giving rise to recombinant (non-parental) combinations of linked genes.

A deletion is a chromosomal mutation involving the loss of a segment of a chromosome. A human disorder resulting from a deletion mutation is cri-du-chat syndrome.

Extra Credit:
24. Bam-Bam has type O blood and can therefore receive only O type blood; no one in the family is able to donate blood to Bam-Bam. Pebbles has type AB blood and can receive all blood types; everyone in the family is able to donate blood to Pebbles. Either Wilma or Fred have type AO blood or BO blood; in either case the only family member able to donate blood to Wilma and Fred is Bam-Bam (No one else in the family has type A or B blood.)

Biology Test 3:
Digestion, Nutrition and Eating Disorders

1a. Answers will vary
        Baconburgers
        Cheeseburgers
        French fries
        etc.
1b. Answers will vary
        They are fried in grease
        Cheese and bacon are high-fat foods , etc.
1c. Sugar, cola, beer.
1d. Answers will vary
        Most commercial soups
1e. This is not considered a balanced meal. A balanced
      diet consists of foods coming from all food groups
      and is low in fat and calories as compared to nutri-
      tional values. A normal healthy diet should not con-
      tain more than 30% of calories coming from fat. The
      average American diet, which is represented by this
      example, is too high in calories and fat calories for
      the nutritional benefits received (although eating
      this meal once in a while or only a part of this meal
      is not itself bad).
2.   See Diagram 4.
      Digestion
        Mouth—mechanical (chewing) breaks down food
          into smaller pieces/softens food and amylase
          breaks down starch, i.e. bread.
        Esophagus—food is moved through this tube and
          the rest of the GI tract through wave-like con-
          tractions, peristalsis; from here it enters the
          stomach.
        Stomach—mechanical contractions of the stomach
          mix the food; HCl lowers the stomach acidity so
          that the pepsin enzymes can effectively break
          down proteins, i.e. meat; food is now called
          chyme.
        Small intestine—chyme enters from stomach; most
          of chemical digestion takes place here; enzymes
          from the small intestine include maltase, su-
          crase, lactase, peptidases, ribonuclease and de-
          oxyribonuclease. Nutrients are absorbed
          through the villi lining the walls, waste materi-
          als proceed to the large intestine.
        Pancreas—releases pancreatic juice (therefore is an

exocrine gland) and also releases insulin, glu-
cagon, and somatostatin (therefore is an endocrine gland).
        Liver—makes bile which is collected and then re-
          leased into the small intestine as needed by the
          gall bladder; bile emulsifies fats so that surface
          area of the lipids/fats increases making diges-
          tion easier/faster.
        Large intestine—absorbs water from the waste
          material; waste proceeds through to the rectum
          to be excreted.
3.   Anorexia nervosa and bulimia nervosa are consid-
      ered abnormal forms of eating because individuals
      suffering from these disorders are not taking in
      enough nutrients to sustain normal functioning of
      their bodies. Anorexia nervosa is an eating disorder
      in which individuals cease to eat and become ob-
      sessed about their weight. This can result from a va-
      riety of factors such as feelings of loss of control
      and distorted self images of their bodies. They view
      themselves as fat when, in fact, they are extremely
      thin and malnutritioned. Women who are anorexics
      can become amenorrheic. Those suffering from bu-
      limia will also be obsessed with their weight. These
      individuals, however, are not always thin. They can
      be of average weight or sometimes even over-
      weight. This illness is characterized by periods of
      binge-eating followed by induced vomiting or the
      use of laxatives. This can cause nutritional prob-
      lems as well as health problems. For example bu-
      limics who induce vomiting may scar their esopha-
      gus tissues due to the acidity of stomach juices and
      may damage teeth enamel for similar reasons. They
      may also follow very strict and strenuous exercise
      routines.

Extra Credit:
1. Normal eating
        Nutritional needs are met (i.e. vitamins, minerals,
          calories, water . . .).
        Food from all food groups are met.
        Growth and weight patterns are normal.
        Eating all 3 meals (i.e. skipping breakfast is NOT
          good).

2. Answers will vary

Biology Test 4:
The Human Respiratory System

1a. *Nose*—entrance for air intake/output. Nasal passages warm up air and contain cilia, which filter out dust, foreign particles, etc.

1b. *Pharynx*—throat; tube that opens posteriorly to esophagus and anteriorly to larynx.

1c. *Larynx*—voice box; short passageway connecting pharynx and trachea.

1d. *Vocal Cord*—muscle folds located within the larynx. Produces sound.

1e. *Trachea*—windpipe; air tube from larynx to bronchi.

1f. *Bronchus*—two primary branches of the trachea about the level of T5 vertebra.

1g. *Lung*—main organ of respiration; one lying on either side of the heart in the thoracic cavity.

1h. *Bronchiole*—branches of the bronchi that further divide into alveoli.

1i. *Alveolus*—air sacs of the lungs where gas exchange occurs.

1j. *Diaphragm*—dome shaped skeletal muscle between the thoracic and abdominal cavities that is the primary muscle of respiration.

2. See Diagram 5.

3a. See Diagram 6.

3b. Hemoglobin is what allows red blood cells to bind oxygen. Without hemoglobin gas exchange would be impaired, since only a small amount of gases can be carried in the blood plasma.

4a. The medulla is responsible for the subconscious control of respiration.

4b. These equations represent how carbon dioxide is diffused in the blood. It shows that carbon dioxide can be dissolved into bicarbonate ions that can be important in controlling the acidity.

4c. If the carbon dioxide level or acidity are high the respiration increases because of chemoreceptors that trigger the increased sympathetic activity.

Extra Credit:

1. Exercise is important because it can increase overall health. Training can improve the cardiovascular system, which can in turn improve respiration.

Biology Test 5:
Molecular Biology

1. b
2. c
3. b
4. a
5. c
6. a
7. d
8. b
9. c
10. b
11. a
12. d
13. b
14. d

15a. Restriction enzymes

15b. Plasmid

15c. Recombinant plasmid

15d. It does not require the use of breeding and hence cuts down the time needed to obtain desired results. This also allows for the potential mixing of genes of differing species of life (because a species is defined by reproductive isolation, the other two techniques are species-limited).

16. 5' ATGTTATA   ACTTGCTGG 3'
    3' TACAATATTGA   ACGACC 5'

17a. Frank, because his DNA fingerprint matches up with those of the child.

17b. In sexual reproduction, half of the DNA of the child comes from each parent.

18. Answer will vary—diagrams should clearly match the samples obtained from Joe and the rapist.

18a. Yes, because the fingerprints are unique to individuals and they match.

18b. Answers will vary.

19a. Intron mutations would not affect gene expression in eukaryotes, since these are removed from the final gene.

19b. During presence of the repressor, the regulatory protein is bound to its regulatory site thereby blocking transcription of the gene's DNA.

Extra Credit:

1. Examples of how biotechnology impacts our lives are seen through the effects of genetic engineering and environment health.

2. Answers will vary.

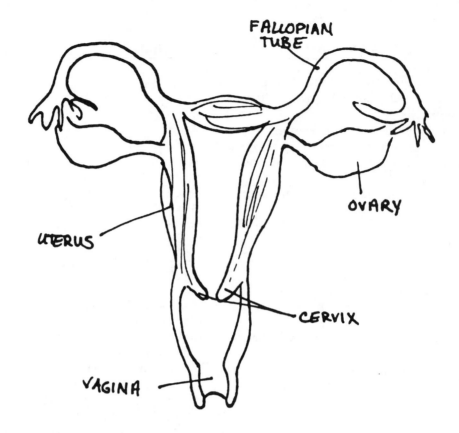

Diagram 1

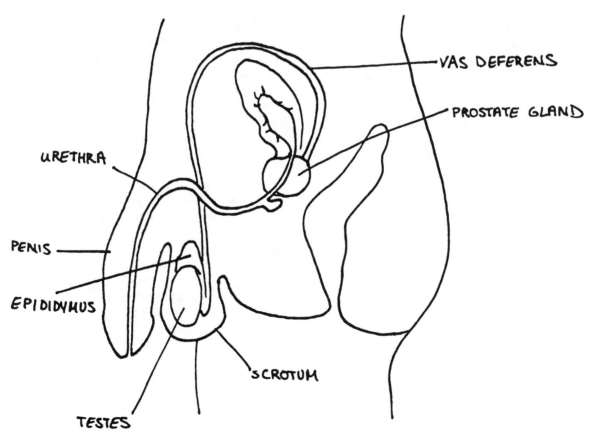

Diagram 2

i.

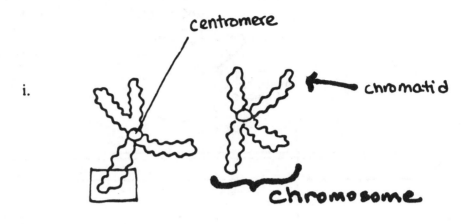

centromere

chromatid

chromosome

ii.

chromatid

iii.

Nucleosome/
Histone + DNA

iv.

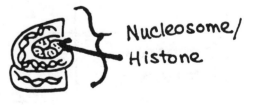

Nucleosome/
Histone

Diagram 3

Phase	Drawing	Events That Occur
Interphase		
	centrioles chromatin T nuclear membrane nucleolus	- chromosomes copied + spread out - centrioles copied
Mitosis,		
Prophase	paired chromatid spindle	- chromosomes come together - nucleolus disappears - nuclear membrane disintegrates - centrioles separate + spindle forms
Metaphase		- chromosomes attach to spindle + line up at center of cell
Anaphase		- centromeres split - microtubules shorten pulling one chromatid to each pole of the cell
Telophase + Cytokinesis	nuclear membrane	- nuclear envelope reforms - spindle breaks apart - cytoplasm divides - result → two identical daughter cells

Table 1

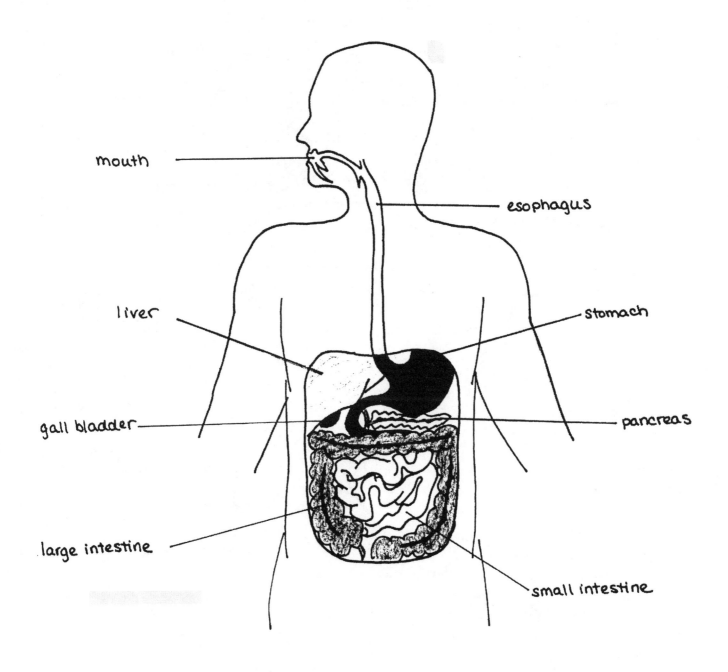

Diagram 4

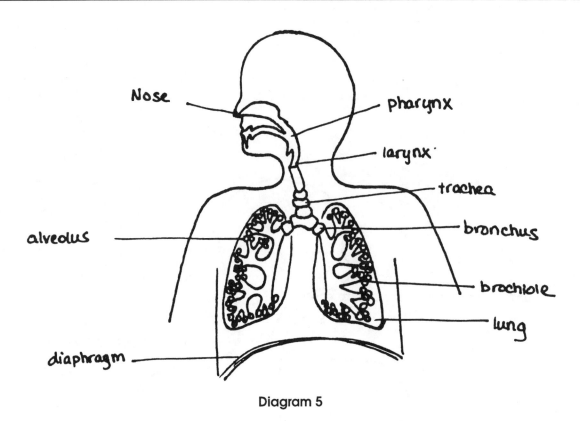

Diagram 5

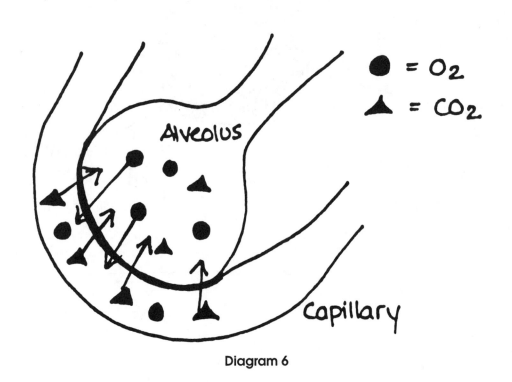

Diagram 6

References

Adamson, J. (1960). *Born free.* New York: Pantheon.

Allyn & Bacon. (1987). *Study skills.* Boston: Author.

Altman, L. K. (1995, May 13). The deadly virus in Zaire: Sifting the many mysteries. *New York Times,* sec. 1, p. 1.

American Association of University Women. (1991). *Shortchanging girls, shortchanging America: A call to action.* Washington, DC: Author.

American Association of University Women Educational Foundation. (1996). *Girls in the middle: Working to succeed.* In J. Applegate. (1995). Cooperative learning in graded tests. *The American Biology Teacher, 57*(6), 363-364.

Applegate, J. (1995). Cooperative learning in graded tests. *The American Biology Teacher, 57*(6), 363-364.

Asterita, M. F. (1985). *The physiology of stress.* New York: Human Sciences Press.

Bailey, S. (1992). *Dana Hall Newsletter.* Wellesley, MA: Dana Hall School.

Blake, S. (1993, April). Are you turning females and minority students away from science? *Science and Children,* pp. 12-15.

Caldwell, M. (1996, January). Ebola tamed—for now. *Discover, 17,* 16-17.

Campbell, P. (1993, March 12). Symposium highlights. *Girls and the Physical Sciences.* Symposium held at the Science and Technology Center, Tufts University. Sponsors: The Wright Center for Innovative Science Education, Tufts University, Medford, MA, and The National Coalition of Girls' Schools, Concord, MA.

Chew, F. (1993). Symposium highlights. *Girls and the Physical Sciences.* Symposium held at the Science and Technology Center, Tufts University. Sponsors: The Wright Center for Innovative Science Education, Tufts University, Medford, MA, and The National Coalition of Girls' Schools, Concord, MA.

Collins, K. (1981). Independent projects: An organized approach. *The American Biology Teacher, 43*(8), 463-465.

Consumer Reports. (1993). *Product testing activities.* Englewood Cliffs: Prentice Hall.

Dawson, D., Horvath, P., & Rulfs, J. (Eds.). (1992). *Biotechnology resources for teachers.* Worcester, MA: Massachusetts Biotechnology Research Institute.

DeRosa, D., & Wolfe, L. (1993). *Boston University CityLab: The mystery of the crooked cell.* Boston: Trustees of Boston University.

Everly, G., & Sobelman, S. (1987). *Assessment of the human stress response.* New York: AMS.

Fallon, P., Katzman, M, & Wooley, S. (1994). The politics of prevention. *Feminist Perspectives on Eating Disorders.* New York: Guilford.

Gardner, A., Mason, C., & Matyas, M. (1989). Equity, excellence, and just plain good teaching. *The American Biology Teacher, 5*(12), 72-77.

Gilligan, C., & Rogers, A. (1993). *Strengthening healthy resistance and courage in girls: A prevention project and a development study.* Cambridge, MA: Harvard Graduate School of Education.

Gleason, J. B., & Snow, C. (1991, December). Adding up the evidence: Why don't more girls go into math and science? *Museum of Science Magazine,* pp. 8-9.

Goldberg, M., & Moulton, S. (1992). Send in the clones. *Biotechnology: The technology of life.* Worcester: Massachusetts Biotechnology Research Institute.

Gornick, V. (1995). Women in science: 100 journeys into the territory (p. 13). *Literary Calvacade.* New York: Simon & Schuster.

Green, E., & Bobrowsky, K. (1971). *Laboratory investigations in biology.* Morriston, NJ: Silver Burdett Ginn.

Guyton, A. C. (1981). *Textbook of medical physiology* (6th ed.). Philadelphia: W. B. Saunders.

Harmon, M. (1993). Symposium highlights. *Girls and the Physical Sciences.* Symposium held at the Science and Technology Center, Tufts University. Sponsors: The Wright Center for Innovative Science Education, Tufts University, Medford, MA, and The National Coalition of Girls' Schools, Concord, MA.

Kahle, J. B. (1991). Women in science: Where do we go from here? In National Coalition of Girls' Schools, *Math and Science for Girls* (pp. 8-23). Concord, MA: National Coalition of Girls' Schools.

Kirk, D. L. (1980). *Biology today.* New York: McGraw-Hill.

Kolata, G. (1994, July 26). Strengths and weaknesses apparent in 2 DNA tests. *The New York Times,* p. A10 (column 5).

Lawrence Hall of Science. (1987). *Fingerprinting teacher's guide.* Berkeley: University of California, Lawrence Hall of Science, GEMS.

McComas, W. F. (1988, September). Variation, adaptation and evolution at the zoo. *The American Biology Teacher, 50*(6), 379-380.

McQuade, W., & Aikman, A. (1974). *Stress.* New York: E. P. Dutton.

Microsoft. (1996). *Microsoft Encarta 96 Encyclopedia, 1993-1995.* Author.

Mosca, G. F., & Shmurak, C. B. (1995, September). An interdisciplinary, gender-equitable mathematics project for the middle school. *Middle School Journal,* pp. 26-29.

National Association of Biology Teachers and Society for Neuroscience. (1996). *Neuroscience Laboratory and Classroom Activities.* Washington, DC: Author.

National Resource Council Committee on Women in Science and Engineering. (1991). Women in science and engineering: Increasing their numbers in the 1990s? *National Academy Press,* pp. 7-27.

New England Consortium for Undergraduate Science Education. (1996). *Achieving gender equity in science classrooms.* Providence, RI: Brown University, Group Independent Study Project.

Pollina, A. (1995, September). Gender balance: Lessons from girls in science and mathematics. *Educational Leadership,* pp. 30-33.

Prentice Hall. (1991). *Biotechnology workbook.* Upper Saddle River, NJ: Author.

Preston, R. (1995, May 22). Back in the hot zone. *The New Yorker, 17*(13), 43-45.

Rutkowski, A. M. (1996). Sickle-cell anemia. *Microsoft Encarta 96 Encyclopedia, 1993-1995.* Microsoft Corporation.

Sadker, M., & Sadker, D. (1994). *Failing at fairness: How our schools cheat girls.* New York: Touchstone.

Saferstein, R. (1995). *Criminalistics: An introduction to forensic science.* Upper Saddle River, NJ: Prentice Hall.

Sanders, Jo. (1994). *Lifting the barriers.* Port Washington, NY: Author.

Sandler, B. (1991, June 16-21). *Math and Science for Girls Symposium.* The National Coalition of Girls' Schools, Wellesley College, Wellesley, MA.

Selye, H. (1974). *Stress without distress.* Philadelphia: Lippincott.

Skolnick, J., Langbort, C., & Day, L. (1982). *How to encourage girls in math and science.* Palo Alto, CA: Dale Seymour Publications.

Spragg, J. (1993). Symposium highlights. *Girls and the Physical Sciences.* Symposium held at the Science and Technology Center, Tufts University. Sponsors: The Wright Center for Innovative Science Education, Tufts University, Medford, MA, and The National Coalition of Girls' Schools, Concord, MA.

Tobias, S. (1985, June). Math anxiety and physics: Some thoughts on learning "difficult" subjects. *Physics Today, 68.*

Wayland High School. (1991). *AP Biology, Wellesley College Greenhouse Lab.* Wayland, MA: Author.

Wolf, N. (1991). *The beauty myth: How images of beauty are used against women.* New York: William Morrow.

Wolfson, Adele. (1993). Symposium highlights. *Girls and the Physical Sciences.* Symposium held at the Science and Technology Center, Tufts University. Sponsors: The Wright Center for Innovative Science Education, Tufts University, Medford, MA, and The National Coalition of Girls' Schools, Concord, MA.